Use R!

Series Editors:
Robert Gentleman   Kurt Hornik   Giovanni Parmigiani

More information about this series at http://www.springer.com/series/6991

James E. Monogan III

Political Analysis Using R

 Springer

James E. Monogan III
Department of Political Science
University of Georgia
Athens, GA, USA

ISSN 2197-5736   ISSN 2197-5744   (electronic)
Use R!
ISBN 978-3-319-23445-8   ISBN 978-3-319-23446-5   (eBook)
DOI 10.1007/978-3-319-23446-5

Library of Congress Control Number: 2015955143

Springer Cham Heidelberg New York Dordrecht London
© Springer International Publishing Switzerland 2015

Printed on acid-free paper

Springer International Publishing AG Switzerland is part of Springer Science+Business Media (www.
springer.com)

This book is dedicated to my father and mother, two of the finest programmers I know.

Preface

The purpose of this volume is twofold: to help readers who are new to political research to learn the basics of how to use R and to provide details to intermediate R users about techniques they may not have used before. R has become prominent in political research because it is free, easily incorporates user-written packages, and offers user flexibility in creating unique solutions to complex problems. All of the examples in this book are drawn from various subfields in Political Science, with data drawn from American politics, comparative politics, international relations, and public policy. The datasets come from the types of sources common to political and social research, such as surveys, election returns, legislative roll call votes, nonprofit organizations' assessments of practices across countries, and field experiments. Of course, while the *examples* are drawn from Political Science, all of the *techniques* described are valid for any discipline. Therefore, this book is appropriate for anyone who wants to use R for social or political research.

All of the *example and homework data*, as well as copies of all of the example code in the chapters, are available through the Harvard Dataverse: **http://dx. doi.org/10.7910/DVN/ARKOTI**. As an overview of the examples, the following list itemizes the data used in this book and the chapters in which the data are referenced:

- 113th U.S. Senate roll call data (Poole et al. 2011). *Chapter 8*
- American National Election Study, 2004 subset used by Hanmer and Kalkan (2013). *Chapters 2 and 7*
- Comparative Study of Electoral Systems, 30-election subset analyzed in Singh (2014a), 60-election subset analyzed in Singh (2014b), and 77-election subset analyzed in Singh (2015). *Chapters 7 and 8*
- Democratization and international border settlements data, 200 countries from 1918–2007 (Owsiak 2013). *Chapter 6*
- Drug policy monthly TV news coverage (Peake and Eshbaugh-Soha 2008). *Chapters 3, 4, and 7*
- Energy policy monthly TV news coverage (Peake and Eshbaugh-Soha 2008). *Chapters 3, 7, 8, and 9*

- Health lobbying data from the U.S. states (Lowery et al. 2008). *Chapter 3*
- Japanese monthly electricity consumption by sector and policy action (Wakiyama et al. 2014). *Chapter 9*
- Kansas Event Data System, weekly actions from 1979–2003 in the Israeli-Palestinian conflict (Brandt and Freeman 2006). *Chapter 9*
- Monte Carlo analysis of strategic multinomial probit of international strategic deterrence model (Signorino 1999). *Chapter 11*
- National Supported Work Demonstration, as analyzed by LaLonde (1986). *Chapters 4, 5, and 8*
- National Survey of High School Biology Teachers, as analyzed by Berkman and Plutzer (2010). *Chapters 6 and 8*
- Nineteenth century militarized interstate disputes data, drawn from Bueno de Mesquita and Lalman (1992) and Jones et al. (1996). Example applies the method of Signorino (1999). *Chapter 11*
- Optimizing an insoluble party electoral competition game (Monogan 2013b). *Chapter 11*
- Political Terror Scale data on human rights, 1993–1995 waves (Poe and Tate 1994; Poe et al. 1999). *Chapter 2*
- Quarterly U.S. monetary policy and economic data from 1959–2001 (Enders 2009). *Chapter 9*
- Salta, Argentina field experiment on e-voting versus traditional voting (Alvarez et al. 2013). *Chapters 5 and 8*
- United Nations roll call data from 1946–1949 (Poole et al. 2011). *Chapter 8*
- U.S. House of Representatives elections in 2010 for Arizona and Tennessee (Monogan 2013a). *Chapter 10*

Like many other statistical software books, each chapter contains example code that the reader can use to practice using the commands with real data. The examples in each chapter are written as if the reader will work through all of the code in one chapter in a single session. Therefore, a line of code may depend on prior lines of code within the chapter. However, no chapter will assume that any code from previous chapters has been run during the current session. Additionally, to distinguish ideas clearly, the book uses fonts and colors to help distinguish input code, output printouts, variable names, concepts, and definitions. Please see Sect. 1.2 on p. 4 for a description of how these fonts are used.

To the reader, are you a beginning or intermediate user? To the course instructor, in what level of class are you assigning this text? This book offers information at a variety of levels. The first few chapters are intended for beginners, while the later chapters introduce progressively more advanced topics. The chapters can be approximately divided into three levels of difficulty, so various chapters can be introduced in different types of courses or read based on readers' needs:

- The book begins with basic information—in fact Chap. 1 assumes that the reader has never installed R or done any substantial data analysis. Chapter 2 continues by describing how to input, clean, and export data in R. Chapters 3–5 describe graphing techniques and basic inferences, offering a description of the techniques as well as code for implementing them R. The content in the first five chapters should be accessible to undergraduate students taking a quantitative methods class, or could be used as a supplement when introducing these concepts in a first-semester graduate methods class.

- Afterward, the book turns to content that is more commonly taught at the graduate level: Chap. 6 focuses on linear regression and its diagnostics, though this material is sometimes taught to undergraduates. Chapter 7 offers code for generalized linear models—models like logit, ordered logit, and count models that are often taught in a course on maximum likelihood estimation. Chapter 8 introduces students to the concept of using *packages* in R to apply advanced methods, so this could be worthwhile in the final required course of a graduate methods sequence or in any upper-level course. Specific topics that are sampled in Chap. 8 are multilevel modeling, simple Bayesian statistics, matching methods, and measurement with roll call data. Chapter 9 introduces a variety of models for time series analysis, so it would be useful as a supplement in a course on that topic, or perhaps even an advanced regression course that wanted to introduce time series.
- The last two chapters, Chaps. 10 and 11, offer an introduction to R programming. Chapter 10 focuses specifically on matrix-based math in R. This chapter actually could be useful in a math for social science class, if students should learn how to conduct linear algebra using software. Chapter 11 introduces a variety of concepts important to writing programs in R: functions, loops, branching, simulation, and optimization.

As a final word, there are several people I wish to thank for help throughout the writing process. For encouragement and putting me into contact with Springer to produce this book, I thank Keith L. Dougherty. For helpful advice and assistance along the way, I thank Lorraine Klimowich, Jon Gurstelle, Eric D. Lawrence, Keith T. Poole, Jeff Gill, Patrick T. Brandt, David Armstrong, Ryan Bakker, Philip Durbin, Thomas Leeper, Kerem Ozan Kalkan, Kathleen M. Donovan, Richard G. Gardiner, Gregory N. Hawrelak, students in several of my graduate methods classes, and several anonymous reviewers. The content of this book draws from past short courses I have taught on R. These courses in turn drew from short courses taught by Luke J. Keele, Evan Parker-Stephen, William G. Jacoby, Xun Pang, and Jeff Gill. My thanks to Luke, Evan, Bill, Xun, and Jeff for sharing this information. For sharing data that were used in the examples in this book, I thank R. Michael Alvarez, Ryan Bakker, Michael B. Berkman, Linda Cornett, Matthew Eshbaugh-Soha, Brian J. Fogarty, Mark Gibney, Virginia H. Gray, Michael J. Hanmer, Peter Haschke, Kerem Ozan Kalkan, Luke J. Keele, Linda Camp Keith, Gary King, Marcelo Leiras, Ines Levin, Jeffrey B. Lewis, David Lowery, Andrew P. Owsiak, Jeffrey S. Peake, Eric Plutzer, Steven C. Poe, Julia Sofía Pomares, Keith T. Poole, Curtis S. Signorino, Shane P. Singh, C. Neal Tate, Takako Wakiyama, Reed M. Wood, and Eric Zusman.

Athens, GA, USA   James E. Monogan III
November 22, 2015

Contents

Chapter 1
Obtaining R and Downloading Packages

This chapter is written for the user who has never downloaded R onto his or her computer, much less opened the program. The chapter offers some brief background on what the program is, then proceeds to describe how R can be downloaded and installed completely free of charge. Additionally, the chapter lists some internet-based resources on R that users may wish to consult whenever they have questions not addressed in this book.

1.1 Background and Installation

R is a platform for the object-oriented statistical programming language S. S was initially developed by John Chambers at Bell Labs, while R was created by Ross Ihaka and Robert Gentleman. R is widely used in statistics and has become quite popular in Political Science over the last decade. The program also has become more widely used in the business world and in government work, so training as an R user has become a marketable skill. R, which is shareware, is similar to S-plus, which is the commercial platform for S. Essentially R can be used as either a matrix-based programming language or as a standard statistical package that operates much like the commercially sold programs Stata, SAS, and SPSS.

Electronic supplementary material: The online version of this chapter (doi: 10.1007/978-3-319-23446-5_1) contains supplementary material, which is available to authorized users.

© Springer International Publishing Switzerland 2015
J.E. Monogan III, *Political Analysis Using R*, Use R!,
DOI 10.1007/978-3-319-23446-5_1

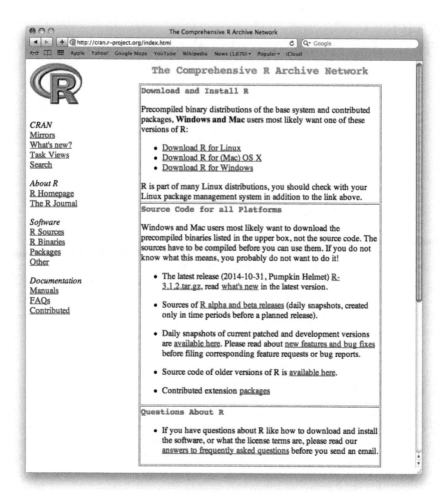

Fig. 1.1 The comprehensive R archive network (CRAN) homepage. The top box, "Download and Install R," offers installation links for the three major operating systems

1.1.1 Where Can I Get R?

The beauty of R is that it is shareware, so it is free to anyone. To obtain R for Windows, Mac, or Linux, simply visit the comprehensive R archive network (CRAN) at http://www.cran.r-project.org/. Figure 1.1 shows the homepage of this website. As can be seen, at the top of the page is an inset labeled *Download and Install R*. Within this are links for installation using the Linux, Mac OS X, and Windows operating systems. In the case of Mac, clicking the link will bring up a downloadable file with the `pkg` suffix that will install the latest version. For Windows, a link named `base` will be presented, which leads to an `exe` file for download and installation. In each operating system, opening the respective file will guide the user through the automated installation process.[1] In this simple procedure, a user can install R on his or her personal machine within five minutes.

As months and years pass, users will observe the release of new versions of R. There are not update patches for R, so as new versions are released, you must completely install a new version whenever you would like to upgrade to the latest edition. Users need not reinstall every single version that is released. However, as time passes, add-on libraries (discussed later in this chapter) will cease to support older versions of R. One potential guide on this point is to upgrade to the newest version whenever a library of interest cannot be installed due to lack of support. The only major inconvenience that complete reinstallation poses is that user-created add-on libraries will have to be reinstalled, but this can be done on an as-needed basis.

1.2   Getting Started: A First Session in R

Once you have installed R, there will be an icon either under the Windows Start menu (with an option of placing a shortcut on the Desktop) or in the Mac Applications folder (with an option of keeping an icon in the workspace Dock). Clicking or double-clicking the icon will start R. Figure 1.2 shows the window associated with the Mac version of the software. You will notice that R does have a few push-button options at the top of the window. Within Mac, the menu bar at the top of the workspace will also feature a few pull-down menus. In Windows, pull down menus also will be presented within the R window. With only a handful of menus and buttons, however, commands in R are entered primarily through user code. Users desiring the fallback option of having more menus and buttons available may wish to install RStudio or a similar program that adds a point-and-click front end to R, but a knowledge of the syntax is essential. Figure 1.3 shows the window associated with the Mac version of RStudio.[2]

Users can submit their code either through script files (the recommended choice, described in Sect. 1.3) or on the command line displayed at the bottom of the R console. In Fig. 1.2, the prompt looks like this:

>

---

[1]The names of these files change as new versions of R are released. As of this printing, the respective files are R-3.1.2-snowleopard.pkg or R-3.1.2-mavericks.pkg for various versions of Mac OS X and R-3.1.2-win.exe for Windows. Linux users will find it easier to install from a terminal. Terminal code is available by following the *Download R for Linux* link on the CRAN page, then choosing a Linux distribution on the next page, and using the terminal code listed on the resulting page. At the time of printing, Debian, various forms of Red Hat, OpenSUSE, and Ubuntu are all supported.

[2]RStudio is available at http://www.rstudio.com.

Fig. 1.2 R Console for a new session

Whenever typing code directly into the command prompt, if a user types a single command that spans multiple lines, then the command prompt turns into a plus sign (+) to indicate that the command is not complete. The plus sign does not indicate any problem or error, but just reminds the user that the previous command is not yet complete. The cursor automatically places itself there so the user can enter commands.

In the electronic edition of this book, input syntax and output printouts from R will be color coded to help distinguish what the user should type in a script file from what results to expect. Input code will be written in blue teletype font. R output will be written in black teletype font. Error messages that R returns will be written in red teletype font. These colors correspond to the color coding R uses for input and output text. While the colors may not be visible in the print edition, the book's text also will distinguish inputs from outputs. Additionally, names of variables will be written in **bold**. Conceptual keywords from statistics and programming, as well as emphasized text, will be written in *italics*. Finally, when the meaning of a command is not readily apparent, identifying initials will be underlined and bolded in the text. For instance, the lm command stands for **l**inear **m**odel.

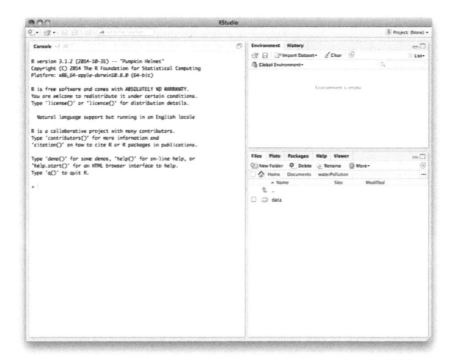

Fig. 1.3 Open window from an RStudio session

When writing R syntax on the command line or in a script file, users should bear a few important preliminaries in mind:

- Expressions and commands in R are case-sensitive. For example, the function var returns the variance of a variable: a simple function discussed in Chap. 4. By contrast, the VAR command from the vars library estimates a Vector Autoregression model—an advanced technique discussed in Chap. 9. Similarly, if a user names a dataset mydata, then it cannot be called with the names MyData, MyData, MYDATA, or myData. R would assume each of these names indicates a different meaning.
- Command lines do not need to be separated by any special character like a semicolon as in Limdep, SAS, or Gauss. A simple hard return will do.
- R ignores anything following the pound character (#) as a comment. This applies when using the command line or script files, but is especially useful when saving notes in script files for later use.
- An object name must start with an alphabetical character, but may contain numeric characters thereafter. A period may also form part of the name of an object. For example, x.1 is a valid name for an object in R.
- You can use the arrow keys on the keyboard to scroll back to previous commands. One push of the up arrow recalls the previously entered command and places it in

the command line. Each additional push of the arrow moves to a command prior to the one listed in the command line, while the down arrow calls the command following the one listed in the command line.

Aside from this handful of important rules, the command prompt in R tends to behave in an intuitive way, returning responses to input commands that could be easily guessed. For instance, at its most basic level R functions as a high-end calculator. Some of the key *arithmetic* commands are: addition (+), subtraction (-), multiplication (*), division (/), exponentiation (^), the modulo function (%%), and integer division (%/%). Parentheses ( ) specify the order of operations. For example, if we type the following input:

```
(3+5/78)^3*7
```

Then R prints the following output:

```
[1]  201.3761
```

As another example, we could ask R what the remainder is when dividing 89 by 13 using the modulo function:

```
89%%13
```

R then provides the following answer:

```
[1]  11
```

If we wanted R to perform integer division, we could type:

```
89%/%13
```

Our output answer to this is:

```
[1]  6
```

The `options` command allows the user to tweak attributes of the output. For example, the `digits` argument offers the option to adjust how many digits are displayed. This is useful, for instance, when considering how precisely you wish to present results on a table. Other useful built-in functions from algebra and trigonometry include: `sin(x)`, `cos(x)`, `tan(x)`, `exp(x)`, `log(x)`, `sqrt(x)`, and `pi`. To apply a few of these functions, first we can expand the number of digits printed out, and then ask for the value of the constant π:

```
options(digits=16)
pi
```

R accordingly prints out the value of π to 16 digits:

```
[1]  3.141592653589793
```

We also may use commands such as `pi` to insert the value of such a constant into a function. For example, if we wanted to compute the sine of a $\frac{\pi}{2}$ radians (or 90°) angle, we could type:

```
sin(pi/2)
```

R correctly prints that $\sin(\frac{\pi}{2}) = 1$:

```
[1]  1
```

1.3   Saving Input and Output

When analyzing data or programming in R, a user will never get into serious trouble provided he or she follows two basic rules:

1. Always leave the original datafiles intact. Any revised version of data should be written into a *new* file. If you are working with a particularly large and unwieldy dataset, then write a short program that winnows-down to what you need, save the cleaned file separately, and then write code that works with the new file.
2. Write all input code in a script that is saved. Users should usually avoid writing code directly into the console. This includes code for cleaning, recoding, and reshaping data as well as for conducting analysis or developing new programs.

If these two rules are followed, then the user can always recover his or her work up to the point of some error or omission. So even if, in data management, some essential information is dropped or lost, or even if a journal reviewer names a predictor that a model should add, the user can always retrace his or her steps. By calling the original dataset with the saved program, the user can make *minor* tweaks to the code to incorporate a new feature of analysis or recover some lost information. By contrast, if the original data are overwritten or the input code is not saved, then the user likely will have to restart the whole project from the beginning, which is a waste of time.

A *script file* in R is simply plain text, usually saved with the suffix .R. To create a new script file in R, simply choose *File→New Document* in the drop down menu to open the document. Alternatively, the console window shown in Fig. 1.2 shows an icon that looks like a blank page at the top of the screen (second icon from the right). Clicking on this will also create a new R script file. Once open, the normal *Save* and *Save As* commands from the *File* menu apply. To open an existing R script, choose *File→Open Document* in the drop down menu, or click the icon at the top of the screen that looks like a page with writing on it (third icon from the right in Fig. 1.2). When working with a script file, any code within the file can be executed in the console by simply highlighting the code of interest, and typing the keyboard shortcut Ctrl+R in Windows or Cmd+Return in Mac. Besides the default script file editor, more sophisticated text editors such as Emacs and RWinEdt also are available.

The product of any R session is saved in the *working directory*. The working directory is the default file path for all files the user wants to read in or write out to. The command getwd (meaning **get w**orking **d**irectory) will print R's current working directory, while setwd (**set w**orking **d**irectory) allows you to change the working directory as desired. Within a Windows machine the syntax for checking, and then setting, the working directory would look like this:

```
getwd()
setwd("C:/temp/")
```

This now writes any output files, be they data sets, figures, or printed output to the folder `temp` in the `C:` drive. Observe that R expects forward slashes to designate subdirectories, which contrasts from Windows's typical use of backslashes. Hence, specifying `C:/temp/` as the working directory points to `C:\temp\` in normal Windows syntax. Meanwhile for Mac or Unix, setting a working directory would be similar, and the path directory is printed exactly as these operating systems designate them with forward slashes:

```
setwd("/Volumes/flashdisk/temp")
```

Note that `setwd` can be called multiple times in a session, as needed. Also, specifying the full path for any file overrides the working directory.

To *save output* from your session in R, try the `sink` command. As a general computing term, a **sink** is an output point for a program where data or results are written out. In R, this term accordingly refers to a file that records all of our printed output. To save your session's ouput to the file `Rintro.txt` within the working directory type:

```
sink("Rintro.txt")
```

Alternatively, if we wanted to override the working directory, in Windows for instance, we could have instead typed:

```
sink("C:/myproject/code/Rintro.txt")
```

Now that we have created an output file, any output that normally would print to the console will instead print to the file `Rintro.txt`. (For this reason, in a first run of new code, it is usually advisable to allow output to print to the screen and then rerun the code later to print to a file.) The `print` command is useful for creating output that can be easily followed. For instance, the command:

```
print("The mean of variable x is...")
```

will print the following in the file `Rintro.txt`:

```
[1] "The mean of variable x is..."
```

Another useful printing command is the `cat` command (short for **cat**enate, to connect things together), which lets you mix objects in R with text. As a preview of simulation tools described in Chap. 11, let us create a variable named x by means of simulation:

```
x <- rnorm(1000)
```

By way of explanation: this syntax draws randomly 1000 times from a standard normal distribution and assigns the values to the vector x. Observe the arrow (`<-`), formed with a *less than* sign and a *hyphen*, which is R's assignment operator. Any time we assign something with the arrow (`<-`) the name on the left (x in this case) allows us to recall the result of the operation on the right (`rnorm(1000)` in this case).[3] Now we can print the mean of these 1000 draws (which should be close to 0 in this case) to our output file as follows:

```
cat("The mean of variable x is...", mean(x), "\n")
```

With this syntax, objects from R can be embedded into the statement you print. The character \n puts in a carriage return. You also can print any statistical output using the either print or cat commands. Remember, your output does not go to the log file unless you use one of the print commands. Another option is to simply copy and paste results from the R console window into Word or a text editor. To turn off the sink command, simply type:

```
sink()
```

1.4 Work Session Management

A key feature of R is that it is an *object-oriented* programming language. Variables, data frames, models, and outputs are all stored in memory as *objects*, or identified (and named) locations in memory with defined features. R stores in working memory any object you create using the name you define whenever you load data into memory or estimate a model. To l̲i̲st̲ the objects you have created in a session use either of the following commands:

```
objects()
ls()
```

To r̲em̲ove all the objects in R type:

```
rm(list=ls(all=TRUE))
```

As a rule, it is a good idea to use the rm command at the start of any new program. If the previous user saved his or her workspace, then they may have used objects sharing the same name as yours, which can create confusion.

To q̲uit R either close the console window or type:

```
q()
```

At this point, R will ask if you wish to save the workspace image. Generally, it is advisable not to do this, as starting with a clean slate in each session is more likely to prevent programming errors or confusion on the versions of objects loaded in memory.

Finally, in many R sessions, we will need to load *packages*, or batches of code and data offering additional functionality not written in R's base code. Throughout this book we will load several packages, particularly in Chap. 8, where

---

[3]The arrow (<-) is the traditional assignment operator, though a single equals sign (=) also can serve for assignments.

our focus will be on example packages written by prominent Political Scientists to implement cutting-edge methods. The necessary commands to load packages are install.packages, a command that automatically downloads and installs a package on a user's copy of R, and library, a command that loads the package in a given session. Suppose we wanted to install the package MCMCpack. This package provides tools for Bayesian modeling that we will use in Chap. 8. The form of the syntax for these commands is:

```
install.packages("MCMCpack")
library(MCMCpack)
```

Package installation is case and spelling sensitive. R will likely prompt you at this point to choose one of the CRAN mirrors from which to download this package: For faster downloading, users typically choose the mirror that is most geographically proximate. The install.packages command only needs to be run once per R installation for a particular package to be available on a machine. The library command needs to be run for every session that a user wishes to use the package. Hence, in the next session that we want to use MCMCpack, we need only type: library(MCMCpack).

1.5 Resources

Given the wide array of base functions that are available in R, much less the even wider array of functionality created by R packages, a book such as this cannot possibly address everything R is capable of doing. This book should serve as a resource introducing how a researcher can use R as a basic statistics program and offer some general pointers about the usage of packages and programming features. As questions emerge about topics not covered in this space, there are several other resources that may be of use:

- Within R, the *Help* pull down menu (also available by typing help.start() in the console) offers several manuals of use, including an "Introduction to R" and "Writing R Extensions." This also opens an HTML-based search engine of the help files.
- UCLA's Institute for Digital Research and Education offers several nice tutorials (http://www.ats.ucla.edu/stat/r/). The CRAN website also includes a variety of online manuals (http://www.cran.r-project.org/other-docs.html).
- Some nice interactive tutorials include swirl, which is a package you install in your own copy of R (more information: http://www.swirlstats.com/), and Try R, which is completed online (http://tryr.codeschool.com/).
- Within the R console, the commands ?, help(), and help.search() all serve to find documentation. For instance, ?lm would find the documentation for the linear model command. Alternatively, help.search("linear model") would search the documentation for a phrase.

- To search the internet for information, Rseek (http://www.rseek.org/, powered by Google) is a worthwhile search engine that searches only over websites focused on R.
- Finally, Twitter users reference R through the hashtag #rstats.

At this point, users should now have R installed on their machine, hold a basic sense of how commands are entered and output is generated, and recognize where to find the vast resources available for R users. In the next six chapters, we will see how R can be used to fill the role of a statistical analysis or econometrics software program.

1.6 Practice Problems

Each chapter will end with a few practice problems. If you have tested all of the code from the in-chapter examples, you should be able to complete these on your own. If you have not done so already, go ahead and install R on your machine for free and try the in-chapter code. Then try the following questions.

1. Compute the following in R:
   (a) -7×2^3
   (b) $\frac{8}{8^2+1}$
   (c) $\cos \pi$
   (d) $\sqrt{81}$
   (e) $\ln e^4$

2. What does the command `cor` do? Find documentation about it and describe what the function does.
3. What does the command `runif` do? Find documentation about it and describe what the function does.
4. Create a vector named `x` that consists of 1000 draws from a standard normal distribution, using code just like you see in Sect. 1.3. Create a second vector named `y` in the same way. Compute the correlation coefficient between the two vectors. What result do you get, and why do you get this result?
5. Get a feel for how to decide when add-on packages might be useful for you. Log in to http://www.rseek.org and look up what the `stringr` package does. What kinds of functionality does this package give you? When might you want to use it?

Chapter 2
Loading and Manipulating Data

We now turn to using R to conduct data analysis. Our first basic steps are simply to load data into R and to clean the data to suit our purposes. Data cleaning and recoding are an often tedious task of data analysis, but nevertheless are essential because miscoded data will yield erroneous results when a model is estimated using them. (In other words, garbage in, garbage out.) In this chapter, we will load various types of data using differing commands, view our data to understand their features, practice recoding data in order to clean them as we need to, merge data sets, and reshape data sets.

Our working example in this chapter will be a subset of Poe et al.'s (1999) Political Terror Scale data on human rights, which is an update of the data in Poe and Tate (1994). Whereas their complete data cover 1976–1993, we focus solely on the year 1993. The eight variables this dataset contains are:

country: A character variable listing the country by name.
democ: The country's score on the Polity III democracy scale. Scores range from 0 (least democratic) to 10 (most democratic).
sdnew: The U.S. State Department scale of political terror. Scores range from 1 (low state terrorism, fewest violations of personal integrity) to 5 (highest violations of personal integrity).
military: A dummy variable coded 1 for a military regime, 0 otherwise.
gnpcats: Level of per capita GNP in five categories: 1 = under \$1000, 2 = \$1000–\$1999, 3 = \$2000–\$2999, 4 = \$3000–\$3999, 5 = over \$4000.
lpop: Logarithm of national population.
civ_war: A dummy variable coded 1 if involved in a civil war, 0 otherwise.
int_war: A dummy variable coded 1 if involved in an international war, 0 otherwise.

Electronic supplementary material: The online version of this chapter (doi: 10.1007/978-3-319-23446-5_2) contains supplementary material, which is available to authorized users.

© Springer International Publishing Switzerland 2015
J.E. Monogan III, *Political Analysis Using R*, Use R!,
DOI 10.1007/978-3-319-23446-5_2

2.1 Reading in Data

Getting data into R is quite easy. There are three primary ways to import data: Inputting the data manually (perhaps written in a script file), reading data from a text-formatted file, and importing data from another program. Since it is a bit less common in Political Science, inputting data manually is illustrated in the examples of Chap. 10, in the context of creating vectors, matrices, and data frames. In this section, we focus on importing data from saved files.

First, we consider how to read in a delimited text file with the read.table command. R will read in a variety of delimited files. (For all the options associated with this command type ?read.table in R.) In text-based data, typically each line represents a unique observation and some designated delimiter separates each variable on the line. The default for read.table is a space-delimited file wherein any blank space designates differing variables. Since our Poe et al. data file, named hmnrghts.txt, is space-separated, we can read our file into R using the following line of code. This data file is available from the Dataverse named on page vii or the chapter content link on page 13. You may need to use setwd command introduced in Chap. 1 to point R to the folder where you have saved the data. After this, run the following code:

```
hmnrghts<-read.table("hmnrghts.txt",
    header=TRUE, na="NA")
```

Note: As was mentioned in the previous chapter, R allows the user to split a single command across multiple lines, which we have done here. Throughout this book, commands that span multiple lines will be distinguished with hanging indentation. Moving to the code itself, observe a few features: One, as was noted in the previous chapter, the left arrow symbol (<-) assigns our input file to an object. Hence, hmnrghts is the name we allocated to our data file, but we could have called it any number of things. Second, the first argument of the read.table command calls the name of the text file hmnrghts.txt. We could have preceded this argument with the file= option—and we would have needed to do so if we had not listed this as the first argument—but R recognizes that the file itself is normally the first argument this command takes. Third, we specified header=TRUE, which conveys that the first row of our text file lists the names of our variables. It is essential that this argument be correctly identified, or else variable names may be erroneously assigned as data or data as variable names.[1] Finally, within the text file, the characters NA are written whenever an observation of a variable is missing. The option na="NA" conveys to R that this is the data set's symbol for a missing value. (Other common symbols of missingness are a period (.) or the number -9999.)

The command read.table also has other important options. If your text file uses a delimiter other than a space, then this can be conveyed to R using the sep option. For instance, including sep="\t" in the previous command would have

---

[1] A closer look at the file itself will show that our header line of variable names actually has one fewer element than each line of data. When this is the case, R assumes that the first item on each line is an observation index. Since that is true in this case, our data are read correctly.

allowed us to read in a tab-separated text file, while `sep=","` would have allowed a comma-separated file. The commands `read.csv` and `read.delim` are alternate versions of `read.table` that merely have differing default values. (Particularly, `read.csv` is geared to **read** **c**omma-**s**eparated **v**alues files and `read.delim` is geared to **read** tab-**delim**ited files, though a few other defaults also change.) Another important option for these commands is `quote`. The defaults vary across these commands for which characters designate string-based variables that use alphabetic text as values, such as the name of the observation (e.g., country, state, candidate). The `read.table` command, by default, uses either single or double quotation marks around the entry in the text file. This would be a problem if double quotes were used to designate text, but apostrophes were in the text. To compensate, simply specify the option `quote = "\""` to only allow double quotes. (Notice the backslash to designate that the double-quote is an argument.) Alternatively, `read.csv` and `read.delim` both only allow double quotes by default, so specifying `quote = "\"'"` would allow either single or double quotes, or `quote = "\'"` would switch to single quotes. Authors also can specify other characters in this option, if need be.

Once you download a file, you have the option of specifying the full path directory in the command to open the file. Suppose we had saved `hmnrghts.txt` into the path directory `C:/temp/`, then we could load the file as follows:

```
hmnrghts <- read.table("C:/temp/hmnrghts.txt",
    header=TRUE, na="NA")
```

As was mentioned when we first loaded the file, another option would have been to use the `setwd` command to **set** the **w**orking **d**irectory, meaning we would not have to list the entire file path in the call to `read.table`. (If we do this, all input and output files will go to this directory, unless we specify otherwise.) Finally, in any GUI-based system (e.g., non-terminal), we could instead type:

```
hmnrghts<-read.table(file.choose(),header=TRUE,na="NA")
```

The `file.choose()` option will open a file browser allowing the user to locate and select the desired data file, which R will then assign to the named object in memory (`hmnrghts` in this case). This browser option is useful in interactive analysis, but less useful for automated programs.

Another format of text-based data is a *fixed width file*. Files of this format do not use a character to delimit variables within an observation. Instead, certain columns of text are consistently dedicated to a variable. Thus, R needs to know which columns define each variable to read in the data. The command for **read**ing a **f**ixed **w**idth **f**ile is `read.fwf`. As a quick illustration of how to load this kind of data, we will load a different dataset—roll call votes from the 113th United States Senate, the term running from 2013 to 2015.[2] This dataset will be revisited in a practice problem

---

[2]These data were gathered by Jeff Lewis and Keith Poole. For more information, see http://www.voteview.com/senate113.htm.

in Chap. 8. To open these data, start by downloading the file `sen113kh.ord` from
the Dataverse listed on page vii or the chapter content link on page 13. Then type:

```
senate.113<-read.fwf("sen113kh.ord",
      widths=c(3,5,2,2,8,3,1,1,11,rep(1,657)))
```

The first argument of `read.fwf` is the name of the file, which we draw from
a URL. (The file extension is `.ord`, but the format is plain text. Try opening
the file in Notepad or TextEdit just to get a feel for the formatting.) The second
argument, `widths`, is essential. For each variable, we must enter the number of
characters allocated to that variable. In other words, the first variable has three
characters, the second has five characters, and so on. This procedure should make
it clear that we must have a codebook for a fixed width file, or inputting the data
is a hopeless endeavor. Notice that the last component in the `widths` argument
is `rep(1,657)`. This means that our data set ends with 657 variables that are
one character long. These are the 657 votes that the Senate cast during that term of
Congress, with each variable recording whether each senator voted yea, nay, present,
or did not vote.

With any kind of data file, including fixed width, if the file itself does not have
names of the variables, we can add these in R. (Again, a good codebook is useful
here.) The commands `read.table`, `read.csv`, and `read.fwf` all include an
option called `col.names` that allows the user to name every variable in the dataset
when reading in the file. In the case of the Senate roll calls, though, it is easier for
us to name the variables afterwards as follows:

```
colnames(senate.113)[1:9]<-c("congress","icpsr","state.code",
      "cd","state.name","party","occupancy","attaining","name")
for(i in 1:657){colnames(senate.113)[i+9]<-paste("RC",i,sep="")}
```

In this case, we use the `colnames` command to set the names of the variables. To
the left of the arrow, by specifying `[1:9]`, we indicate that we are only naming the
first nine variables. To the right of the arrow, we use one of the *most fundamental*
commands in R: the c̲ombine command (`c`), which combines several elements into
a vector. In this case, our vector includes the names of the variables in text. On the
second line, we proceed to name the 657 roll call votes `RC1`, `RC2`, ..., `RC657`.
To save typing we make this assignment using a `for` loop, which is described in
more detail in Chap. 11. Within the `for` loop, we use the `paste` command, which
simply prints our text (`"RC"`) and the index number `i`, sep̲arated by nothing (hence
the empty quotes at the end). Of course, by default, R assigns generic variable names
(`V1`, `V2`, etc.), so a reader who is content to use generic names can skip this step,
if preferred. (Bear in mind, though, that if we name the first nine variables like we
did, the first roll call vote would be named `V10` without our applying a new name.)

2.1.1 Reading Data from Other Programs

Turning back to our human rights example, you also can import data from many other statistical programs. One of the most important libraries in R is the `foreign` package, which makes it very easy to bring in data from other statistical packages, such as SPSS, Stata, and Minitab.[3] As an alternative to the text version of the human rights data, we also could load a Stata-formatted data file, `hmnrghts.dta`.

Stata files generally have a file extension of **dta**, which is what the `read.dta` command refers to. (Similarly, `read.spss` will **read** an **SPSS**-formatted file with the `.sav` file extension.) To open our data in Stata format, we need to download the file `hmnrghts.dta` from the Dataverse linked on page vii or the chapter content linked on page 13. Once we save it to our hard drive, we can either set our working directory, list the full file path, or use the `file.choose()` command to access our data . For example, if we downloaded the file, which is named `hmnrghts.dta`, into our `C:\temp\` folder, we could open it by typing:

```
library(foreign)
setwd("C:/temp/")
hmnrghts.2 <- read.dta("hmnrghts.dta")
```

Any data in Stata format that you select will be converted to R format. One word of warning, by default if there are value labels on Stata-formatted data, R will import the labels as a string-formatted variable. If this is an issue for you, try importing the data without value labels to save the variables using the numeric codes. See the beginning of Chap. 7 for an example of the `convert.factors=FALSE` option. (One option for data sets that are not excessively large is to load two copies of a Stata dataset—one with the labels as text to serve as a codebook and another with numerical codes for analysis.) It is always good to see exactly how the data are formatted by inspecting the spreadsheet after importing with the tools described in Sect. 2.2.

2.1.2 Data Frames in R

R distinguishes between *vectors*, *lists*, *data frames*, and *matrices*. Each of these is an object of a different class in R. Vectors are indexed by length, and matrices are indexed by rows and columns. Lists are not pervasive to basic analyses, but are handy for complex storage and are often thought of as *generic* vectors where each element can be any class of object. (For example, a list could be a vector of

---

[3]The `foreign` package is so commonly used that it now downloads with any new R installation. In the unlikely event, though, that the package will not load with the `library` command, simply type `install.packages("foreign")` in the command prompt to download it. Alternatively, for users wishing to import data from *Excel*, two options are present: One is to save the Excel file in comma-separated values format and then use the `read.csv` command. The other is to install the `XLConnect` library and use the `readWorksheetFromFile` command.

model results, or a mix of data frames and maps.) A data frame is a matrix that R designates as a data set. With a data frame, the columns of the matrix can be referred to as variables. After reading in a data set, R will treat your data as a data frame, which means that you can refer to any variable within a data frame by adding $VARIABLENAME to the name of the data frame.[4] For example, in our human rights data we can print out the variable country in order to see which countries are in the dataset:

```
hmnrghts$country
```

Another option for calling variables, though an *inadvisable* one, is to use the attach command. R allows the user to load multiple data sets at once (in contrast to some of the commercially available data analysis programs). The attach command places one dataset at the forefront and allows the user to call directly the names of the variables without referring the name of the data frame. For example:

```
attach(hmnrghts)
country
```

With this code, R would recognize country in isolation as part of the attached dataset and print it just as in the prior example. The problem with this approach is that R may store objects in memory with the *same name* as some of the variables in the dataset. In fact, when recoding data the user should *always* refer to the data frame by name, otherwise R confusingly will create a copy of the variable in memory that is distinct from the copy in the data frame. For this reason, I generally recommend against attaching data. If, for some circumstance, a user feels attaching a data frame is unavoidable, then the user can conduct what needs to be done with the attached data and then use the detach command as soon as possible. This command works as would be expected, removing the designation of a working data frame and no longer allowing the user to call variables in isolation:

```
detach(hmnrghts)
```

2.1.3   Writing Out Data

To export data you are using in R to a text file, use the functions write.table or write.csv. Within the foreign library, write.dta allows the user to write out a Stata-formatted file. As a simple example, we can generate a matrix with four observations and six variables, counting from 1 to 24. Then we can write this to a comma-separated values file, a space-delimited text file, and a Stata file:

```
x <- matrix(1:24, nrow=4)
write.csv(x, file="sample.csv")
write.table(x, file="sample.txt")
write.dta(as.data.frame(x), file="sample.dta")
```

---

[4]More technically, data frames are objects of the S3 class. For all S3 objects, attributes of the object (such as variables) can be called with the dollar sign ($).

Note that the command `as.data.frame` converts matrices to data frames, a distinction described in the prior section. The command `write.dta` expects the object to be of the `data.frame` class. Making this conversion is unnecessary if the object is already formatted as data, rather than a matrix. To check your effort in saving the files, try removing x from memory with the command `rm(x)` and then restoring the data from one of the saved files.

To keep up with where the saved data files are going, the files we write out will be saved in our *working directory*. To **get** the **w**orking **d**irectory (that is, have R tell us what it is), simply type: `getwd()`. To change the working directory where output files will be written, we can **set** the **w**orking **d**irectory, using the same `setwd` command that we considered when opening files earlier. All subsequently saved files will be output into the specified directory, unless R is explicitly told otherwise.

2.2   Viewing Attributes of the Data

Once data are input into R, the first task should be to inspect the data and make sure they have loaded properly. With a relatively small dataset, we can simply print the whole data frame to the screen:

```
hmnrghts
```

Printing the entire dataset, of course, is not recommended or useful with large datasets. Another option is to look at the names of the variables and the first few lines of data to see if the data are structured correctly through a few observations. This is done with the `head` command:

```
head(hmnrghts)
```

For a quick list of the names of the variables in our dataset (which can also be useful if exact spelling or capitalization of variable names is forgotten) type:

```
names(hmnrghts)
```

A route to getting a comprehensive look at the data is to use the `fix` command:

```
fix(hmnrghts)
```

This presents the data in a spreadsheet allowing for a quick view of observations or variables of interest, as well as a chance to see that the data matrix loaded properly. An example of this data editor window that `fix` opens is presented in Fig. 2.1. The user has the option of editing data within the spreadsheet window that `fix` creates, though unless the revised data are written to a new file, there will be no permanent record of these changes.[5] Also, it is key to note that before continuing an R session

---

[5]The `View` command is similar to `fix`, but does not allow editing of observations. If you prefer to only be able to see the data without editing values (perhaps even by accidentally leaning on your keyboard), then `View` might be preferable.

country	democ	sdnew	military	gnpcats	lpop	civ_war	int_war
afganistan	NA	5	1	<1000	16.67	1	0
albania	8	2	0	<1000	15.04	0	0
algeria	0	5	0	1000–1999	17.12	0	0
angola	0	5	0	<1000	16.2	1	0
argentina	8	2	0	>4000	17.33	0	0
australia	10	1	0	>4000	16.69	0	0
austria	10	1	0	>4000	15.88	0	0
bahamas	NA	1	0	>4000	12.51	0	0
bahrain	0	2	0	>4000	13.25	0	0
bangladesh	9	3	0	<1000	18.62	0	0
barbados	NA	1	0	>4000	12.49	0	0
belgium	10	1	0	>4000	16.12	0	0
belize	NA	1	0	2000–2999	12.22	0	0
benin	9	1	0	<1000	15.46	0	0
bhutan	0	4	0	<1000	14.35	0	0
bolivia	8	3	0	<1000	15.9	0	0
botswana	10	1	0	2000–2999	14.15	0	0
brazil	10	4	0	3000–3999	18.89	0	0
brunei	NA	1	0	<NA>	12.54	0	0
bulgaria	8	2	0	1000–1999	16.01	0	0
burkina faso	0	2	1	<1000	16.1	0	0
burma	0	5	1	<1000	17.59	1	0
burundi	0	5	0	<1000	15.6	1	0
cameroon	0	3	0	<1000	16.36	0	0
canada	10	1	0	>4000	17.15	0	0
cape verde	NA	1	0	<1000	12.87	0	0

Fig. 2.1 R data editor opened with the `fix` command

with more commands, you must close the data editor window. The console is frozen as long as the `fix` window is open.

We will talk more about descriptive statistics in Chap. 4. In the meantime, though, it can be informative to see some of the basic descriptive statistics (including the mean, median, minimum, and maximum) as well as a count of the number of missing observations for each variable:

```
summary(hmnrghts)
```

Alternatively, this information can be gleaned for only a single variable, such as logged population:

```
summary(hmnrghts$lpop)
```

2.3 Logical Statements and Variable Generation

As we turn to cleaning data that are loaded in R, an essential toolset is the group of logical statements. Logical (or Boolean) statements in R are evaluated as to whether they are TRUE or FALSE. Table 2.1 summarizes the common logical operators in R.

Table 2.1 Logical operators in R

Operator	Means
<	Less than
<=	Less than or equal to
>	Greater than
>=	Greater than or equal to
==	Equal to
!=	Not equal to
&	And
|	Or

Note that the Boolean statement "is equal to" is designated by two equals signs (==), whereas a single equals sign (=) instead serves as an assignment operator.

To apply some of these Boolean operators from Table 2.1 in practice, suppose, for example, we wanted to know which countries were in a civil war and had an above average democracy score in 1993. We could generate a new variable in our working dataset, which I will call dem.civ (though the user may choose the name). Then we can view a table of our new variable and list all of the countries that fit these criteria:

```
hmnrghts$dem.civ <- as.numeric(hmnrghts$civ_war==1 &
    hmnrghts$democ>5.3)
table(hmnrghts$dem.civ)
hmnrghts$country[hmnrghts$dem.civ==1]
```

On the first line, hmnrghts$dem.civ defines our new variable within the human rights dataset.[6] On the right, we have a two-part Boolean statement: The first asks whether the country is in a civil war, and the second asks if the country's democracy score is higher than the average of 5.3. The ampersand (&) requires that both statements must simultaneously be true for the whole statement to be true. All of this is embedded within the as.numeric command, which encodes our Boolean output **as** a **numeric** variable. Specifically, all values of TRUE are set to 1 and FALSE values are set to 0. Such a coding is usually more convenient for modeling purposes. The next line gives us a table of the relative frequencies of 0s and 1s. It turns out that only four countries had above-average democracy levels and were involved in a civil war in 1993. To see which countries, the last line asks R to print the names of countries, but the square braces following the vector indicate which observations to print: Only those scoring 1 on this new variable.[7]

---

[6]Note, though, that any new variables we create, observations we drop, or variables we recode only change the data in *working memory*. Hence, our original data file on disk remains unchanged and therefore safe for recovery. Again, we must use one of the commands from Sect. 2.1.3 if we want to save a second copy of the data including all of our changes.

[7]The output prints the four country names, and four values of NA. This means in four cases, one of the two component statements was TRUE but the other statement could not be evaluated because the variable was missing.

Another sort of logical statement in R that can be useful is the is statement. These statements ask whether an observation or object meets some criterion. For example, is.na is a special case that asks whether an observation is missing or not. Alternatively, statements such as is.matrix or is.data.frame ask whether an object is of a certain class. Consider three examples:

```
table(is.na(hmnrghts$democ))
is.matrix(hmnrghts)
is.data.frame(hmnrghts)
```

The first statement asks for each observation whether the value of democracy is missing. The table command then aggregates this and informs us that 31 observations are missing. The next two statements ask whether our dataset hmnrghts is saved as a matrix, then as a data frame. The is.matrix statement returns FALSE, indicating that matrix-based commands will not work on our data, and the is.data.frame statement returns TRUE, which indicates that it is stored as a data frame. With a sense of logical statements in R, we can now apply these to the task of cleaning data.

2.4 Cleaning Data

One of the first tasks of data cleaning is deciding how to deal with *missing data*. R designates missing values with NA. It translates missing values from other statistics packages into the NA missing format. However a scholar deals with missing data, it is important to be mindful of the relative proportion of unobserved values in the data and what information may be lost. One (somewhat crude) option to deal with missingness would be to prune the dataset through listwise deletion, or removing every observation for which a single variable is not recorded. To create a new data set that prunes in this way, type:

```
hmnrghts.trim <- na.omit(hmnrghts)
```

This diminishes the number of observations from 158 to 127, so a tangible amount of information has been lost.

Most modeling commands in R give users the option of estimating the model over complete observations only, implementing listwise deletion on the fly. As a warning, listwise deletion is actually the default in the base commands for linear and generalized linear models, so data loss can fly under the radar if the user is not careful. Users with a solid background on regression-based modeling are urged to consider alternative methods for dealing with missing data that are superior to listwise deletion. In particular, the mice and Amelia libraries implement the useful technique of multiple imputation (for more information see King et al. 2001; Little and Rubin 1987; Rubin 1987).

If, for some reason, the user needs to redesignate missing values as having some numeric value, the is.na command can be useful. For example, if it were beneficial to list missing values as -9999, then these could be coded as:

```
hmnrghts$democ[is.na(hmnrghts$democ)]<- -9999
```

In other words, all values of democracy for which the value is missing will take on the value of −9999. *Be careful*, though, as R and all of its modeling commands will now regard the formerly missing value as a valid observation and will insert the misleading value of −9999 into any analysis. This sort of action should only be taken if it is required for data management, a special kind of model where strange values can be dummied-out, or the rare case where a missing observation actually can take on a meaningful value (e.g., a budget dataset where missing items represent a $0 expenditure).

2.4.1 Subsetting Data

In many cases, it is convenient to subset our data. This may mean that we only want observations of a certain type, or it may mean we wish to winnow-down the number of variables in the data frame, perhaps because the data include many variables that are of no interest. If, in our human rights data, we only wanted to focus on countries that had a democracy score from 6–10, we could call this subset dem.rights and create it as follows:

```
dem.rights <- subset(hmnrghts, subset=democ>5)
```

This creates a 73 observation subset of our original data. Note that observations with a *missing* (NA) value of **democ** will not be included in the subset. Missing observations also would be excluded if we made a greater than or equal to statement.[8]

As an example of variable selection, if we wanted to focus only on democracy and wealth, we could keep only these two variables and an index for all observations:

```
dem.wealth<-subset(hmnrghts,select=c(country, democ, gnpcats))
```

An alternative means of selecting which variables we wish to keep is to use a minus sign after the select option and list only the columns we wish to drop. For example, if we wanted all variables except the two indicators of whether a country was at war, we could write:

```
no.war <- subset(hmnrghts,select=-c(civ_war,int_war))
```

Additionally, users have the option of calling both the subset and select options if they wish to choose a subset of variables over a specific set of observations.

---

[8]This contrasts from programs like Stata, which treat missing values as positive infinity. In Stata, whether missing observations are included depends on the kind of Boolean statement being made. R is more consistent in that missing cases are always excluded.

2.4.2 Recoding Variables

A final aspect of data cleaning that often arises is the need to recode variables. This
may emerge because the functional form of a model requires a transformation of a
variable, such as a logarithm or square. Alternately, some of the values of the data
may be misleading and thereby need to be recoded as missing or another value. Yet
another possibility is that the variables from two datasets need to be coded on the
same scale: For instance, if an analyst fits a model with survey data and then makes
forecasts using Census data, then the survey and Census variables need to be coded
the same way.

For mathematical transformations of variables, the syntax is straightforward and
follows the form of the example below. Suppose we want the actual population of
each country instead of its logarithm:

```
hmnrghts$pop <- exp(hmnrghts$lpop)
```

Quite simply, we are applying the exponential function (exp) to a logged value to
recover the original value. Yet any type of mathematical operator could be substituted in for exp. A variable could be squared (^2), logged (log()), have
the square root taken (sqrt()), etc. Addition, subtraction, multiplication, and
division are also valid—either with a scalar of interest or with another variable.
Suppose we wanted to create an ordinal variable coded 2 if a country was in both a
civil war and an international war, 1 if it was involved in either, and 0 if it was not
involved in any wars. We could create this by adding the civil war and international
war variables:

```
hmnrghts$war.ord<-hmnrghts$civ_war+hmnrghts$int_war
```

A quick table of our new variable, however, reveals that no nations had both kinds
of conflict going in 1993.

Another common issue to address is when data are presented in an undesirable
format. Our variable **gnpcats** is actually coded as a text variable. However, we
may wish to recode this as a numeric ordinal variable. There are two means of
accomplishing this. The first, though taking several lines of code, can be completed
quickly with a fair amount of copy-and-paste:

```
hmnrghts$gnp.ord <- NA
hmnrghts$gnp.ord[hmnrghts$gnpcats=="<1000"]<-1
hmnrghts$gnp.ord[hmnrghts$gnpcats=="1000-1999"]<-2
hmnrghts$gnp.ord[hmnrghts$gnpcats=="2000-2999"]<-3
hmnrghts$gnp.ord[hmnrghts$gnpcats=="3000-3999"]<-4
hmnrghts$gnp.ord[hmnrghts$gnpcats==">4000"]<-5
```

Here, a blank variable was created, and then the values of the new variable filled-in
contingent on the values of the old using Boolean statements.

A second option for recoding the GNP data can be accomplished through John
Fox's **c**ompanion to **a**pplied **r**egression (car) library. As a user-written library, we
must download and install it before the first use. The installation of a library is
straightforward. First, type:

```
install.packages("car")
```

Once the library is installed (again, a step which need not be repeated unless R is reinstalled), the following lines will generate our recoded per capita GNP measure:

```
library(car)
hmnrghts$gnp.ord.2<-recode(hmnrghts$gnpcats,'"<1000"=1;
    "1000-1999"=2;"2000-2999"=3;"3000-3999"=4;">4000"=5')
```

Be careful that the `recode` command is delicate. Between the apostrophes, all of the reassignments from old values to new are defined separated by semicolons. A single space between the apostrophes will generate an error. Despite this, `recode` can save users substantial time on data cleaning. The basic syntax of `recode`, of course, could be used to create dummy variables, ordinal variables, or a variety of other recoded variables. So now two methods have created a new variable, each coded 1 to 5, with 5 representing the highest per capita GNP.

Another standard type of recoding we might want to do is to create a dummy variable that is coded as 1 if the observation meets certain conditions and 0 otherwise. For example, suppose instead of having categories of GNP, we just want to compare the highest category of GNP to all the others:

```
hmnrghts$gnp.dummy<-as.numeric(hmnrghts$gnpcats==">4000")
```

As with our earlier example of finding democracies involved in a civil war, here we use a logical statement and modify it with the `as.numeric` statement, which turns each `TRUE` into a 1 and each `FALSE` into a 0.

Categorical variables in R can be given a special designation as *factors*. If you designate a categorical variable as a factor, R will treat it as such in statistical operation and create dummy variables for each level when it is used in a regression. If you import a variable with no numeric coding, R will automatically call the variable a *character* vector, and convert the character vector into a factor in most analysis commands. If we prefer, though, we can designate that a variable is a factor ahead of time and open up a variety of useful commands. For example, we can designate `country` as a factor:

```
hmnrghts$country <- as.factor(hmnrghts$country)
levels(hmnrghts$country)
```

Notice that R allows the user to put the same quantity (in this case, the variable **country**) on both sides of an assignment operator. This recursive assignment takes the old values of a quantity, makes the right-hand side change, and then replaces the new values into the same place in memory. The `levels` command reveals to us the different recorded values of the factor.

To change which level is the first level (e.g., to change which category R will use as the reference category in a regression) use the `relevel` command. The following code sets "united states" as the reference category for **country**:

```
hmnrghts$country<-relevel(hmnrghts$country,"united states")
levels(hmnrghts$country)
```

Now when we view the levels of the factor, "united states" is listed as the first level, and the first level is always our reference group.

2.5 Merging and Reshaping Data

Two final tasks that are common to data management are merging data sets and reshaping panel data. As we consider examples of these two tasks, let us consider an update of Poe et al.'s (1999) data: Specifically, Gibney et al. (2013) have continued to code data for the Political Terror Scale. We will use the 1994 and 1995 waves of the updated data. The variables in these waves are:

Country: A character variable listing the country by name.
COWAlpha: Three-character country abbreviation from the Correlates of War dataset.
COW: Numeric country identification variable from the Correlates of War dataset.
WorldBank: Three-character country abbreviation used by the World Bank.
Amnesty.1994/Amnesty.1995: Amnesty International's scale of political terror. Scores range from 1 (low state terrorism, fewest violations of personal integrity) to 5 (highest violations of personal integrity).
StateDept.1994/StateDept.1995: The U.S. State Department scale of political terror. Scores range from 1 (low state terrorism, fewest violations of personal integrity) to 5 (highest violations of personal integrity).

For the last two variables, the name of the variable depends on which wave of data is being studied, with the suffix indicating the year. Notice that these data have four identification variables: This is designed explicitly to make these data easier for researchers to use. Each index makes it easy for a researcher to link these political terror measures to information provided by either the World Bank or the Correlates of War dataset. This should show how ubiquitous the act of merging data is to Political Science research.

To this end, let us practice *merging data*. In general, merging data is useful when the analyst has two separate data frames that contain information about the same observations. For example, if a Political Scientist had one data frame with economic data by country and a second data frame containing election returns by country, the scholar might want to merge the two data sets to link economic and political factors within each country. In our case, suppose we simply wanted to link each country's political terror score from 1994 to its political terror score from 1995. First, download the data sets `pts1994.csv` and `pts1995.csv` from the Dataverse on page vii or the chapter content link on page 13. As before, you may need to use `setwd` to point R to the folder where you have saved the data. After this, run the following code to load the relevant data:

```
hmnrghts.94<-read.csv("pts1994.csv")
hmnrghts.95<-read.csv("pts1995.csv")
```

These data are comma separated, so `read.csv` is the best command in this case.

If we wanted to take a look at the first few observations of our 1994 wave, we could type `head(hmnrghts.94)`. This will print the following:

	Country	COWAlpha	COW	WorldBank
1	United States	USA	2	USA
2	Canada	CAN	20	CAN
3	Bahamas	BHM	31	BHS
4	Cuba	CUB	40	CUB
5	Haiti	HAI	41	HTI
6	Dominican Republic	DOM	42	DOM

	Amnesty.1994	StateDept.1994
1	1	NA
2	1	1
3	1	2
4	3	3
5	5	4
6	2	2

Similarly, head(hmnrghts.95) will print the first few observations of our 1995 wave:

	Country	COWAlpha	COW	WorldBank
1	United States	USA	2	USA
2	Canada	CAN	20	CAN
3	Bahamas	BHM	31	BHS
4	Cuba	CUB	40	CUB
5	Haiti	HAI	41	HTI
6	Dominican Republic	DOM	42	DOM

	Amnesty.1995	StateDept.1995
1	1	NA
2	NA	1
3	1	1
4	4	3
5	2	3
6	2	2

As we can see from our look at the top of each data frame, the data are ordered similarly in each case, and our four index variables have the same name in each respective data set. We only need one index to merge our data, and the other three are redundant. For this reason, we can drop three of the index variables from the 1995 data:

```
hmnrghts.95<-subset(hmnrghts.95,
    select=c(COW,Amnesty.1995,StateDept.1995))
```

We opted to delete the three text indices in order to merge on a numeric index. This choice is arbitrary, however, because R has no problem merging on a character variable either. (Try replicating this exercise by merging on COWAlpha, for example.)

To combine our 1994 and 1995 data, we now turn to the merge command.[9] We type:

```
hmnrghts.wide<-merge(x=hmnrghts.94,y=hmnrghts.95,by=c("COW"))
```

Within this command, the option x refers to one dataset, while y is the other. Next to the by option, we name an identification variable that uniquely identifies each observation. The by command actually allows users to name multiple variables if several are needed to uniquely identify each observation: For example, if a researcher was merging data where the unit of analysis was a country-year, a country variable and a year variable might be essential to identify each row uniquely. In such a case the syntax might read, by=c("COW","year"). As yet another option, if the two datasets had the same index, but the variables were named differently, R allows syntax such as, by.x=c("COW"), by.y=c("cowCode"), which conveys that the differently named index variables are the name.

Once we have merged our data, we can preview the finished product by typing head(hmnrghts.wide). This prints:

```
  COW                 Country COWAlpha WorldBank Amnesty.1994
1   2           United States      USA       USA            1
2  20                  Canada      CAN       CAN            1
3  31                 Bahamas      BHM       BHS            1
4  40                    Cuba      CUB       CUB            3
5  41                   Haiti      HAI       HTI            5
6  42      Dominican Republic      DOM       DOM            2
  StateDept.1994 Amnesty.1995 StateDept.1995
1             NA            1             NA
2              1           NA              1
3              2            1              1
4              3            4              3
5              4            2              3
6              2            2              2
```

As we can see, the 1994 and 1995 scores for Amnesty and StateDept are recorded in one place for each country. Hence, our merge was successful. By default, R excludes any observation from either dataset that does not have a *linked* observation (e.g., equivalent value) from the other data set. So if you use the defaults and the new dataset includes the same number of rows as the two old datasets, then all observations were linked and included. For instance, we could type:

```
dim(hmnrghts.94); dim(hmnrghts.95); dim(hmnrghts.wide)
```

This would quickly tell us that we have 179 observations in both of the inputs, as well as the output dataset, showing we did not lose any observations. Other options within merge are all.x, all.y, and all, which allow you to specify whether to force

---

[9]Besides the merge, the dplyr package offers several data-joining commands that you also may find of use, depending on your needs.

the inclusion of all observations from the dataset x, the dataset y, and from either dataset, respectively. In this case, R would encode NA values for observations that did not have a linked case in the other dataset.

As a final point of data management, sometimes we need to *reshape* our data. In the case of our merged data set, hmnrghts.wide, we have created a panel data set (e.g., a data set consisting of repeated observations of the same individuals) that is in *wide format*. Wide format means that each row in our data defines an individual of study (a country) while our repeated observations are stored in separate variables (e.g., Amnesty.1994 and Amnesty.1995 record Amnesty International scores for two separate years). In most models of panel data, we need our data to be in *long format*, or stacked format. Long format means that we need two index variables to identify each row, one for the individual (e.g., country) and one for time of observation (e.g., year). Meanwhile, each variable (e.g., Amnesty) will only use one column. R allows us to reshape our data from wide to long, or from long to wide. Hence, whatever the format of our data, we can reshape it to our needs.

To reshape our political terror data from wide format to long, we use the reshape command:

```
hmnrghts.long<-reshape(hmnrghts.wide,varying=c("Amnesty.1994",
    "StateDept.1994","Amnesty.1995","StateDept.1995"),
    timevar="year",idvar="COW",direction="long",sep=".")
```

Within the command, the first argument is the name of the data frame we wish to reshape. The varying term lists all of the variables that represent repeated observations over time. *Tip:* Be sure that repeated observations of the same variable have the same *prefix* name (e.g., Amnesty or StateDept) and then the *suffix* (e.g., 1994 or 1995) consistently reports time. The timevar term allows us to specify the name of our new time index, which we call year. The idvar term lists the variable that uniquely identifies individuals (countries, in our case). With direction we specify that we want to convert our data into long format. Lastly, the sep command offers R a cue of what character separates our prefixes and suffixes in the repeated observation variables: Since a period (.) separates these terms in each of our Amnesty and StateDept variables, we denote that here.

A preview of the result can be seen by typing head(hmnrghts.long). This prints:

```
          COW            Country COWAlpha WorldBank year
2.1994      2      United States      USA       USA 1994
20.1994    20             Canada      CAN       CAN 1994
31.1994    31            Bahamas      BHM       BHS 1994
40.1994    40               Cuba      CUB       CUB 1994
41.1994    41              Haiti      HAI       HTI 1994
42.1994    42 Dominican Republic      DOM       DOM 1994
          Amnesty StateDept
2.1994          1        NA
20.1994         1         1
```

```
31.1994          1              2
40.1994          3              3
41.1994          5              4
42.1994          2              2
```

Notice that we now have only one variable for `Amnesty` and one for `StateDept`. We now have a new variable named `year`, so between `COW` and `year`, each row uniquely identifies each country-year. Since the data are naturally sorted, the top of our data only show 1994 observations. Typing `head(hmnrghts.long[hmnrghts.long$year==1995,])` shows us the first few 1995 observations:

```
            COW                 Country COWAlpha WorldBank year
2.1995       2         United States       USA       USA 1995
20.1995     20                Canada       CAN       CAN 1995
31.1995     31               Bahamas       BHM       BHS 1995
40.1995     40                  Cuba       CUB       CUB 1995
41.1995     41                 Haiti       HAI       HTI 1995
42.1995     42 Dominican Republic        DOM       DOM 1995
            Amnesty StateDept
2.1995            1        NA
20.1995          NA         1
31.1995           1         1
40.1995           4         3
41.1995           2         3
42.1995           2         2
```

As we can see, all of the information is preserved, now in long (or stacked) format.

As a final illustration, suppose we had started with a data set that was in long format and wanted one in wide format. To try this, we will reshape `hmnrghts.long` and try to recreate our original wide data set. To do this, we type:

```
hmnrghts.wide.2<-reshape(hmnrghts.long,
    v.names=c("Amnesty","StateDept"),
    timevar="year",idvar="COW",direction="wide",sep=".")
```

A few options have now changed: We now use the `v.names` command to indicate the variables that include repeated observations. The `timevar` parameter now needs to be a variable within the dataset, just as `idvar` is, in order to separate individuals from repeated time points. Our `direction` term is now `wide` because we want to convert these data into wide format. Lastly, the `sep` command specifies the character that R will use to separate prefixes from suffixes in the final form. By typing `head(hmnrghts.wide.2)` into the console, you will now see that this new dataset recreates the original wide dataset.

This chapter has covered the variety of means of importing and exporting data in R. It also has discussed data management issues such as missing values, subsetting, recoding data, merging data, and reshaping data. With the capacity to clean and manage data, we now are ready to start analyzing our data. We next proceed to data visualization.

2.6 Practice Problems

As a practice dataset, we will download and open a subset of the 2004 American
National Election Study used by Hanmer and Kalkan (2013). This dataset is named
hanmerKalkanANES.dta, and it is available from the Dataverse referenced on
page vii or in the chapter content link on page 13. These data are in Stata format, so
be sure to load the correct library and use the correct command when opening. (*Hint:*
When using the proper command, be sure to specify the convert.factors=F
option within it to get an easier-to-read output.) The variables in this dataset all
relate to the 2004 U.S. presidential election, and they are: a respondent identification
number (**caseid**), retrospective economic evaluations (**retecon**), assessment of George
W. Bush's handling of the war in Iraq (**bushiraq**), an indicator for whether the
respondent voted for Bush (**presvote**), partisanship on a seven-point scale (**partyid**),
ideology on a seven-point scale (**ideol7b**), an indicator of whether the respondent is
white (**white**), an indicator of whether the respondent is female (**female**), age of the
respondent (**age**), level of education on a seven-point scale (**educ1_7**), and income on
a 23-point scale (**income**). (The variable **exptrnout2** can be ignored.)

1. Once you have loaded the data, do the following to check your work:

    (a) If you ask R to return the variable names, what does the list say? Is it correct?
    (b) Using the head command, what do the first few lines look like?
    (c) If you use the fix command, do the data look like an appropriate spreadsheet?

2. Use the summary command on the whole data set. What can you learn immediately? How many missing observations do you have?
3. Try subsetting the data in a few ways:

    (a) Create a copy of the dataset that removes all missing observations with listwise
        deletion. How many observations remain in this version?
    (b) Create a second copy that only includes the respondent identification number,
        retrospective economic evaluations, and evaluation of Bush's handling of Iraq.

4. Create a few new variables:

    (a) The seven-point partisanship scale (**partyid**) is coded as follows: 0 = Strong
        Democrat, 1 = Weak Democrat, 2 = Independent Leaning Democrat, 3 =
        Independent No Leaning, 4 = Independent Leaning Republican, 5 = Weak
        Republican, and 6 = Strong Republican. Create two new indicator variables.
        The first should be coded 1 if the person identifies as Democrat in any way
        (including independents who lean Democratic), and 0 otherwise. The second
        new variable should be coded 1 if the person identifies as Republican in any
        way (including independents who lean Republican), and 0 otherwise. For each
        of these two new variables, what does the summary command return for
        them?
    (b) Create a new variable that is the squared value of the respondent's age in years.
        What does the summary command return for this new variable?
    (c) Create a new version of the income variable that has only four categories.
        The first category should include all values of **income** than range from 1–12,

the second from 13–17, the third from 18–20, and the last from 21–23. Use the `table` command to see the frequency of each category.

(d) <u>Bonus:</u> Use the `table` command to compare the 23-category version of income to the four-category version of income. Did you code the new version correctly?

Chapter 3
Visualizing Data

Visually presenting data and the results of models has become a centerpiece of modern political analysis. Many of Political Science's top journals, including the *American Journal of Political Science*, now ask for figures in lieu of tables whenever both can convey the same information. In fact, Kastellec and Leoni (2007) make the case that figures convey empirical results better than tables. Cleveland (1993) and Tufte (2001) wrote two of the leading volumes that describe the elements of good quantitative visualization, and Yau (2011) has produced a more recent take on graphing. Essentially these works serve as style manuals for graphics.[1] Beyond the suggestions these scholars offer for the sake of readers, viewing one's own data visually conveys substantial information about the data's univariate, bivariate, and multivariate features: Does a variable appear skewed? Do two variables substantively appear to correlate? What is the proper functional relationship between variables? How does a variable change over space or time? Answering these questions for oneself as an analyst and for the reader generally can raise the quality of analysis presented to the discipline.

On the edge of this graphical movement in quantitative analysis, R offers state-of-the-art data and model visualization. Many of the commercial statistical programs have tried for years to catch up to R's graphical capacities. This chapter showcases these capabilities, turning first to the plot function that is automatically available as part of the base package. Second, we discuss some of the other graphing commands offered in the base library. Finally, we turn to the lattice library, which allows the user to create Trellis Graphics—a framework for visualization

---

Electronic supplementary material: The online version of this chapter (doi: 10.1007/978-3-319-23446-5_3) contains supplementary material, which is available to authorized users.

[1] Other particularly key historical figures in the development of graphical measures include Halley (1686), Playfair (1786/2005), and Tukey (1977). A more comprehensive history is presented by Beniger and Robyn (1978).

© Springer International Publishing Switzerland 2015
J.E. Monogan III, *Political Analysis Using R*, Use R!,
DOI 10.1007/978-3-319-23446-5_3

developed by Becker, Cleveland, and others to put Cleveland's (1993) suggestions into practice. Although space does not permit it here, users are also encouraged to look up the ggplot2 packages, which offers additional graphing options. Chang (2013), in particular, offers several examples of graphing with ggplot2.

In this chapter, we work with two example datasets. The first is on health lobbying in the 50 American states, with a specific focus on the proportion of firms from the health finance industry that are registered to lobby (Lowery et al. 2008). A key predictor variable is the total number of health finance firms open for business, which includes organizations that provide health plans, business services, employer health coalitions, and insurance. The dataset also includes the lobby participation rate by state, or number of lobbyists as a proportion of the number of firms, not only in health finance but for all health-related firms and in six other subareas. These are cross-sectional data from the year 1997. The complete variable list is as follows:

stno: Numeric index from 1–50 that orders the states alphabetically.

raneyfolded97: Folded Ranney Index of state two-party competition in 1997.[2]

healthagenda97: Number of bills related to health considered by the state legislature in 1997.

supplybusiness: Number of health finance establishments.

businesssupplysq: Squared number of health finance establishments.

partratebusness: Lobby participation rate for health finance—number of registrations as a percentage of the number of establishments.

predictbuspartrate: Prediction of health finance participation rate as a quadratic function of number of health finance establishments. (No control variables in the prediction.)

partratetotalhealth: Lobby participation rate for all of health care (including seven subareas).

partratedpc: Lobby participation rate for direct patient care.

partratepharmprod: Lobby participation rate for drugs and health products.

partrateprofessionals: Lobby participation rate for health professionals.

partrateadvo: Lobby participation rate for health advocacy.

partrategov: Lobby participation rate for local government.

rnmedschoolpartrate: Lobby participation rate for health education.

Second, we analyze Peake and Eshbaugh-Soha's (2008) data on the number of television news stories related to energy policy in a given month. In this data frame, the variables are:

Date: Character vector of the month and year observed.

Energy: Number of energy-related stories broadcast on nightly television news by month.

Unemploy: The unemployment rate by month.

Approval: Presidential approval by month.

oilc: Price of oil per barrel.

---

[2]Nebraska and North Carolina are each missing observations of the Ranney index.

freeze1: An indicator variable coded 1 during the months of August–November 1971, when wage and price freezes were imposed. Coded 0 otherwise.

freeze2: An indicator variable coded 1 during the months of June–July 1973, when price wage and price freezes were imposed. Coded 0 otherwise.

embargo: An indicator variable coded 1 during the months of October 1973–March 1974, during the Arab oil embargo. Coded 0 otherwise.

hostages: An indicator variable coded 1 during the months of November 1979–January 1981, during the Iran hostage crisis. Coded 0 otherwise.

Presidential speeches: Additional indicators are coded as 1 during the month a president delivered a major address on energy policy, and 0 otherwise. The indicators for the respective speeches are called: **rmn1173, rmn1173a, grf0175, grf575, grf575a, jec477, jec1177, jec479, grf0175s, jec479s,** and **jec477s**.

3.1   Univariate Graphs in the `base` Package

As a first look at our data, displaying a single variable graphically can convey a sense of the distribution of the data, including its mode, dispersion, skew, and kurtosis. The `lattice` library actually offers a few more commands for univariate visualization than `base` does, but we start with the major built-in univariate commands. Most graphing commands in the `base` package call the `plot` function, but `hist` and `boxplot` are noteworthy exceptions.

The `hist` command is useful to simply gain an idea of the relative frequency of several common values. We start by loading our data on energy policy television news coverage. Then we create a **hist**ogram of this time series of monthly story counts with the `hist` command. First, download Peake and Eshbaugh-Soha's data on energy policy coverage, the file named `PESenergy.csv`. The file is available from the Dataverse named on page vii or the chapter content link on page 33. You may need to use `setwd` to point R to the folder where you have saved the data. After this, run the following code:

```
pres.energy<-read.csv("PESenergy.csv")
hist(pres.energyEnergy,xlab="Television Stories",main="")
abline(h=0,col='gray60')
box()
```

The result this code produces is presented in Fig. 3.1. In this code, we begin by reading Peake and Eshbaugh-Soha's (2008) data. The data file itself is a comma-separated values file with a header row of variable names, so the defaults of `read.csv` suit our purposes. Once the data are loaded, we plot a histogram of our variable of interest using the `hist` command: `pres.energy$Energy` calls the variable of interest from its data frame. We use the `xlab` option, which allows us to define the label R prints on the horizontal axis. Since this axis shows us the values of the variable, we simply wish to see the phrase "Television Stories," describing in brief what these numbers mean. The `main` option defines a title printed over the top of the figure. In this case, the only way to impose a blank title is to include quotes with no content between them. A neat feature of plotting in the `base` package is

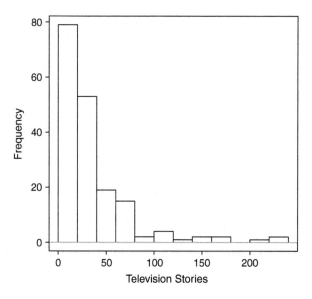

Fig. 3.1 Histogram of the monthly count of television news stories related to energy

that a few commands can add additional information to a plot that has already been drawn. The `abline` command is a flexible and useful tool. (The name **a-b line** refers to the linear formula $y = a + bx$. Hence, this command can draw lines with a slope and intercept, or it can draw a horizontal or vertical line.) In this case, `abline` adds a horizontal line along the 0 point on the vertical axis, hence `h=0`. This is added to clarify where the base of the bars in the figure is. Finally, the `box()` command encloses the whole figure in a box, often useful in printed articles for clarifying where graphing space ends and other white space begins. As the histogram shows, there is a strong concentration of observations at and just above 0, and a clear positive skew to the distribution. (In fact, these data are reanalyzed in Fogarty and Monogan (2014) precisely to address some of these data features and discuss useful means of analyzing time-dependent media counts.)

Another univariate graph is a box-and-whisker plot. R allows us to obtain this solely for the single variable, or for a subset of the variable based on some other available measure. First drawing this for a single variable:

```
boxplot(pres.energy$Energy,ylab="Television Stories")
```

The result of this is presented in panel (a) of Fig. 3.2. In this case, the values of the monthly counts are on the vertical axis; hence, we use the `ylab` option to label the vertical axis (or **y**-axis **lab**el) appropriately. In the figure, the bottom of the box represents the first quartile value (25th percentile), the large solid line inside the box represents the median value (second quartile, 50th percentile), and the top of the box represents the third quartile value (75th percentile). The whiskers, by default, extend to the lowest and highest values of the variable that are no more than 1.5 times the interquartile range (or difference between third and first quartiles) away

from the box. The purpose of the whiskers is to convey the range over which the
bulk of the data fall. Data falling outside of this range are portrayed as dots at their
respective values. This boxplot fits our conclusion from the histogram: small values
including 0 are common, and the data have a positive skew.

Box-and-whisker plots also can serve to offer a sense of the conditional
distribution of a variable. For our time series of energy policy coverage, the first
major event we observe is Nixon's November 1973 speech on the subject. Hence,
we might create a simple indicator where the first 58 months of the series (through
October 1973) are coded 0, and the remaining 122 months of the series (November
1973 onward) are coded 1. Once we do this, the boxplot command allows us to
condition on a variable:

```
pres.energy$post.nixon<-c(rep(0,58),rep(1,122))
boxplot(pres.energy$Energy~pres.energy$post.nixon,
    axes=F,ylab="Television Stories")
axis(1,at=c(1,2),labels=c("Before Nov. 1973",
    "After Nov. 1973"))
axis(2)
box()
```

This output is presented in panel (b) of Fig. 3.2. The first line of code defines our
pre v. post November 1973 variable. Notice here that we again define a vector
with c. Within c, we use the rep command (for **rep**eat). So rep(0,58) produces
58 zeroes, and rep(1,122) produces 122 ones. The second line draws our
boxplots, but we add two important caveats relative to our last call to boxplot:
First, we list pres.energy$Energy~pres.energy$post.nixon as our
data argument. The argument before the tilde (~) is the variable for which we want
the distribution, and the argument afterward is the conditioning variable. Second,
we add the axes=F command. (We also could write axes=FALSE, but R accepts
F as an abbreviation.) This gives us more control over how the horizontal and

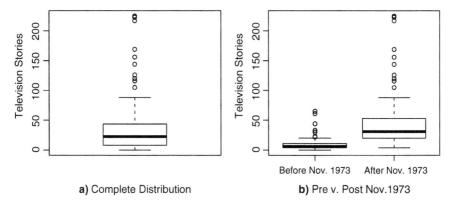

a) Complete Distribution   b) Pre v. Post Nov.1973

Fig. 3.2 Box-and-whisker plots of the distribution of the monthly count of television new stories
related to energy. Panel (**a**) shows the complete distribution, and panel (**b**) shows the distributions
for the subsets before and after November 1973

vertical axes are presented. In the subsequent command, we add axis 1 (the bottom
horizontal axis), adding text labels at the tick marks of 1 and 2 to describe the values
of the conditioning variable. Afterward, we add axis 2 (the left vertical axis), and a
box around the whole figure. Panel (b) of Fig. 3.2 shows that the distribution before
and after this date is fundamentally different. Much smaller values persist before
Nixon's speech, while there is a larger mean and a greater spread in values afterward.
Of course, this is only a first look and the effect of Nixon's speech is confounded
with a variety of factors—such as the price of oil, presidential approval, and the
unemployment rate—that contribute to this difference.

3.1.1 Bar Graphs

Bar graphs can be useful whenever we wish to illustrate the value some statistic
takes for a variety of groups as well as for visualizing the relative proportions of
nominal or ordinally measured data. For an example of barplots, we turn now to
the other example data set from this chapter, on health lobbying in the 50 American
states. Lowery et al. offer a bar graph of the means across all states of the lobbying
participation rate—or number of lobbyists as a percentage of number of firms—
for all health lobbyists and for seven subgroups of health lobbyists (2008, Fig. 3).
We can recreate that figure in R by taking the means of these eight variables and
then applying the `barplot` function to the set of means. First we must load
the data. To do this, download Lowery et al.'s data on lobbying, the file named
`constructionData.dta`. The file is available from the Dataverse named on
page vii or the chapter content link on page 33. Again, you may need to use `setwd`
to point R to the folder where you have saved the data. Since these data are in Stata
format, we must use the `foreign` library and then the `read.dta` command:

```
library(foreign)
health.fin<-read.dta("constructionData.dta")
```

To create the actual figure itself, we can create a subset of our data that only
includes the eight predictors of interest and then use the `apply` function to obtain
the mean of each variable.

```
part.rates<-subset(health.fin,select=c(
     partratetotalhealth,partratedpc,
     partratepharmprod,partrateprofessionals,partrateadvo,
     partratebusness,partrategov,rnmedschoolpartrate))
lobby.means<-apply(part.rates,2,mean)
names(lobby.means)<-c("Total Health Care",
     "Direct Patient Care","Drugs/Health Products",
     "Health Professionals","Health Advocacy","
     Health Finance","Local Government","Health Education")
```

In this case, `part.rates` is our subsetted data frame that only includes the eight
lobby participation rates of interest. On the last line, the `apply` command allows
us to take a matrix or data frame (`part.rates`) and apply a function of interest
(`mean`) to either the rows or the columns of the data frame. We want the mean of

each variable, and the columns of our data set represent the variables. The 2 that is
the second component of this command therefore tells apply that we want to apply
mean to the *columns* of our data. (By contrast, an argument of 1 would apply to the
rows. Row-based computations would be handy if we needed to compute some new
quantity for each of the 50 states.) If we simply type lobby.means into the R
console now, it will print the eight means of interest for us. To set up our figure
in advance, we can attach an English-language name to each quantity that will be
reported in our figure's margin. We do this with the names command, and then
assign a vector with a name for each quantity.

To actually draw our bar graph, we use the following code:

```
par(mar=c(5.1, 10 ,4.1 ,2.1))
barplot(lobby.means,xlab="Percent Lobby Registration",
     xlim=c(0,26),horiz=T,cex.names=.8,las=1)
text(x=lobby.means,y=c(.75,1.75,3,4.25,5.5,6.75,8,9),
     labels=paste(round(lobby.means,2)),pos=4)
box()
```

The results are plotted in Fig. 3.3. The first line calls the par command, which
allows the user to change a wide array of defaults in the graphing space. In our

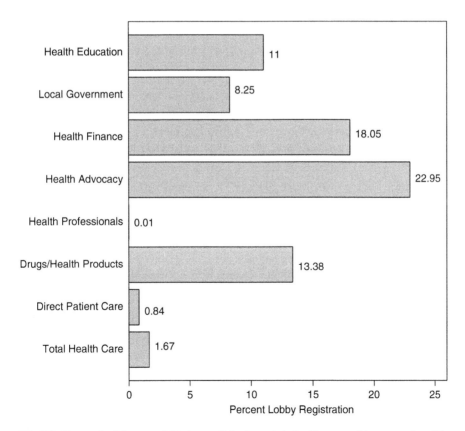

Fig. 3.3 Bar graph of the mean lobbying participation rate in health care and in seven sub-guilds
across the 50 U.S. states, 1997

case, we need a bigger left margin, so we used the `mar` option to change this, setting the second value to the relatively large value of 10. (In general, the margins are listed as bottom, left, top, then right.) Anything adjusted with `par` is reset to the defaults after the plotting window (or device, if writing directly to a file) is closed. Next, we actually use the `barplot` command. The main argument is `lobby.means`, which is the vector of variable means. The default for `barplot` is to draw a graph with vertical lines. In this case, though, we set the option `horiz=T` to get horizontal bars. We also use the options `cex.names` (**c**haracter **ex**pansion for axis **names**) and `las=1` (**l**abel **a**xis **s**tyle) to shrink our bar labels to 80 % of their default size and force them to print horizontally, respectively.[3] The `xlab` command allows us to describe the variable for which we are showing the means, and the `xlim` (**x**-axis **lim**its) command allows us to set the space of our horizontal axis. Finally, we use the `text` command to print the mean for each lobby registration rate at the end of the bar. The `text` command is useful any time we wish to add text to a graph, be these numeric values or text labels. This command takes x coordinates for its position along the horizontal axis, y coordinates for its position along the vertical axis, and `labels` values for the text to print at each spot. The `pos=4` option specifies to print the text to the right of the given point (alternatively 1, 2, and 3 would specify below, left, and above, respectively), so that our text does not overlap with the bar.

3.2 The `plot` Function

We turn now to `plot`, the workhorse graphical function in the `base` package. The `plot` command lends itself naturally to bivariate plots. To see the total sum of arguments that one can call using `plot`, type `args(plot.default)`, which returns the following:

```
function (x, y=NULL, type="p", xlim=NULL, ylim=NULL,
    log="", main=NULL, sub=NULL, xlab=NULL, ylab=NULL,
    ann=par("ann"), axes=TRUE, frame.plot=axes,
    panel.first=NULL, panel.last=NULL, asp=NA, ...)
```

Obviously there is a lot going on underneath the generic `plot` function. For the purpose of getting started with figure creation in R we want to ask what is essential. The answer is straightforward: one variable x must be specified. Everything else has either a default value or is not essential. To start experimenting with `plot`, we continue to use the 1997 state health lobbying data loaded in Sect. 3.1.1.

With `plot`, we can plot the variables separately with the command `plot(varname)`, though this is definitively less informative than the kinds of

---

[3]The default `las` value is 0, which prints labels parallel to the axis. 1, our choice here, prints them horizontally. 2 prints perpendicular to the axis, and 3 prints them vertically.

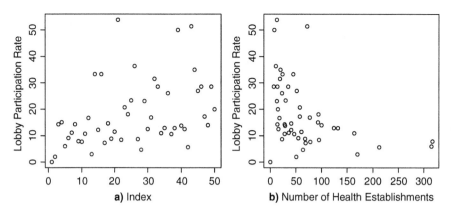

Fig. 3.4 Lobby participation rate of the health finance industry alone and against the number of health finance business establishments. (**a**) Index. (**b**) Number of Health Establishments

graphs just presented in Sect. 3.1. That said, if we simply wanted to see all of the observed values of the lobby participation rate by state of health finance firms (partratebusness), we simply type:

```
plot(health.fin$partratebusness,
     ylab="Lobby Participation Rate")
```

Figure 3.4a is returned in the R graphics interface. Note that this figure plots the lobby participation rate against the row number in the data frame: With cross-sectional data this index is essentially meaningless. By contrast, if we were studying time series data, and the data were sorted on time, then we could observe how the series evolves over time. Note that we use the ylab option because otherwise the default will label our vertical axis with the tacky-looking health.fin$partratebusness. (Try it, and ask yourself what a journal editor would think of how the output looks.)

Of course, we are more often interested in bivariate relationships. We can explore these easily by incorporating a variable x on the horizontal axis (usually an *independent* variable) and a variable y on the vertical axis (usually a *dependent* variable) in the call to plot:

```
plot(y=health.fin$partratebusness,x=health.fin$supplybusiness,
     ylab="Lobby Participation Rate",
     xlab="Number of Health Establishments")
```

This produces Fig. 3.4b, where our horizontal axis is defined by the number of health finance firms in a state, and the vertical axis is defined by the lobby participation rate of these firms in the respective state. This graph shows what appears to be a decrease in the participation rate as the number of firms rises, perhaps in a curvilinear relationship.

One useful tool is to plot the functional form of a bivariate model onto the scatterplot of the two variables. In the case of Fig. 3.4b, we may want to compare how a linear function versus a quadratic, or squared, function of the number of firms fits the outcome of lobby participation rate. To do this, we can fit two linear regression models, one that includes a linear function of number of firms, and the other that includes a quadratic function. Additional details on regression models are discussed later on in Chap. 6. Our two models in this case are:

```
finance.linear<-lm(partratebusness~supplybusiness,
    data=health.fin)
summary(finance.linear)
finance.quadratic<-lm(partratebusness~supplybusiness+
    I(supplybusiness^2),data=health.fin)
summary(finance.quadratic)
```

The lm (**l**inear **m**odel) command fits our models, and the summary command summarizes our results. Again, details of lm will be discussed in Chap. 6. With the model that is a linear function of number of firms, we can simply feed the name of our fitted model (finance.linear) into the command abline in order to add our fitted regression line to the plot:

```
plot(y=health.fin$partratebusness,x=health.fin$supplybusiness,
    ylab="Lobby Participation Rate",
    xlab="Number of Health Establishments")
abline(finance.linear)
```

As mentioned before, the abline command is particularly flexible. A user can specify a as the intercept of a line and b as the slope. A user can specify h as the vertical-axis value where a horizontal line is drawn, or v as the horizontal-axis value where a vertical line is drawn. Or, in this case, a regression model with one predictor can be inserted to draw the best-fitting regression line. The results are presented in Fig. 3.5a.

Alternatively, we could redraw this plot with the quadratic relationship sketched on it. Unfortunately, despite abline's flexibility, it cannot draw a quadratic

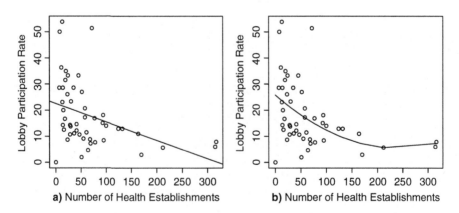

Fig. 3.5 Lobby participation rate of the health finance industry against the number of health establishments, linear and quadratic models. (**a**) Linear function. (**b**) Quadratic function

relationship by default. The easiest way to plot a complex functional form is to save the predicted values from the model, reorder the data based on the predictor of interest, and then use the lines function to add a connected line of all of the predictions. Be sure the data are properly ordered on the predictor, otherwise the line will appear as a jumbled mess. The code in this case is:

```
plot(y=health.fin$partratebusness,x=health.fin$supplybusiness,
     ylab="Lobby Participation Rate",
     xlab="Number of Health Establishments")
finance.quadratic<-lm(partratebusness~supplybusiness+
     I(supplybusiness^2), data=health.fin)
health.fin$quad.fit<-finance.quadratic$fitted.values
health.fin<-health.fin[order(health.fin$supplybusiness),]
lines(y=health.fin$quad.fit,x=health.fin$supplybusiness)
```

This outcome is presented in Fig. 3.5b. While we will not get into lm's details yet, notice that I(supplybusiness^2) is used as a predictor. I means "as is", so it allows us to compute a mathematical formula on the fly. After redrawing our original scatterplot, we estimate our quadratic model and save the fitted values to our data frame as the variable quad.fit. On the fourth line, we reorder our data frame health.fin according to the values of our input variable supplybusiness. This is done by using the order command, which lists vector indices in order of increasing value. Finally, the lines command takes our predicted values as the vertical coordinates (y) and our values of the number of firms as the horizontal coordinates (x). This adds the line to the plot showing our quadratic functional form.

3.2.1 Line Graphs with plot

So far, our analyses have relied on the plot default of drawing a scatterplot. In time series analysis, though, a line plot over time is often useful for observing the properties of the series and how it changes over time. (Further information on this is available in Chap. 9.) Returning to the data on television news coverage of energy policy first raised in Sect. 3.1, let us visualize the outcome of energy policy coverage and an input of oil price.

Starting with number of energy stories by month, we create this plot as follows:

```
plot(x=pres.energy$Energy,type="l",axes=F,
     xlab="Month", ylab="Television Stories on Energy")
axis(1,at=c(1,37,73,109,145),labels=c("Jan. 1969",
     "Jan. 1972","Jan. 1975","Jan. 1978","Jan. 1981"),
     cex.axis=.7)
axis(2)
abline(h=0,col="gray60")
box()
```

This produces Fig. 3.6a. In this case, our data are already sorted by month, so if we only specify x with no y, R will show all of the values in correct temporal

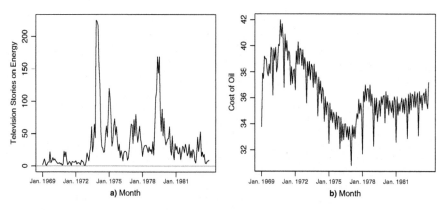

Fig. 3.6 Number of television news stories on energy policy and the price of oil per barrel, respectively, by month. (**a**) News coverage. (**b**) Oil price

order.[4] To designate that we want a line plot instead of a scatterplot of points, we insert the letter l in the type="l" option. In this case, we have turned off the axes because the default tick marks for month are not particularly meaningful. Instead, we use the axis command to insert a label for the first month of the year every 3 years, offering a better sense of real time. Notice that in our first call to axis, we use the cex.axis option to shrink our labels to 70 % size. This allows all five labels to fit in the graph. (By trial and error, you will see that R drops axis labels that will not fit rather than overprint text.) Finally, we use abline to show the zero point on the vertical axis, since this is a meaningful number that reflects the complete absence of energy policy coverage in television news. As our earlier figures demonstrated, we see much more variability and a higher mean after the first 4 years. The figure of the price of oil per barrel can be created in a similar way:

```
plot(x=pres.energy$oilc,type="l",axes=F,xlab="Month",
    ylab="Cost of Oil")
axis(1,at=c(1,37,73,109,145),labels=c("Jan. 1969",
    "Jan. 1972","Jan. 1975","Jan. 1978","Jan. 1981"),
    cex.axis=.7)
axis(2)
box()
```

Again, the data are sorted, so only one variable is necessary. Figure 3.6b presents this graph.

---

[4]Alternatively, though, if a user had some time index in the data frame, a similar plot could be produced by typing something to the effect of: pres.energy$Time<-1:180; plot(y=pres.energy$Energy,x=pres.energy$Time,type="l").

3.2.2 *Figure Construction with* plot: *Additional Details*

Having tried our hand with plots from the base package, we will now itemize in detail the basic functions and options that bring considerable flexibility to creating figures in R. Bear in mind that R actually offers the useful option of beginning with a blank slate and adding items to the graph bit-by-bit.

The Coordinate System: In Fig. 3.4, we were not worried about establishing the coordinate system because the data effectively did this for us. But often, you will want to establish the dimensions of the figure before plotting anything— especially if you are building up from the blank canvas. The most important point here is that your x and y must be of the same length. This is perhaps obvious, but missing data can create difficulties that will lead R to balk.

Plot Types: We now want to plot these series, but the plot function allows for different types of plots. The different types that one can include within the generic plot function include:

- type="p" This is the default and it plots the x and y coordinates as *points*.
- type="l" This plots the x and y coordinates as *lines*.
- type="n" This plots the x and y coordinates as *nothing* (it sets up the coordinate space only).
- type="o" This plots the x and y coordinates as *points and lines* overlaid (i.e., it "overplots").
- type="h" This plots the x and y coordinates as *histogram-like vertical lines*. (Also called a *spike plot*.)
- type="s" This plots the x and y coordinates as *stair-step like lines*.

Axes: It is possible to turn off the axes, to adjust the coordinate space by using the xlim and ylim options, and to create your own labels for the axes.

axes= Allows you to control whether the axes appear in the figure or not. If you have strong preferences about how your axes are created, you may turn them off by selecting axes=F within plot and then create your own labels using the separate axis command:

- axis(side=1,at=c(2,4,6,8,10,12),labels=c("Feb", "Apr","June","Aug","Oct","Dec"))

xlim=,ylim= For example, if we wanted to expand the space from the R default, we could enter:

- plot(x=ind.var, y=dep.var, type="o", xlim=c(-5, 17),ylim=c(-5, 15))

xlab="",ylab="" Creates labels for the x- and y-axis.

Style: There are a number of options to adjust the style in the figure, including changes in the line type, line weight, color, point style, and more. Some common commands include:

`asp=`   Defines the **asp**ect ratio of the plot. Setting `asp=1` is a powerful and useful option that allows the user to declare that the two axes are measured on the same scale. See Fig. 5.1 on page 76 and Fig. 8.4 on page 153 as two examples of this option.

`lty=`   Selects the type of line (solid, dashed, short-long dash, etc.).

`lwd=`   Selects the line width (fat or skinny lines).

`pch=`   Selects the plotting symbol, can either be a numbered symbol (`pch=1`) or a letter (`pch="D"`).

`col=`   Selects the color of the lines or points in the figure.

`cex=`   **C**haracter **ex**pansion factor that adjusts the size of the text and symbols in the figure. Similarly, `cex.axis` adjusts axis annotation size, `cex.lab` adjusts font size for axis labels, `cex.main` adjusts the font size of the title, and `cex.sub` adjusts subtitle font size.

Graphing Parameters: The `par` function brings added functionality to plotting in R by giving the user control over the graphing **par**ameters. One noteworthy feature of `par` is that it allows you to plot multiple calls to `plot` in a single graphic. This is accomplished by selecting `par(new=T)` while a plot window (or device) is still open and before the next call to `plot`. Be *careful*, though. Any time you use this strategy, include the `xlim` and `ylim` commands in each call to make sure the graphing space stays the same. Also be careful that graph margins are not changing from one call to the next.

3.2.3   Add-On Functions

There are also a number of add-on functions that one can use once the basic coordinate system has been created using `plot`. These include:

`arrows(x1, y1, x2, y2)`   Create arrows within the plot (useful for labeling particular data points, series, etc.).

`text(x1, x2, "text")`   Create text within the plot (modify size of text using the character expansion option `cex`).

`lines(x, y)`   Create a plot that connects lines.

`points(x, y)`   Create a plot of points.

`polygon()`   Create a polygon of any shape (rectangles, triangles, etc.).

`legend(x, y, at = c("", ""), labels=c("", ""))`   Create a legend to identify the components in the figure.

`axis(side)`   Add an axis with default or customized labels to one of the sides of a plot. Set the side to 1 for bottom, 2 for left, 3 for top, and 4 for right.

`mtext(text, side)`   Command to add **m**argin **text**. This lets you add an axis label to one of the sides with more control over how the label is presented. See the code that produces Fig. 7.1 on page 108 for an example of this.

3.3 Using `lattice` Graphics in R

As an alternative to the `base` graphics package, you may want to consider the `lattice` add-on package. These produce `trellis` graphics from the S language, which tend to make better displays of grouped data and numerous observations. A few nice features of the `lattice` package are that the graphs have viewer-friendly defaults, and the commands offer a `data=` option that does not require the user to list the data frame with every call to a variable.

To start, the first time we use the `lattice` library, we must install it. Then, on every reuse of the package, we must call it with the `library` command.

```
install.packages("lattice")
library(lattice)
```

To obtain a scatterplot similar to the one we drew with `plot`, this can be accomplished in `lattice` using the `xyplot` command:

```
xyplot(partratebusness~supplybusiness,data=health.fin,
    col="black",ylab="Lobby Participation Rate",
    xlab="Number of Health Establishments")
```

Figure 3.7a displays this graph. The syntax differs from the `plot` function somewhat: In this case, we can specify an option, `data=health.fin`, that allows us to type the name of the relevant data frame once, rather than retype it for each variable. Also, both variables are listed together in a single argument using the form, `vertical.variable~horizontal.variable`. In this case, we also specify the option, `col="black"` for the sake of producing a black-and-white figure. By default `lattice` colors results cyan in order to allow readers to easily separate data information from other aspects of the display, such as axes and labels (Becker et al. 1996, p. 153). Also, by default, `xyplot` prints tick marks on the third and fourth axes to provide additional reference points for the viewer.

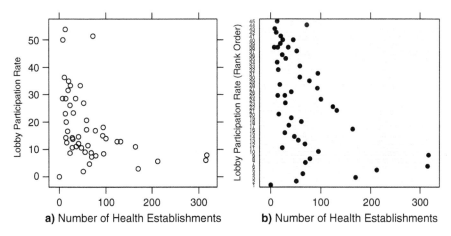

Fig. 3.7 Lobby participation rate of the health finance industry against the number of health establishments, (**a**) scatterplot and (**b**) dotplot

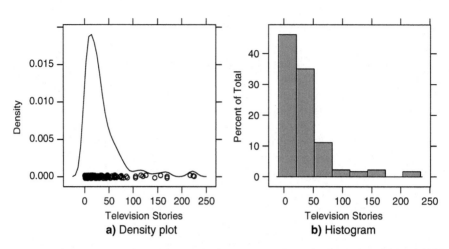

Fig. 3.8 (**a**) Density plot and (**b**) histogram showing the univariate distribution of the monthly count of television news stories related to energy

The lattice package also contains functions that draw graphs that are similar to a scatterplot, but instead use a rank-ordering of the vertical axis variable. This is how the stripplot and dotplot commands work, and they offer another view of a relationship and its robustness. The dotplot command may be somewhat more desirable as it also displays a line for each rank-ordered value, offering a sense that the scale is different. The dotplot syntax looks like this:

```
dotplot(partratebusness~supplybusiness,
    data=health.fin,col="black",
    ylab="Lobby Participation Rate (Rank Order)",
    xlab="Number of Health Establishments")
```

Figure 3.7b displays this result. The stripplot function uses similar syntax.

Lastly, the lattice library again gives us an option to look at the distribution of a single variable by plotting either a histogram or a density plot. Returning to the presidential time series data we first loaded in Sect. 3.1, we can now draw a density plot using the following line of code:

```
densityplot(~Energy,data=pres.energy,
    xlab="Television Stories",col="black")
```

This is presented in Fig. 3.8a. This output shows points scattered along the base, each representing the value of an observation. The smoothed line across the graph represents the estimated relative density of the variable's values.

Alternatively, a histogram in lattice can be drawn with the histogram function:

```
histogram(~Energy, data=pres.energy,
    xlab="Television Stories", col="gray60")
```

This is printed in Fig. 3.8b. In this case, color is set to col="gray60". The default again is for cyan-colored bars. For a good grayscale option in this case, a medium gray still allows each bar to be clearly distinguished. A final interesting feature of `histogram` is left to the reader: The function will draw conditional histogram distributions. If you still have the `post.nixon` variable available that we created earlier, you might try typing `histogram(~Energy|post.nixon,data=pres.energy)`, where the vertical pipe (`|`) is followed by the conditioning variable.

3.4 Graphic Output

A final essential point is a word on how users can export their R graphs into a desired word processor or desktop publisher. The first option is to save the screen output of a figure. On Mac machines, user may select the figure output window and then use the dropdown menu *File→Save As...* to save the figure as a PDF file. On Windows machines, a user can simply right-click on the figure output window itself and then choose to save the figure as either a metafile (which can be used in programs such as Word) or as a postscript file (for use in LaTeX). Also by right-clicking in Windows, users may copy the image and paste it into Word, PowerPoint, or a graphics program.

A second option allows users more precision over the final product. Specifically, the user can write the graph to a graphics device, of which there are several options. For example, in writing this book, I exported Fig. 3.5a by typing:

```
postscript("lin.partrate.eps",horizontal=FALSE,width=3,
    height=3,onefile=FALSE,paper="special",pointsize=7)
plot(y=health.fin$partratebusness,x=health.fin$supplybusiness,
    ylab="Lobby Participation Rate",
    xlab="Number of Health Establishments")
abline(finance.linear)
dev.off()
```

The first line calls the `postscript` command, which created a file called `lin.partrate.eps` that I saved the graph as. Among the key options in this command are `width` and `height`, each of which I set to three inches. The `pointsize` command shrank the text and symbols to neatly fit into the space I allocated. The `horizontal` command changes the orientation of the graphic from landscape to portrait orientation on the page. Change it to `TRUE` to have the graphic adopt a landscape orientation. Once `postscript` was called, all graphing commands wrote to the file *and not to the graphing window*. Hence, it is typically a good idea to perfect a graph before writing it to a graphics device. Thus, the `plot` and `abline` commands served to write all of the output to the file. Once I was finished writing to the file, the `dev.off()` command closed the file so that no other graphing commands would write to it.

Of course postscript graphics are most frequently used by writers who use the desktop publishing language of LaTeX. Writers who use more traditional word processors such as Word or Pages will want to use other graphics devices. The

available options include: jpeg, pdf, png, and tiff.[5] To use any of these four·
graphics devices, substitute a call for the relevant function where postscript
is in the previous code. Be sure to type ?png to get a feel for the syntax of these
alternative devices, though, as each of the five has a slightly different syntax.

As a special circumstance, graphs drawn from the lattice package use a
different graphics device, called trellis.device. It is technically possible to
use the other graphics devices to write to a file, but unadvisable because the device
options (e.g., size of graph or font size) will not be passed to the graph. In the case
of Fig. 3.7b, I generated the output using the following code:

```
trellis.device("postscript",file="dotplot.partrate.eps",
    theme=list(fontsize=list(text=7,points=7)),
    horizontal=FALSE,width=3,height=3,
    onefile=FALSE,paper="special")
dotplot(partratebusness~supplybusiness,
    data=health.fin,col='black',
    ylab="Lobby Participation Rate (Rank Order)",
    xlab="Number of Health Establishments")
dev.off()
```

The first argument of the trellis.device command declares which driver the
author wishes to use. Besides postscript, the author can use jpeg, pdf, or
png. The second argument lists the file to write to. Font and character size must
be set through the theme option, and the remaining arguments declare the other
preferences about the output.

This chapter has covered univariate and bivariate graphing functions in R.
Several commands from both the base and lattice packages have been
addressed. This is far from an exhaustive list of R's graphing capabilities, and
users are encouraged to learn more about the available options. This primer should,
however, serve to introduce users to various means by which data can be visualized
in R. With a good sense of how to get a feel for our data's attributes visually, the
next chapter turns to numerical summaries of our data gathered through descriptive
statistics.

3.5 Practice Problems

In addition to their analysis of energy policy coverage introduced in this chapter,
Peake and Eshbaugh-Soha (2008) also study drug policy coverage. These data
similarly count the number of nightly television news stories in a month focusing
on drugs, from January 1977 to December 1992. Their data is saved in comma-
separated format in the file named drugCoverage.csv. Download their data
from the Dataverse named on page vii or the chapter content link on page 33. The
variables in this data set are: a character-based time index showing month and year

---

[5]My personal experience indicates that png often looks pretty clear and is versatile.

(**Year**), news coverage of drugs (**drugsmedia**), an indicator for a speech on drugs that Ronald Reagan gave in September 1986 (**rwr86**), an indicator for a speech George H.W. Bush gave in September 1989 (**ghwb89**), the president's approval rating (**approval**), and the unemployment rate (**unemploy**).

1. Draw a histogram of the monthly count of drug-related stories. You may use either of the histogram commands described in the chapter.
2. Draw two boxplots: One of drug-related stories and another of presidential approval. How do these figures differ and what does that tell you about the contrast between the variables?
3. Draw two scatterplots:

   (a) In the first, represent the number of drug-related stories on the vertical axis, and place the unemployment rate on the horizontal axis.
   (b) In the second, represent the number of drug-related stories on the vertical axis, and place presidential approval on the horizontal axis.
   (c) How do the graphs differ? What do they tell you about the data?
   (d) Bonus: Add a linear regression line to each of the scatterplots.

4. Draw two line graphs:

   (a) In the first, draw the number of drug-related stories by month over time.
   (b) In the second, draw presidential approval by month over time.
   (c) What can you learn from these graphs?

5. Load the `lattice` library and draw a density plot of the number of drug-related stories by month.
6. Bonus: Draw a bar graph of the frequency of observed unemployment rates. (*Hint:* Try using the `table` command to create the object you will graph.) Can you go one step further and draw a bar graph of the percentage of time each value is observed?

Chapter 4
Descriptive Statistics

Before developing any models with or attempting to draw any inferences from a data set, the user should first get a sense of the features of the data. This can be accomplished through the data visualization methods described in Chap. 3, as well as through descriptive statistics of a variable's central tendency and dispersion, described in this chapter. Ideally, the user will perform both tasks, regardless of whether the results become part of the final published product. A traditional recommendation to analysts who estimate functions such as regression models is that the first table of the article ought to describe the descriptive statistics of all input variables and the outcome variable. While some journals have now turned away from using scarce print space on tables of descriptive statistics, a good data analyst will always create this table for him or herself. Frequently this information can at least be reported in online appendices, if not in the printed version of the article.

As we work through descriptive statistics, the working example in this chapter will be policy-focused data from LaLonde's (1986) analysis of the National Supported Work Demonstration, a 1970s program that helped long-term unemployed individuals find private sector jobs and covered the labor costs of their employment for a year. The variables in this data frame are:

treated: Indicator variable for whether the participant received the treatment.
age: Measured in years.
education: Years of education.
black: Indicator variable for whether the participant is African-American.
married: Indicator variable for whether the participant is married.
nodegree: Indicator variable for not possessing a high school diploma.

Electronic supplementary material: The online version of this chapter (doi: 10.1007/978-3-319-23446-5_4) contains supplementary material, which is available to authorized users.

© Springer International Publishing Switzerland 2015
J.E. Monogan III, *Political Analysis Using R*, Use R!,
DOI 10.1007/978-3-319-23446-5_4

re74: Real earnings in 1974.
re75: Real earnings in 1975.
re78: Real earnings in 1978.
hispanic: Indicator variable for whether the participant is Hispanic.
u74: Indicator variable for unemployed in 1974.
u75: Indicator variable for unemployed in 1975.

4.1 Measures of Central Tendency

Our first task will be to calculate centrality measures, which give us a sense of a typical value of a distribution. The most common measures of central tendency are the mean, median, and mode. The inter-quartile range, offering the middle 50 % of the data, is also informative. To begin with some example calculations, we first must load LaLonde's data (named LL). These are available as part of the **C**oarsened **E**xact **M**atching package (cem), which we will discuss at greater length in Chap. 8. As with any other user-defined package, our first task is to install the package:

```
install.packages("cem")
library(cem)
data(LL)
```

After installing the package, we load the library, as we will have to do in every session in which we use the package. Once the library is loaded, we can load the data simply by calling the data command, which loads this saved data frame from the cem package into working memory. We conveniently can refer to the data frame by the name LL[1].

For all of the measures of central tendency that we compute, suppose we have a single variable x, with n different values: $x_1, x_2, x_3, \ldots, x_n$. We also could sort the values from smallest to largest, which is designated differently with *order statistics* as: $x_{(1)}, x_{(2)}, x_{(3)}, \ldots x_{(n)}$. In other words, if someone asked you for the second order statistic, you would tell them the value of $x_{(2)}$, the second smallest value of the variable.

With a variable like this, the most commonly used measure of centrality is the sample *mean*. Mathematically, we compute this as the average of the observed values:

$$\bar{x} = \frac{x_1 + x_2 + \cdots + x_n}{n} = \frac{1}{n} \sum_{i=1}^{n} x_i \tag{4.1}$$

Within R, we can apply Eq. (4.1)'s formula using the mean function. So if x in this case was the income participants in the National Supported Work Demonstration earned in 1974, we would apply the function to the variable re74:

---

[1] These data also are available in comma-separated format in the file named LL.csv. This data file can be downloaded from the Dataverse on page vii or the chapter content link on page 53.

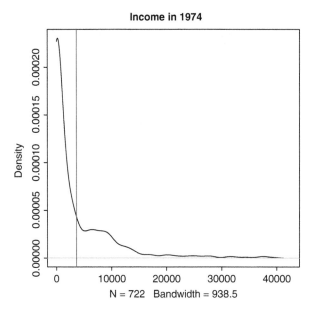

Fig. 4.1 Density plot of real earnings in 1974 from the National Supported Work Demonstration data

```
mean(LL$re74)
```

R responds by printing [1] 3630.738, so we can report the sample mean as $\bar{x} = 3630.738$.

Of course, it is advisable to continue to visualize the data using the tools from Chap. 3. Besides computing the mean of real earnings in 1974, we also can learn a lot just from drawing a density plot. We could do this using the lattice code described in the last chapter or with a little more user control as follows:

```
dens.74<-density(LL$re74,from=0)
plot(dens.74,main="Income in 1974")
abline(v=mean(LL$re74),col="red")
```

On the first line, the density command allows us to compute the density of observations at each value of income. With the from option, we can specify that the minimum possible value of income is 0 (and the to option would have let us set a maximum). On the second line, we simply plot this density object. Lastly, we use abline to add a vertical line where our computed mean of $3,630.74 is located.

The resulting graph is shown in Fig. 4.1. This figure is revealing: The bulk of the data fall below the mean. The mean is as high as it is because a handful of very large incomes (shown in the long right tail of the graph) are drawing it upward. With the picture, we quickly get a sense of the overall distribution of the data.

Turning back to statistical representations, another common measure of central tendency is the sample *median*. One advantage of computing a median is that it is more robust to extreme values than the mean. Imagine if our sample had somehow included Warren Buffett—our estimate of mean income would have increased substantially just with one observation. The median, by contrast, would move very little in response to such an extreme observation. Our formula for computing a median with observed data turns to the order statistics we defined above:

$$\tilde{x} = \begin{cases} x_{\left(\frac{n+1}{2}\right)} & \text{where } n \text{ is odd} \\ \frac{1}{2}\left(x_{\left(\frac{n}{2}\right)} + x_{\left(1+\frac{n}{2}\right)}\right) & \text{where } n \text{ is even} \end{cases} \tag{4.2}$$

Note that notation for the median is somewhat scattered, and $\tilde{x}$ is one of the several commonly used symbols. Formally, whenever we have an odd number of values, we simply take the middle order statistic (or middle value when the data are sorted from smallest to largest). Whenever we have an even number of values, we take the two middle order statistics and average between them. (E.g., for ten observations, split the difference between $x_{(5)}$ and $x_{(6)}$ to get the median.) R will order our data, find the middle values, and take any averages to report the median if we simply type:

```
median(LL$re74)
```

In this case, R prints [1] 823.8215, so we can report $\tilde{x} = 823.8215$ as the median income for program participants in 1974. Observe that the median value is *much* lower than the mean value, \$2,806.92 lower, to be exact. This is consistent with what we saw in Fig. 4.1: We have a positive skew to our data, with some extreme values pulling the mean up somewhat. Later, we will further verify this by looking at quantiles of our distribution.

A third useful measure of central tendency reports a range of central values. The *inter-quartile range* is the middle 50 % of the data. Using order statistics, we compute the lower and upper bounds of this quantity as:

$$\text{IQR}_x = \left[x_{\left(\frac{n}{4}\right)}, x_{\left(\frac{3n}{4}\right)}\right] \tag{4.3}$$

The two quantities reported are called the first and third *quartiles*. The first quartile is a value for which 25 % of the data are less than or equal to the value. Similarly, 75 % of the data are less than or equal to the third quartile. In this way, the middle 50 % of the data falls between these two values. In R, there are two commands we can type to get information on the inter-quartile range:

```
summary(LL$re74)
IQR(LL$re74)
```

The summary command is useful because it presents the median and mean of the variable in one place, along with the minimum, maximum, first quartile, and third quartile. Our output from R looks like this:

```
Min. 1st Qu.  Median    Mean 3rd Qu.     Max.
 0.0     0.0   823.8  3631.0  5212.0  39570.0
```

This is handy for getting three measures of central tendency at once, though note that the values of the mean and median by default are rounded to fewer digits that the separate commands reported. Meanwhile, the interquartile range can be read from the printed output as $IQR_x = [0, 5212]$. Normally, we would say that at least 50 % of participants had an income between \$0 and \$5212. In this case, though, we know no one earned a negative income, so 75 % of respondents fell into this range. Finally, the IQR command reports the difference between the third and first quartiles, in this case printing: [1] 5211.795. This command, then, simply reports the spread between the bottom and top of the interquartile range, again with less rounding that we would have gotten by using the numbers reported by summary.

In most circumstances, rounding and the slight differences in outputs that these commands produce pose little issue. However, if more digits are desired, the user can control a variety of *global options* that shape the way R presents results with the options command that was mentioned in Chap. 1. The digits argument specifically shapes the number of digits presented. So, for example, we could type:

```
options(digits=9)
summary(LL$re74)
```

Our output would then look like this:

```
 Min.  1st Qu.    Median       Mean   3rd Qu.       Max.
0.000    0.000   823.822   3630.740  5211.790  39570.700
```

Hence, we can see that discrepancies are a function of rounding. Bear in mind, though, that changes with the options command apply to *all* outputs in the session. For instance, it turns out that if we re-ran the mean command the output would now show even more digits than we had before.

We also could get a general summary of all variables in a data set at once just by typing the name of the data frame alone into the summary command:

```
summary(LL)
```

This reports the same descriptive statistics as before, but for all variables at once. If any observations are missing a value for a variable, this command will print the number of NA values for the variable. Beware, though, not all of the quantities reported in this table are meaningful. For indicator variables such as **treated, black, married, nodegree, hispanic, u74**, and **u75**, remember that the variables are not continuous. The mean essentially reports the proportion of respondents receiving a 1 rather than a 0, and the count of any missing values is useful. However, the other information is not particularly informative.

4.1.1 Frequency Tables

For variables that are measured nominally or ordinally, the best summary of information is often a simple table showing the frequency of each value. In R, the table command reports this for us. For instance, our data include a simple indicator coded 1 if the respondent is African-American and 0 otherwise. To get the relative frequencies of this variable, we type:

```
table(LL$black)
```

This prints the output:

```
   0    1
 144  578
```

Hence, 144 respondents are not African-American, and 578 respondents are African-American. With a nominal indicator such as this, the only valid measure of central tendency is the *mode*, which is the most common value a variable takes on. In this case, the most frequent value is a 1, so we could say that the mode is African-American.

As another example, these data measure education in years. Measured in this way, we could think of this as a continuous variable. Yet, the number of values this variable takes on is somewhat limited, as no one in the sample has fewer than three or more than 16 years of education. We therefore may wish to look at a frequency table for this variable as well. Also, even if the mean and the median are informative values, we may wish to compute the mode to know what the most common number of years of education is in these data. To compute the frequency table and to have R automatically return the mode, we type:

```
table(LL$education)
which.max(table(LL$education))
```

The table we see is:

3	4	5	6	7	8	9	10	11	12	13	14	15	16
1	6	5	7	15	62	110	162	195	122	23	11	2	1

At a glance, few respondents never went to high school at all, and only a handful have more than a high school education. We also could scan the table to observe that the mode is 11 years of education, which describes 195 respondents. However, if we have many more categories than we do for **education**, doing this will become difficult. Hence, feeding our table into the which.max command returns **which** label in the table that has the **max**imum frequency. Our resulting printout is:

```
11
 9
```

The first line, 11, prints the value label of the cell with the highest frequency—this is our mode. The second line adds the additional detail that the value of 11 is the ninth cell of the table (a detail we usually can ignore).

Another way we could present our frequencies is in a bar plot based on the above table. We could do this with the following code:

```
barplot(table(LL$education),xlab="Years of Education",
     ylab="Frequency",cex.axis=.9,cex.names=.9,ylim=c(0,200))
abline(h=0,col='gray60')
box()
```

On the first line, we specify that we are drawing a bar plot of table(LL$edu cation). Notice that we use cex.axis and cex.names to reduce the size

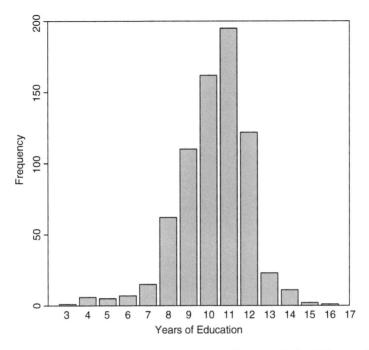

Fig. 4.2 Distribution of number of years of education from the National Supported Work Demonstration data

of the text on the vertical and horizontal axis, respectively. Afterward, we add a baseline at 0 and draw a box around the full figure. The result is shown in Fig. 4.2. With this plot, we can easily spot that the highest bar, our mode, is at 11 years of education. The graph also gives us a quick sense of the spread of the other values.

As a side point, suppose an analyst wanted not just a table of frequencies, but the percentage of values in each category. This could be accomplished simply by dividing the table by the number of cases and multiplying by 100. So for the percent of respondents falling into each category on the education variable, we type:

```
100*table(LL$education)/sum(table(LL$education))
```

R then will print:

```
         3          4          5          6
 0.1385042  0.8310249  0.6925208  0.9695291
         7          8          9         10
 2.0775623  8.5872576 15.2354571 22.4376731
        11         12         13         14
27.0083102 16.8975069  3.1855956  1.5235457
        15         16
 0.2770083  0.1385042
```

This output now shows the percentage of observations falling into each category.

4.2   Measures of Dispersion

Besides getting a sense of the center of our variable, we also would like to know
how spread out our observations are. The most common measures of this are the
variance and standard deviation, though we also will discuss the median average
deviation as an alternative measure. Starting with the sample variance, our formula
for this quantity is:

$$\text{Var}(x) = s_x^2 = \frac{(x_1 - \bar{x})^2 + (x_2 - \bar{x})^2 + \cdots + (x_n - \bar{x})^2}{n-1} = \frac{1}{n-1}\sum_{i=1}^{n}(x_i - \bar{x})^2$$

(4.4)

In R, we obtain this quantity with the function `var`. For income in 1974, we type:

```
var(LL$re74)
```

This prints the value: `[1] 38696328`. Hence, we can write Var$(x) = 38696328$.
Of course, the variance is in a squared metric. Since we may not want to think of
the spread in terms of "38.7 million squared dollars," we will turn to alternative
measures of dispersion as well. That said, the variance is an essential quantity that
feeds into a variety of other calculations of interest.

The standard deviation is simply the square root of the variance:

$$\text{SD}(x) = s_x = \sqrt{\text{Var}(x)} = \sqrt{\frac{1}{n-1}\sum_{i=1}^{n}(x_i - \bar{x})^2}$$

(4.5)

This simple transformation of the variance has the nice property of putting our
measure of dispersion back onto the original scale. We could either take the square
root of a computed variance, or allow R to do all steps of the calculation for us:

```
sd(LL$re74)
```

In this case, R prints: `[1] 6220.637`. Hence, $s_x = 6220.637$. When a variable
is shaped like a normal distribution (which our income variable is not), a useful
approximation is the 68-95-99.7 rule. This means that approximately 68 % of our
data fall within one standard deviation of the mean, 95 % within two standard
deviations, and 99.7 % within three standard deviations. For income in 1974, a heavy
concentration of incomes at $0 throws this rule off, but with many other variables it
will observationally hold.

A very different measure of dispersion is the *median absolute deviation*. We
define this as:

$$\text{MAD}(x) = \text{median}(|x_i - \text{median}(x)|)$$

(4.6)

In this case, we use the median as our measure of centrality, rather than the mean.
Then we compute the absolute difference between each observation and the median.
Lastly, we compute the median *of the deviations*. This offers us a sense of a typical
deviation from the median. In R the command is typed:

```
mad(LL$re74)
```

Here, R returns a value of 1221.398. Like the standard deviation, this is on the scale of the original variable, in dollars. Unlike the standard deviation, this statistic turns out to be much smaller in this case. Again, extreme values can really run-up variances and standard deviations, just as they can distort a mean. The median absolute deviation, by contrast, is less sensitive to extreme values.

4.2.1 Quantiles and Percentiles

As a final topic, *quantiles* and *percentiles* allow us to gain a sense of a variable's overall distribution. Quantiles are the relative placement of data values in a sorted list, scaled $[0, 1]$. For a value q the quantile for that value would be the order statistic $x_{(q \cdot n)}$. Percentiles are the same thing, scaled $[0, 100]$, so for a value p the pth percentile would be $x_{\left(\frac{p \cdot n}{100}\right)}$. Hence, the median is the 0.5 quantile and the 50th percentile. Special cases of quantiles include the previously introduced *quartiles* (dividing the data into four groups), *quintiles* (dividing into five groups), and *deciles* (dividing into ten groups).

In R, the command quantile can give us any quantile we wish. By default, R prints the quantiles for $q \in \{0.00, 0.25, 0.50, 0.75, 1.00\}$. We have the option of specifying whichever quantiles we want, though. The syntax is:

```
quantile(LL$re74)
quantile(LL$re74, c(0,.1,.2,.3,.4,.5,.6,.7,.8,.9,1))
```

The first command prints our default quantiles, though it reports them with the rescaled percentile labels:

0%	25%	50%	75%	100%
0.0000	0.0000	823.8215	5211.7946	39570.6797

Essentially, this information repeats the quartile information that summary provided us earlier. On our second line of code, we add a vector of 11 quantiles of interest to request deciles, which give us the cut points for each additional 10 % of the data. This result is:

0%	10%	20%	30%
0.0000	0.0000	0.0000	0.0000
40%	50%	60%	70%
0.0000	823.8215	1837.2208	3343.5705
80%	90%	100%	
6651.6747	10393.2177	39570.6797	

This is revealing as it shows that at least 40 % of our respondents had an income of \$0 in 1974. Further, going from the 90th percentile to the 100th percentile (or maximum), we see a jump from \$10,393 to \$39,570, suggesting that some particularly extreme values are in the top 10 % of our data. Hence, these data do have a substantial positive skew to them, explaining why our computed median is so different from the mean.

In this chapter, we have covered the various means by which we can compute measures of centrality and dispersion in R. We have also discussed frequency tables and quantiles. Together with the graphing techniques of Chap. 3, we now have a big basket of tools for assessing and reporting the attributes of a data set. In the coming chapter, we will turn to drawing inferences from our data.

4.3 Practice Problems

Consider again Peake and Eshbaugh-Soha's (2008) analysis of drug policy coverage, which was introduced in the practice problems for Chap. 3. Recall that the comma-separated data file is named `drugCoverage.csv`. If you do not have it downloaded already, please visit the Dataverse (see page vii) or this chapter's online content (see page 53). Again, the variables are: a character-based time index showing month and year (**Year**), news coverage of drugs (**drugsmedia**), an indicator for a speech on drugs that Ronald Reagan gave in September 1986 (**rwr86**), an indicator for a speech George H.W. Bush gave in September 1989 (**ghwb89**), the president's approval rating (**approval**), and the unemployment rate (**unemploy**).

1. What can you learn simply by applying the `summary` command to the full data set? What jumps out most clearly from this output? Are there any missing values in these data?
2. Using the `mean` function, compute the following:

   • What is the mean of the indicator for George H.W. Bush's 1989 speech? Given that this variable only takes on values of 0 and 1, how would you interpret this quantity?
   • What is the mean level of presidential approval? How would you interpret this quantity?

3. What is the median level of media coverage of drug-related issues?
4. What is the interquartile range of media coverage of drug-related issues?
5. Report two frequency tables:

   • In the first, report the frequency of values for the indicator for Ronald Reagan's 1986 speech.
   • In the second, report the frequency of values for the unemployment rate in a given month.
   • What is the modal value of unemployment? In what percentage of months does the mode occur?

6. What are the variance, standard deviation, and median absolute deviation for news coverage of drugs?
7. What are the 10th and 90th percentiles of presidential approval in this 1977–1992 time frame?

Chapter 5
Basic Inferences and Bivariate Association

In this chapter, we begin to use *inferential statistics* and *bivariate statistics*. In Chap. 4, we were content simply to characterize the properties of a single variable in the sample at hand. Usually in Political Science, though, our motivation as researchers will be to argue whether a claim can be generalized. Hence, inferential statistics are designed to draw inferences about a broader population. Further, we frequently want to measure the level of association between variables, and bivariate statistics serve as measures of the degree to which two variables are associated with each other.

In later chapters, linear regression models, generalized linear models, time series models, and other models that we estimate offer the opportunity to draw an inference about a broader population. They also allow us to evaluate bivariate or multivariate relationships among variables. For now, we focus on a handful of stepping stone inferential and bivariate statistics: Tests about means, associations between two categorical variables (via cross-tabulations), and correlations between two continuous variables.

In this chapter, our working example data will be the same data from LaLonde's (1986) analysis of the National Supported Work Demonstration. Information about the features of these data can be reviewed at the start of Chap. 4. In this case, every member of our sample is someone who was long-term unemployed. Hence, as we draw inferences, it would not be fair to try to conclude something about the entire population of the USA in the mid-1970s because these data do not compose a sample of that population. For the purposes of our working example, we will attempt to draw conclusions about the population of long-term unemployed persons in the USA. More information on how this sample was drawn is available in LaLonde (1986),

Electronic supplementary material: The online version of this chapter (doi: 10.1007/978-3-319-23446-5_5) contains supplementary material, which is available to authorized users.

and the reader is urged to read about *random sampling* if more information is desired
about the theory of statistical inference.

5.1   Significance Tests for Means

Before computing any inferential statistics, we must load LaLonde's data once
again. Users who have already installed the cem library can simply type:

```
library(cem)
data(LL)
```

Users who did not install cem in Chap. 4 will need to type install.packages
("cem") before the two preceding lines of code will work properly. Once these
data are loaded in memory, again by the name LL, we can turn to applied analysis[1].
   We begin by testing hypotheses about the mean of a population (or multiple
populations). We first consider the case where we want to test whether the mean
of some population of interest differs from some value of interest. To conduct this
significance test, we need: (1) our estimate of the sample mean, (2) the standard
error of our mean estimate, and (3) a null and alternative hypothesis. The sample
mean is defined earlier in Eq. (4.1), and the standard error of our estimate is simply
the standard deviation of the variable [defined in Eq. (4.5)] divided by the square
root of our sample size, $s_x/\sqrt{n}$.
   When defining our null and alternative hypotheses, we define the null hypothesis
based on some value of interest that we would like to rule out as a possible value of
the population parameter. Hence, if we say:

$$H_0: \quad \mu = \mu_0$$

This means that our null hypothesis (H_0) is that the population mean (μ) is equal
to some numeric value we set (μ_0). Our *research hypothesis* is the alternative
hypothesis we would like to reject this null in favor of. We have three choices for
potential research hypotheses:

$$H_A: \quad \mu > \mu_0$$

$$H_A: \quad \mu < \mu_0$$

$$H_A: \quad \mu \neq \mu_0$$

The first two are called one-tailed tests and indicate that we believe the population
mean should be, respectively, greater than or less than the proposed value μ_0. Most
research hypotheses should be considered as one of the one-tailed tests, though
occasionally the analyst does not have a strong expectation on whether the mean

---

[1] As before, these data also are available in comma-separated format in the file named LL.csv.
This data file can be downloaded from the Dataverse on page vii or the chapter content link on
page 63.

should be bigger or smaller. The third alternative listed defines the two-tailed test, which asks whether the mean is simply different from (or not equal to) the value μ_0.

Once we have formulated our hypothesis, we compute a t-ratio as our *test statistic* for the hypothesis. Our test statistic includes the sample mean, standard error, and the population mean defined by the null hypothesis (μ_0). This formula is:

$$t = \frac{\bar{x} - \mu_0}{\text{SE}(\bar{x}|H_0)} = \frac{\bar{x} - \mu_0}{s_x / \sqrt{n}} \tag{5.1}$$

This is distributed Student's-t with $n - 1$ degrees of freedom under the null (and asymptotically normal).[2] Once we have this test statistic, we compute our *p-value* as follows:

$$p - \text{value} = \begin{cases} P(t^* \leq t | H_0) & H_A : \mu < \mu_0 \\ P(t^* \geq t | H_0) & H_A : \mu > \mu_0 \\ P(|t^* - \mu_0| \geq |t - \mu_0||H_0) & H_A : \mu \neq \mu_0 \end{cases}$$

In this case, assume t^* is the actual value of our statistic that we compute. The typical action in this case is to have a pre-defined *confidence level* and decide whether to reject the null hypothesis or not based on whether the p-value indicates that rejection can be done with that level of confidence. For instance, if an analyst was willing to reject a null hypothesis if he or she could do so with 90 % confidence, then if $p < 0.10$, he or she would reject the null and conclude that the research hypothesis is correct. Many users also proceed to report the p-value so that readers can draw conclusions about significance themselves.

R makes all of these calculations very straightforward, doing all of this in a single line of user code. Suppose that we had a hypothesis that, in 1974, the population of long-term unemployed Americans had a lower income than \$6,059, a government estimate of the mean income for the overall population of Americans. In this case, our hypothesis is:

$$H_0: \quad \mu = 6059$$

$$H_A: \quad \mu < 6059$$

This is a one-tailed test because we do not even entertain the idea that the long-term unemployed could have an on-average higher income than the general population. Rather, we simply ask whether the mean of our population of interest is discernibly lower than \$6,059 or not. To test this hypothesis in R, we type:

```
t.test(LL$re74, mu=6059, alternative="less")
```

---

[2]This statistic has a t distribution because the sample mean has a normally distributed *sampling distribution* and the sample standard error has a χ^2 sampling distribution with $n - 1$ degrees of freedom. The ratio of these two distributions yields a t distribution.

The first argument of the t.test lists our variable of interest, LL$re74, for which R automatically computes the sample mean and standard error. Second, the mu=6059 argument lists the value of interest from our null hypothesis. Be sure to include this argument: If you forget, the command will still run assuming you want mu=0, which is silly in this case. Finally, we specify our alternative hypothesis as "less". This means we believe the population mean to be less than the null quantity presented. The result of this command prints as:

```
One Sample t-test

data:  LL$re74
t = -10.4889, df = 721, p-value < 2.2e-16
alternative hypothesis: true mean is less than 6059
95 percent confidence interval:
     -Inf 4012.025
sample estimates:
mean of x
 3630.738
```

This presents a long list of information: At the end, it reports the sample mean of 3630.738. Earlier, it shows us the value of our t-ratio is -10.4889, along with the fact that our t distribution has 721 degrees of freedom. As for the p-value, when R prints p-value < 2.2e-16, this means that p is so minuscule that it is smaller than R's level of decimal precision, much less any common significance threshold. Hence, we can reject the null hypothesis and conclude that long-term unemployed Americans had a significantly lower income than \$6,059 in 1974.

5.1.1   Two-Sample Difference of Means Test, Independent Samples

As an alternative to using one sample to draw an inference about the relevant population mean, we may have *two* samples and want to test whether the two populations means are equal. In this case, if we called the set of observations from one sample x and the observations from the second sample y, then we would formulate our null hypothesis as:

$$H_0: \quad \mu_x = \mu_y$$

Again, we will pair this with one of the three alternative hypotheses:

$$H_A: \quad \mu_x < \mu_y$$

$$H_A: \quad \mu_x > \mu_y$$

$$H_A: \quad \mu_x \neq \mu_y$$

Again, the first two possible alternative hypotheses are one-tailed tests where we have a clear expectation as to which population's mean should be bigger. The third possible alternative simply evaluates whether the means are different. When building our test statistic from this null hypothesis, we rely on the fact that H_0 also implies $\mu_x - \mu_y = 0$. Using this fact, we construct our t-ratio as:

$$t = \frac{(\bar{x} - \bar{y}) - (\mu_x - \mu_y)}{\text{SE}(\bar{x} - \bar{y}|H_0)} \tag{5.2}$$

The last question is how we calculate the standard error. Our calculation depends on whether we are willing to assume that the variance is the same in each population. Under the assumption of unequal variance, we compute the standard error as:

$$\text{SE}(\bar{x} - \bar{y}|H_0) = \sqrt{\frac{s_x^2}{n_x} + \frac{s_y^2}{n_y}} \tag{5.3}$$

Under the assumption of equal variance, we have:

$$\text{SE}(\bar{x} - \bar{y}|H_0) = \sqrt{\frac{(n_x - 1)s_x^2 + (n_y - 1)s_y^2}{n_x + n_y - 2}} \sqrt{\frac{1}{n_x} + \frac{1}{n_y}} \tag{5.4}$$

As an example, we can conduct a test with the last observation of income in the National Supported Work Demonstration, which was measured in 1978. Suppose our hypothesis is that income in 1978 was higher among individuals who received the treatment of participating in the program (y) than it was among those who were control observations and did not get to participate in the program (x). Our hypothesis in this case is:

$$H_0: \quad \mu_x = \mu_y$$
$$H_A: \quad \mu_x < \mu_y$$

Again, this is a one-tailed test because we are not entertaining the idea that the treatment could have reduced long-term income. Rather, the treatment either increased income relative to the control observations, or it had no discernible effect. R allows us to conduct this two-sample t-test using either assumption. The commands for unequal and equal variances, respectively, are:

```
t.test(re78~treated,data=LL,alternative="less",var.equal=F)
t.test(re78~treated,data=LL,alternative="less",var.equal=T)
```

The first argument, `re78~treated`, is in functional notation and indicates that income in 1978 is being separated based on values of the treatment indicator. The `data` option allows us to name the dataset so that we do not have to call it for each variable. When we state `alternative="less"`, we are declaring our alternative hypothesis to mean that the average income for the lower value of

treated (group 0, the control) should be lower than the average for the higher value of **treated** (group 1, the treated group). The only difference between the commands is that the first sets var.equal=F so that variances are assumed unequal, and the second sets var.equal=T so that variances are assumed equal.

The results print as follows. For the assumption of unequal variances, we see:

```
Welch Two Sample t-test

data:   re78 by treated
t = -1.8154, df = 557.062, p-value = 0.035
alternative hypothesis: true difference in means is less
   than 0
95 percent confidence interval:
     -Inf -81.94117
sample estimates:
mean in group 0 mean in group 1
      5090.048        5976.352
```

Meanwhile for the equal variance assumption, we see:

```
Two Sample t-test

data:   re78 by treated
t = -1.8774, df = 720, p-value = 0.03043
alternative hypothesis: true difference in means is less
  than 0
95 percent confidence interval:
     -Inf -108.7906
sample estimates:
mean in group 0 mean in group 1
      5090.048        5976.352
```

The results are pretty similar, as would be expected. Both report the same estimates of the means for the control group (5090.048) and treated group (5976.352). However, because the standard error is computed differently, we get slightly different t values in each case (and a differently calculated degrees of freedom for the unequal variances). The p-value is slightly larger when assuming unequal variances, but in this case either option yields a similar conclusion. Hence, in either case, we reject the null hypothesis at the 95 % confidence level and conclude that for the treated group income was higher in 1978 than for the control group. It should be noted that one limitation of a test like this is that we have not controlled for any of the other variables known to influence income, and the treatment assignment was not random in this case. Chapters 6–8 offer several examples of methods designed to control statistically for other predictors. Specifically, in Sect. 8.3 we revisit this exact example with a more advanced technique.

5.1.2 Comparing Means with Dependent Samples

A third mean-related test statistic we may want to compute is a difference of means with a dependent sample (e.g., comparing matched samples). In other words, suppose we have a situation in which each observation in sample 1 matches with an observation in sample 2. This could mean we are studying the same person before and after an event, a person doing the same task with different treatments, using a twin study, or using matching methods to pair treated observations to control observations. In this case, we should no longer treat each sample as independent, but compute differences for each pairing and analyze the differences. An easy way to think of this would be to create a new variable, $w_i = x_i - y_i$ where x and y are matched for each case i. In this case, our null hypothesis is $H_0 : \mu_w = 0$, and our alternative hypothesis can be any of the three choices:

$$H_A: \quad \mu_w < 0$$

$$H_A: \quad \mu_w > 0$$

$$H_A: \quad \mu_w \neq 0$$

The test statistic in this case is given by Eq. (5.5), computed for the new variable w.

$$t = \frac{\bar{w} - 0}{\text{SE}(\bar{w}|H_0)} = \frac{\bar{w}}{s_w/\sqrt{n}} \tag{5.5}$$

As can be seen, this is effectively the same test statistic as in Eq. (5.1) with w as the variable of interest and 0 as the null value. The user technically could create the w variable him or herself and then simply apply the code for a single-sample significance test for a mean.

More quickly, though, this procedure could be automated by inserting two separate variables for the linked observations into the t-test command. Suppose, for instance, that we wanted to know if our control observations saw a rise in their income from 1974 to 1978. It is possible that wages may not increase over this time because these numbers are recorded in real terms. However, if wages did increase, then observing how they changed for the control group can serve as a good baseline for comparing change in the treated group's wages in the same time frame. To conduct this paired sample t-test for our control observations, we type:

```
LL.0<-subset(LL,treated==0)
t.test(LL.0$re74,LL.0$re78,paired=T,alternative="less")
```

In the first line we create a subset only of our control observations. In the second line, our first argument is the measure of income in 1974, and the second is income in 1978. Third, we specify the option `paired=T`: This is *critical*, otherwise R will assume each variable forms an independent sample, but in our case this is a paired sample where each individual has been observed twice. (To this end, by typing `paired=F` instead, this gives us the syntax for a two-sample t-test if our separate samples are in differing columns of data.) Finally, `alternative="less"` means that we expect the mean of the first observation, in 1974, to be lower than the mean of the second, in 1978. Our results are:

```
Paired t-test

data:   LL.0$re74 and LL.0$re78
t = -3.8458, df = 424, p-value = 6.93e-05
alternative hypothesis: true difference in means is
less than 0
95 percent confidence interval:
    -Inf -809.946
sample estimates:
mean of the differences
              -1417.563
```

This output tells us that earnings were on average \$1,417.56 lower in 1974 than in 1978. Our t-ratio is $t = -3.8458$, and the corresponding p-value is $p = 0.00007$. Hence at any common confidence threshold, we can reject the null hypothesis and conclude that incomes were higher in 1978 than in 1974 among long-term unemployed who did not receive the treatment.

Just as a final comparison, we could compute the same sort of test on the treated group as follows:

```
LL.1<-subset(LL,treated==1)
t.test(LL.1$re74,LL.1$re78,paired=T,alternative="less")
```

The results are somewhat similar:

```
Paired t-test

data:   LL.1$re74 and LL.1$re78
t = -4.7241, df = 296, p-value = 1.788e-06
alternative hypothesis: true difference in means is
less than 0
95 percent confidence interval:
    -Inf -1565.224
sample estimates:
mean of the differences
              -2405.353
```

We observe a bigger growth of \$2,405.35 among the treated observations, and this result is also statistically discernible. This larger growth rate is encouraging for the long-term earnings potential of the program. For bonus points, the reader is encouraged to look up difference-in-differences techniques and consider how they might apply to studies with a design such as this.

5.2 Cross-Tabulations

In situations where we want to analyze the association between two nominal or ordinal variables, a cross-tabulation is often a good tool for inference. A cross tabulation tests the hypothesis that an independent categorical variable affects the conditional distribution of a dependent categorical variable. The researcher asks: Will certain values of the dependent variable be noticeably more or less frequent when moving from one category of an independent variable to another? In assessing this effect, the analyst should always break down relative percentages of categories of the dependent variable within categories of the independent variable. Many people make a mistake by breaking down percentages within categories of the dependent variable; such a mistake prevents a researcher from substantively evaluating the stated hypothesis that the independent variable causes the dependent variable and not the reverse. The results of a cross-tabulation substantively compare the percentages of the same value of the dependent variable across categories of the independent variable.

Some common mistakes to avoid: First, once again, avoid breaking down percentages by the dependent variable. Second, avoid comparing the largest percentage in each category of an independent variable. The hypothesis states that the frequency of the dependent variable will vary by value of the independent variable; it does not argue what value of the dependent variable will be most frequent. Lastly, avoid drawing inferences based on the pure magnitude of percentages; the researcher's task is to look at differences in the distribution. For example, if vote choice is the dependent variable, and 66 % of Republicans support the Democratic candidate, while 94 % of Democrats support the Democratic candidate, the researcher should not focus on majority support from both parties. Instead, the researcher should observe that a 28 percentage point difference implies that partisanship has an important effect on how individuals vote.

Consider two examples from the LaLonde dataset. First, we can simply ask whether being unemployed in 1974 (u74) served as a good predictor of being unemployed in 1975 (u75). We would have to think that an individual's prior work status shapes current work status. To build a cross-tabulation in R we need to install the gmodels package and then load the library. Once we have done this, we can use the CrossTable function:

```
install.packages("gmodels")
library(gmodels)
CrossTable(y=LL$u75,x=LL$u74,prop.c=F,prop.t=F,
    prop.chisq=F,chisq=T,format="SPSS")
```

In this code, y specifies the column variable, and x specifies the row variable. This means our dependent variable makes up the columns and the independent makes up the rows. Because we want the conditional distribution of the dependent variable for each given value of the independent variable, the options prop.c, prop.t, and prop.chisq are all set to FALSE (referring to **prop**ortion of the **c**olumn, **t**otal sample, and contribution to the **chisq**uare statistic). This means that each cell only contains the raw frequency and the row-percentage, which corresponds to the distribution conditional on the independent variable. The option chisq=T reports Pearson's Chi-squared (χ^2) test. Under this test, the null hypothesis is that the two variables are independent of each other. The alternative hypothesis is that knowing the value of one variable changes the expected distribution of the other.[3] By setting the format option to SPSS, rather than SAS, we are presented with percentages in our cells, rather than proportions.

The results of this command are printed below:

```
   Cell Contents
|-------------------------|
|                   Count |
|             Row Percent |
|-------------------------|


Total Observations in Table:   722


                | LL$u75
    LL$u74 |         0 |         1 | Row Total |
-----------|-----------|-----------|-----------|
         0 |       386 |         9 |       395 |
           |   97.722% |    2.278% |   54.709% |
-----------|-----------|-----------|-----------|
         1 |        47 |       280 |       327 |
           |   14.373% |   85.627% |   45.291% |
-----------|-----------|-----------|-----------|
Column Total |      433 |       289 |       722 |
-----------|-----------|-----------|-----------|


Statistics for All Table Factors


Pearson's Chi-squared test
-----------------------------------------------------------
Chi^2 =  517.7155      d.f. =  1      p =  1.329138e-114

Pearson's Chi-squared test with Yates' continuity
correction
-----------------------------------------------------------
Chi^2 =  514.2493      d.f. =  1      p =  7.545799e-114


      Minimum expected frequency: 130.8906
```

---

[3]Note that this is a symmetric test of association. The test itself has no notion of which is the dependent or independent variable.

As we can see, among those who were employed in 1974 (**u74**=0), 97.7 % were employed in 1975. Among those who were unemployed in 1974 (**u75**=1), 14.4 % were employed in 1975.[4] This corresponds to an 83.3 percentage point difference between the categories. This vast effect indicates that employment status in 1 year does, in fact, beget employment status in the following year. Further, our test statistic is $\chi^2_{1df} = 517.7155$ with a minuscule corresponding p-value. Hence, we reject the null hypothesis that employment status in 1974 is independent from employment status in 1975 and conclude that employment status in 1974 conditions the distribution of employment status in 1975.

As a more interesting question, we might ask whether receiving the treatment from the National Supported Work Demonstration shapes employment status in 1975. We would test this hypothesis with the code:

```
CrossTable(y=LL$u75,x=LL$treated,prop.c=F,prop.t=F,
    prop.chisq=F,chisq=T,format="SPSS")
```

The output from this command is:

```
   Cell Contents
|-------------------------|
|                   Count |
|             Row Percent |
|-------------------------|


Total Observations in Table:   722
```

	LL$u75		
LL$treated	0	1	Row Total
0	247	178	425
	58.118%	41.882%	58.864%
1	186	111	297
	62.626%	37.374%	41.136%
Column Total	433	289	722

```
Statistics for All Table Factors
```

---

[4]To get more meaningful levels than 0 and 1 in this case, we would need to create copies of the variables **u74** and **u75** that recorded each value as text (e.g., "Unemployed" and "Employed"). The `recode` command from the `car` library offers a straightforward way of doing this, if desired.

```
Pearson's Chi-squared test
-------------------------------------------------------------
Chi^2 =  1.480414      d.f. =  1      p =  0.2237097


Pearson's Chi-squared test with Yates' continuity
correction
-------------------------------------------------------------
Chi^2 =  1.298555      d.f. =  1      p =  0.2544773


      Minimum expected frequency: 118.8823
```

Substantively, the effects are in the expected direction. Among control observations (**treated**=0), 58.1 % were employed in 1975. Among treated observations (**treated**=1), 62.6 % were employed in 1975. Hence we see a 4.5 percentage point bump in employment among treated observations over control observations. However, our test statistic is $\chi^2_{1df} = 1.4804$. The corresponding p-value is $p = 0.2237$. Hence, if we set our confidence threshold at 90 % or anything higher, we would fail to reject the null hypothesis and conclude that there was no discernible relationship between the treatment and employment status.

5.3   Correlation Coefficients

As a preview to the next chapter, we conclude our look at bivariate statistics by showing how to calculate a correlation coefficient in R. Correlation coefficients are calculated as a measure of association between two continuous variables. We specifically focus on Pearson's r, the correlation coefficient for a linear relationship. This value shows how well the independent variable linearly predicts the dependent variable. This measure will range between -1 and 1. A correlation coefficient of 0 suggests the absence of any linear relationship between the two variables. (Though, importantly, a nonlinear relationship also might yield $r = 0$ and some erroneous conclusions.) A value of 1 would imply a perfect positive relationship, and a value of -1 would indicate a perfect negative relationship. The square of a Pearson's r (r^2) calculates the amount of variance explained by the predictor.

The formula for a Pearson correlation coefficient is essentially the covariance of two variables, x and y, divided by the standard deviation of each variable:

$$r = \frac{\sum_{i=1}^{n}(x_i - \bar{x})(y_i - \bar{y})}{\sqrt{\sum_{i=1}^{n}(x_i - \bar{x})}\sqrt{\sum_{i=1}^{n}(y_i - \bar{y})}} \tag{5.6}$$

Within R, this quantity is computed with the `cor` command.[5]

Suppose we wanted to evaluate whether the number of years of education served as a good predictor of our first measure of income, in 1974. We could type:

```
cor(LL$education,LL$re74)
cor(LL$education,LL$re74)^2
```

The first line computes the actual correlation coefficient itself. R returns a printout of: [1] 0.08916458. Hence, our correlation coefficient is $r = 0.0892$. The second line recalculates the correlation and squares the result for us all at once. This tells us that $r^2 = 0.0080$. The implication of this finding is that by knowing a respondent's number of years of education, we could explain 0.8 % of the variance in 1974 income. On its face, this seems somewhat weak, but as a general word of advice always gauge r^2 (or multiple R^2, in the next chapter) values by comparing them with other findings in the same area. Some sorts of models will routinely explain 90 % of the variance, while others do well to explain 5 % of the variance.

As a final example, we can consider the idea that income begets income. Consider how well income in 1975 correlates with income in 1978. We compute this by typing:

```
cor(LL$re75,LL$re78)
cor(LL$re75,LL$re78)^2
```

The first line returns the correlation coefficient between these two variables, printing: [1] 0.1548982. Our estimate of $r = 0.1549$ indicates that high values of income in 1975 do generally correspond to high values of income in 1978. In this case, the second line returns $r^2 = 0.0240$. This means we can explain 2.4 % of the variance of income in 1978 by knowing what someone earned in 1975.

Remember that the graphing tools from Chap. 3 can help us understand our data, including any results that we quantify such as correlation coefficients. If we are wondering why earlier income does not do a better job of predicting later income, we could draw a scatterplot as follows:

```
plot(x=LL$re75,y=LL$re78,xlab="1975 Income",ylab="1978 Income",
     asp=1,xlim=c(0,60000),ylim=c(0,60000),pch=".")
```

Notice that we have used the `asp=1` option to set the **asp**ect ratio of the two axes at 1. This guarantees that the scale of the two axes is held to be the same—which is appropriate since both variables in the figure are measured in inflation-adjusted dollars. The output is reported in Fig. 5.1. As can be seen, many of the observations cluster at zero in one or both of the years, so there is a limited degree to which a linear relationship characterizes these data.

We now have several basic inferences in hand: t-tests on means and χ^2 tests for cross-tabulations. Difference in means tests, cross-tabulations, and correlation

---

[5]The `cor` command also provides a `method` option for which available arguments are `pearson`, `kendall` (which computes Kendall's τ, a rank correlation), and `spearman` (which computes Spearman's ρ, another rank correlation). Users are encouraged to read about the alternate methods before using them. Here, we focus on the default Pearson method.

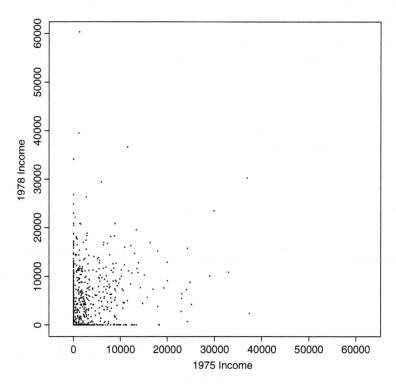

Fig. 5.1 Scatterplot of income in 1975 and 1978 from National Supported Work Demonstration data

coefficients have also given us a good sense of evaluating bivariate relationships. In the next chapter, we turn to multivariate statistics, specifically using linear regression methods. This will build on the linear techniques that correlation coefficients use and allow us to introduce the concept of statistical control.

5.4 Practice Problems

Please load the `foreign` library and download Alvarez et al.'s (2013) data, which are saved in the Stata-formatted file `alpl2013.dta`. This file is available from the Dataverse named on page vii or the chapter content named on page 63. These data are from a field experiment in Salta, Argentina in which some voters cast ballots through e-voting, and others voted in the traditional setting. The variables are: an indictor for whether the voter used e-voting or traditional voting (**EV**), age group (**age_group**), education (**educ**), white collar worker (**white_collar**), not a full time worker (**not_full_time**), male (**male**), a count variable for number of six possible technological devices used (**tech**), an ordinal scale for political knowledge (**pol_info**), a character vector naming the polling place (**polling_place**), whether the respondent thinks poll workers are qualified (**capable_auth**), whether the voter evaluated the voting experience positively (**eval_voting**), whether the voter evaluated the speed of voting as quick (**speed**), whether the voter is sure his or her vote is being counted (**sure_counted**), whether the voter thought voting was easy (**easy_voting**), whether the voter is confident in ballot secrecy (**conf_secret**), whether the voter thinks Salta's elections are clean (**how_clean**), whether the voter thinks e-voting should replace traditional voting (**agree_evoting**), and whether the voter prefers selecting candidates from different parties electronically (**eselect_cand**).

1. Consider the number of technological devices. Test the hypothesis that the average Salta voter has used more than three of these six devices. (Formally: $H_0 : \mu = 3; H_A : \mu > 3$.)
2. Conduct two independent sample difference of means tests:

   a. Is there any difference between men and women in how many technological devices they have used?
   b. Is there any difference in how positively voters view the voting experience (**eval_voting**) based on whether they used e-voting or traditional voting (**EV**)?

3. Construct two cross-tabulations:

   a. Construct a cross-tabulation where the dependent variable is how positively voters view the voting experience (**eval_voting**) and the independent variable is whether they used e-voting or traditional voting (**EV**). Does the distribution of voting evaluation depend on whether the voter used e-voting? This cross-tabulation addressed the same question as is raised in #2.b. Which approach is more appropriate here?
   b. Construct a cross-tabulation where the dependent variable is how positively voters view the voting experience (**eval_voting**) and the independent variable is the ordinal scale of political knowledge (**pol_info**). Does the distribution of voting evaluation change with the voter's level of political knowledge?

4. Consider the correlation between level of education (**educ**) and political knowledge (**pol_info**):

   a. Compute Pearson's r between these two variables.
   b. Many argue that, with two ordinal variables, a more appropriate correlation measure is Spearman's ρ, which is a rank correlation. Compute ρ and contrast the results from r.

Chapter 6
Linear Models and Regression Diagnostics

The linear regression model estimated with ordinary least squares (OLS) is a workhorse model in Political Science. Even when a scholar uses a more advanced method that may make more accurate assumptions about his or her data—such as probit regression, a count model, or even a uniquely crafted Bayesian model—the researcher often draws from the basic form of a model that is linear in the parameters. By a similar token, many of the R commands for these more advanced techniques use functional syntax that resembles the code for estimating a linear regression. Therefore, an understanding of how to use R to estimate, interpret, and diagnose the properties of a linear model lends itself to sophisticated use of models with a similar structure.

This chapter proceeds by describing the lm (linear model) command in R, which estimates a linear regression model with OLS, and the command's various options. Then, the chapter describes how to conduct regression diagnostics of a linear model. These diagnostics serve to evaluate whether critical assumptions of OLS estimation hold up, or if our results may be subject to bias or inefficiency.

Throughout the chapter, the working example is an analysis of the number of hours high school biology teachers spend teaching evolution. The model replicates work by Berkman and Plutzer (2010, Table 7.2), who argue that this policy outcome is affected by state-level factors (such as curriculum standards) and teacher attributes (such as training). The data are from the National Survey of High School Biology Teachers and consist of 854 observations of high school biology teachers who were surveyed in the spring of 2007. The outcome of interest is the number of hours a teacher devotes to human and general evolution in his or her high school biology class (**hrs_allev**), and the twelve input variables are as follows:

Electronic supplementary material: The online version of this chapter (doi: 10.1007/978-3-319-23446-5_6) contains supplementary material, which is available to authorized users.

© Springer International Publishing Switzerland 2015
J.E. Monogan III, *Political Analysis Using R*, Use R!,
DOI 10.1007/978-3-319-23446-5_6

phase1: An index of the rigor of ninth & tenth grade evolution standards in 2007 for the state the teacher works in. This variable is coded on a standardized scale with mean 0 and standard deviation 1.

senior_c: An ordinal variable for the seniority of the teacher. Coded -3 for 1–2 years experience, -2 for 3–5 years, -1 for 6–10 years, 0 for 11–20 years, and 1 for 21+ years.

ph_senior: An interaction between standards and seniority.

notest_p: An indicator variable coded 1 if the teacher reports that the state does not have an assessment test for high school biology, 0 if the state does have such a test.

ph_notest_p: An interaction between standards and no state test.

female: An indicator variable coded 1 if the teacher is female, 0 if male. Missing values are coded 9.

biocred3: An ordinal variable for how many biology credit hours the teacher has (both graduate and undergraduate). Coded 0 for 24 hours or less, 1 for 25–40 hours, and 2 for 40+ hours.

degr3: The number of science degrees the teacher holds, from 0 to 2.

evol_course: An indicator variable coded 1 if the instructor took a specific college-level course on evolution, 0 otherwise.

certified: An indicator coded 1 if the teacher has normal state certification, 0 otherwise.

idsci_trans: A composite measure, ranging from 0 to 1, of the degree to which the teacher thinks of him or herself as a scientist.

confident: Self-rated expertise on evolutionary theory. Coded -1 for "less" than many other teachers, 0 for "typical" of most teachers, 1 for "very good" compared to most high school biology teachers, and 2 for "exceptional" and on par with college-level instructors.

6.1   Estimation with Ordinary Least Squares

To start, we need to load the survey data, which we will name `evolution`. In this example, we load a Stata-formatted data set. This is easily possible through the `foreign` library, which provides us with the `read.dta` command:[1]

```
rm(list=ls())
library(foreign)
evolution<-read.dta("BPchap7.dta",convert.factors=FALSE)
```

---

[1] Berkman and Plutzer's data file, named `BPchap7.dta`, is available from the Dataverse linked on page vii or the chapter content linked on page 79. Remember that you may need to use the `setwd` command to point to where you have saved the data.

As a rule, we want to start by viewing the descriptive statistics from our data set. At minimum, use the `summary` command, and perhaps some of the other commands described in Chaps. 3 and 4:

```
summary(evolution)
```

In addition to the descriptive statistics `summary` gives us, it will also list the number of missing observations we have on a given variable (under `NA's`), if any are missing. The default condition for most modeling commands in R is to delete any case that is missing an observation on any variable in a model. Hence, the researcher needs to be aware not only of variation in relevant variables, but also how many cases lack an observation.[2] Additionally, researchers should be careful to notice anything in the descriptive statistics that deviates from a variable's values that are listed in the codebook. For example, in this case the variable **female** has a maximum value of 9. If we know from our codebook that 0 and 1 are the only valid observed values of this variable, then we know that anything else is either a miscode or (in this case) a missing value.

Before proceeding, we need to reclassify the missing observations of **female**:

```
evolution$female[evolution$female==9]<-NA
summary(evolution)
evolution<-subset(evolution,!is.na(female))
```

This command recodes only the values of **female** coded as a 9 as missing. As the subsequent call to `summary` shows, the 13 values coded as a 9 are now listed as missing, so they will automatically be omitted in our subsequent analysis. To make sure any computations we make focus only on the observations over which we fit the model, we subset our data to exclude the missing observations. As an alternative to using `subset` here, if we had missing values on multiple variables, we instead may have wanted to type: `evolution<-na.omit(evolution)`.

Having cleaned our data, we now turn to the model of hours spent teaching evolution described at the start of the chapter. We estimate our linear model using OLS:

```
mod.hours<-lm(hrs_allev~phase1*senior_c+phase1*notest_p+
     female+biocred3+degr3+evol_course+certified+idsci_trans+
     confident,data=evolution)
summary(mod.hours)
```

The standard syntax for specifying the formula for a model is to list the outcome variable to the left of the tilde (~), and the input variables on the right-hand side separated by plus signs. Notice that we did include two special terms: `phase1*senior_c` and `phase1*notest_p`. Considering the first, `phase1*senior_c`, this *interactive notation* adds three terms to our model: **phase1**, **senior_c**, and the product of the two. Such interactive models allow for

---

[2]A theoretically attractive alternative to *listwise deletion* as a means of handling missing data is *multiple imputation*. See Little and Rubin (1987), Rubin (1987), and King et al. (2001) for more details.

conditional effects of a variable.[3] The data option of lm allows us to call variables
from the same dataset without having to refer to the dataset's name with each
variable. Other prominent options for the lm command include subset, which
allows the user to analyze only a portion of a dataset, and weights, which allows
the user to estimate a linear model with weighted least squares (WLS). Observe that
we had to name our model upon estimation, calling it mod.hours by choice, and
to obtain the results of our estimation, we need to call our model with the summary
command. The output of summary(mod.hours) looks like this:

```
Call:
lm(formula=hrs_allev~phase1*senior_c+phase1*notest_p+
    female+biocred3+degr3+evol_course+certified+idsci
    _trans+
    confident,data=evolution)

Residuals:
    Min      1Q  Median      3Q      Max
-20.378  -6.148  -1.314   4.744   32.148

Coefficients:
                 Estimate Std. Error t value Pr(>|t|)
(Intercept)       10.2313     1.1905   8.594  < 2e-16 ***
phase1             0.6285     0.3331   1.886   0.0596 .
senior_c          -0.5813     0.3130  -1.857   0.0636 .
notest_p           0.4852     0.7222   0.672   0.5019
female            -1.3546     0.6016  -2.252   0.0246 *
biocred3           0.5559     0.5072   1.096   0.2734
degr3             -0.4003     0.3922  -1.021   0.3077
evol_course        2.5108     0.6300   3.985 7.33e-05 ***
certified         -0.4446     0.7212  -0.617   0.5377
idsci_trans        1.8549     1.1255   1.648   0.0997 .
confident          2.6262     0.4501   5.835 7.71e-09 ***
phase1:senior_c   -0.5112     0.2717  -1.881   0.0603 .
phase1:notest_p   -0.5362     0.6233  -0.860   0.3899
---
Signif. codes:  0 *** 0.001 ** 0.01 * 0.05 . 0.1   1

Residual standard error: 8.397 on 828 degrees of freedom
Multiple R-squared:  0.1226,Adjusted R-squared:  0.1099
F-statistic: 9.641 on 12 and 828 DF,  p-value: < 2.2e-16
```

---

[3]See Brambor et al. (2006) for further details on interaction terms. Also, note that
an equivalent specification of this model could be achieved by replacing phase1*
senior_c and phase1*notest_p with the terms phase1+senior_c+ph_senior+
notest_p+ph_notest_p. We are simply introducing each of the terms separately in this way.

Table 6.1 Linear model of hours of class time spent teaching evolution by high school biology teachers (OLS estimates)

Predictor	Estimate	Std. Error	t value	$Pr(> |t|)$
Intercept	10.2313	1.1905	8.59	0.0000
Standards index 2007	0.6285	0.3331	1.89	0.0596
Seniority (centered)	−0.5813	0.3130	−1.86	0.0636
Standards × seniority	−0.5112	0.2717	−1.88	0.0603
Believes there is no test	0.4852	0.7222	0.67	0.5019
Standards × believes no test	−0.5362	0.6233	−0.86	0.3899
Teacher is female	−1.3546	0.6016	−2.25	0.0246
Credits earned in biology (0–2)	0.5559	0.5072	1.10	0.2734
Science degrees (0–2)	−0.4003	0.3922	−1.02	0.3077
Completed evolution class	2.5108	0.6300	3.99	0.0001
Has normal certification	−0.4446	0.7212	−0.62	0.5377
Identifies as scientist	1.8549	1.1255	1.65	0.0997
Self-rated expertise (−1 to +2)	2.6262	0.4501	5.84	0.0000

Notes: $N = 841$. $R^2 = 0.1226$. $F_{12,828} = 9.641$ ($p < 0.001$). Data from Berkman and Plutzer (2010)

The top of the printout repeats the user-specified model command and then provides some descriptive statistics for the residuals. The table that follows presents the results of primary interest: The first column lists every predictor in the model, including an intercept. The second column presents the OLS estimate of the partial regression coefficient. The third column presents the t-ratio for a null hypothesis that the partial regression coefficient is zero, and the fourth column presents a two-tailed p-value for the t-ratio. Finally, the table prints dots and stars based on the thresholds that the two-tailed p-value crosses.[4] Below the table, several fit statistics are reported: The standard error of regression (or residual standard error), the R^2 and adjusted R^2 values, and the F-test for whether the model as a whole explains a significant portion of variance. The results of this model also are presented more formally in Table 6.1.[5]

---

[4]Users are reminded that for one-tailed tests, in which the user wishes to test that the partial coefficient specifically is either greater than or less than zero, the p-value will differ. If the sign of the coefficient matches the alternative hypothesis, then the corresponding p-value is half of what is reported. (Naturally, if the sign of the coefficient is opposite the sign of the alternative hypothesis, the data do not fit with the researcher's hypothesis.) Additionally, researchers may want to test a hypothesis in which the null hypothesis is something other than zero: In this case, the user can construct the correct t-ratio using the reported estimate and standard error.

[5]Researchers who write their documents with LaTeX can easily transfer the results of a linear model from R to a table using the xtable library. (HTML is also supported by xtable.) On first use, install with: install.packages("xtable"). Once installed, simply entering library(xtable); xtable(mod.hours) would produce LaTeX-ready code for a table that is similar to Table 6.1. As another option for outputting results, see the rtf package about how to output results into Rich Text Format.

Many researchers, rather than reporting the *t*-ratios and *p*-values presented in the default output of lm will instead report *confidence intervals* of their estimates. One must be careful in the interpretation of confidence intervals, so readers unfamiliar with these are urged to consult a statistics or econometrics textbook for more information (such as Gujarati and Porter 2009, pp. 108–109). To construct such a **conf**idence **int**erval in R, the user must choose a confidence level and use the confint command:

```
confint(mod.hours,level=0.90)
```

The level option is where the user specifies the confidence level. 0.90 corresponds to 90 % confidence, while level=0.99, for instance, would produce a 99 % confidence interval. The results of our 90 % confidence interval are reported as follows:

```
                            5 %          95 %
(Intercept)          8.27092375  12.19176909
phase1               0.07987796   1.17702352
senior_c            -1.09665413  -0.06587642
notest_p            -0.70400967   1.67437410
female              -2.34534464  -0.36388231
biocred3            -0.27927088   1.39099719
degr3               -1.04614354   0.24552777
evol_course          1.47336072   3.54819493
certified           -1.63229086   0.74299337
idsci_trans          0.00154974   3.70834835
confident            1.88506881   3.36729476
phase1:senior_c     -0.95856134  -0.06377716
phase1:notest_p     -1.56260919   0.49020149
```

Among other features, one useful attribute of these is that a reader can examine a 90 % (for instance) confidence interval and reject any null hypothesis that proposes a value outside of the interval's range for a two-tailed test. For example, the interval for the variable **confident** does not include zero, so we can conclude with 90 % confidence that the partial coefficient for this variable is different from zero.[6]

6.2 Regression Diagnostics

We are only content to use OLS to estimate a linear model if it is the Best Linear Unbiased Estimator (BLUE). In other words, we want to obtain estimates that on average yield the true population parameter (unbiased), and among unbiased

---

[6]In fact, we also could conclude that the coefficient is *greater* than zero at the 95 % confidence level. For more on how confidence intervals can be useful for one-tailed tests as well, see Gujarati and Porter (2009, p. 115).

estimators we want the estimator that minimizes the error variance of our estimates (best or efficient). Under the Gauss–Markov theorem, OLS is BLUE and valid for inferences if four assumptions hold:

1. Fixed or exogenous input values. In other words the predictors (X) must be independent of the error term. $\text{Cov}(X_{2i}, u_i) = \text{Cov}(X_{3i}, u_i) = \cdots = \text{Cov}(X_{ki}, u_i) = 0$.
2. Correct functional form. In other words, the conditional mean of the disturbance must be zero.
   $$E(u_i|X_{2i}, X_{3i}, \ldots, X_{ki}) = 0.$$
3. Homoscedasticity or constant variance of the disturbances (u_i). $\text{Var}(u_i) = \sigma^2$.
4. There is no autocorrelation between disturbances. $\text{Cov}(u_i, u_j) = 0$ for $i \neq j$.

While we never observe the values of disturbances, as these are population terms, we can predict residuals $(\hat{u})$ after estimating a linear model. Hence, we typically will use residuals in order to assess whether we are willing to make the Gauss–Markov assumptions. In the following subsections, we conduct regression diagnostics to assess the various assumptions and describe how we might conduct remedial measures in R to correct for apparent violations of the Gauss–Markov assumptions. The one exception is that we do not test the assumption of *no autocorrelation* because we cannot reference our example data by time or space. See Chap. 9 for examples of autocorrelation tests and corrections. Additionally, we describe how to diagnose whether the errors have a normal distribution, which is essential for statistical inference. Finally, we consider the presence of two notable data features— multicollinearity and outlier observations—that are not part of the Gauss–Markov assumptions but nevertheless are worth checking for.

6.2.1 Functional Form

It is critical to have the correct functional form in a linear model; otherwise, its results will be *biased*. Therefore, upon estimating a linear model we need to assess whether we have specified the model correctly, or whether we need to include nonlinear aspects of our predictors (such as logarithms, square roots, squares, cubes, or splines). As a rule, an essential diagnostic for any linear model is to do a scatterplot of the residuals $(\hat{u})$. These plots ought to be done against both the fitted values $(\hat{Y})$ and against the predictors (X). To construct a plot of residuals against fitted values, we would simply reference attributes of the model we estimated in a call to the plot command:

```
plot(y=mod.hours$residuals,x=mod.hours$fitted.values,
     xlab="Fitted Values",ylab="Residuals")
```

Notice that mod.hours$residuals allowed us to reference the model's residuals $(\hat{u})$, and mod.hours$fitted.values allowed us to call the predicted values $(\hat{Y})$. We can reference many features with the dollar sign ($). Type names(mod.hours) to see everything that is saved. Turning to our output plot, it is presented in Fig. 6.1. As analysts, we should check this plot for a few features: Does the local average of the residuals tend to stay around zero? If the

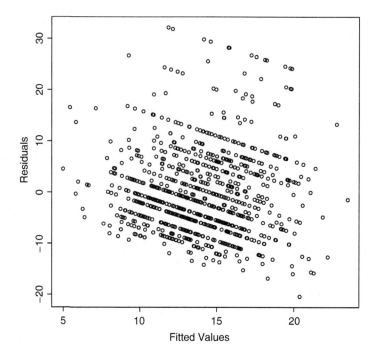

Fig. 6.1 Scatterplot of residuals against fitted values from model of hours of teaching evolution

residuals show a clear pattern of rising or falling over any range, then the functional form of some variable may be wrong. Does the spread of the residuals differ at any portion in the graph? If so, there may be a heteroscedasticity issue. One apparent feature of Fig. 6.1 is that the residuals appear to hit a diagonal "floor" near the bottom of the cloud. This emerges because a teacher cannot spend fewer than zero hours teaching evolution. Hence, this natural floor reflects a limit in the dependent variable. A functional form limitation such as this is often best addressed within the Generalized Linear Model framework, which will be considered in the next chapter.

Another useful tool is to draw figures of the residuals against one or more predictors. Figure 6.2 shows two plots of the residuals from our model against the composite scale of the degree to which the teacher self-identifies as a scientist. Figure 6.2a shows the basic plot using the raw data, which a researcher should always look at. In this case, the predictor of interest takes on 82 unique values, but many observations take on the same values, particularly at the upper end of the scale. In cases like this, many points on the plot will be superimposed on each other. By *jittering* the values of **idsci_trans**, or adding a small randomly drawn number, it becomes easier to see where a preponderance of the data are. Figure 6.2b shows a revised plot that jitters the predictor. The risk of the jittered figure is that moving the data can distort a true pattern between the predictor and residuals. However, in a case of an ordinal (or perhaps semi-ordinal) input variable, the two subfigures

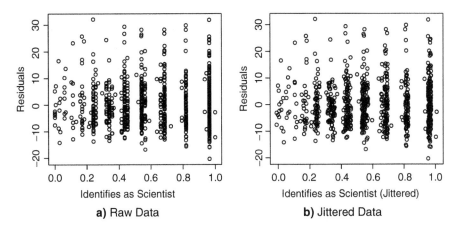

Fig. 6.2 Scatterplot of residuals against the degree to which a teacher identifies as a scientist.
(**a**) Raw data. (**b**) Jittered data

can complement each other to offer the fullest possible picture. The two scatterplots
from Fig. 6.2 are produced as follows:

```
plot(y=mod.hours$residuals,x=evolution$idsci_trans,
    xlab="Identifies as Scientist",ylab="Residuals")
plot(y=mod.hours$residuals,x=jitter(evolution$idsci_trans,
    amount=.01),xlab="Identifies as Scientist (Jittered)",
    ylab="Residuals")
```

Much like the residual-to-fitted value plot of Fig. 6.1, we examine the residual-to-
predictor plots of Fig. 6.2 for changes in the local mean as well as differences in the
spread of the residuals, each contingent on the predictor value. On functional form,
there is little to suggest that the running mean is changing markedly across values.
Hence, as with the residual-to-fitted plot, we see little need to respecify our model
with a nonlinear version of this predictor. However, the spread of the residuals looks
a bit concerning, so we will revisit this issue in the next section.

In addition to graphical methods, one common test statistic for diagnosing a
misspecified functional form is Ramsey's RESET test (regression specification error
test). This test proceeds by reestimating the original model, but this time including
the fitted values from the original model in some nonlinear form (such as a quadratic
or cubic formula). Using an F-ratio to assess whether the new model explains
significantly more variance than the old model serves as a test of whether a different
form of one or more predictors should be included in the model. We can conduct
this test for a potential cubic functional form as follows:

```
evolution$fit<-mod.hours$fitted.values
reset.mod<-lm(hrs_allev~phase1*senior_c+phase1*notest_p+
    female+biocred3+degr3+evol_course+certified+idsci_trans+
    confident+I(fit^2)+I(fit^3), data=evolution)
anova(mod.hours, reset.mod)
```

The first line of code saves the fitted values from the original model as a variable in the data frame. The second line adds squared and cubed forms of the fitted values into the regression model. By embedding these terms within the I function (again meaning, "as **is**"), we can algebraically transform the input variable on the fly as we estimate the model. Third, the anova command (for **an**alysis **of var**iance) presents the results of an F-test that compares the original model to the model including a quadratic and cubic form of the fitted values. In this case, we get a result of $F_{2826} = 2.5626$, with a p-value of $p = 0.07772$. This indicates that the model with the cubic polynomial of fitted values does fit significantly better at the 90 % level, implying another functional form would be better.

To determine which predictor could be the culprit of the misspecified functional form, we can conduct Durbin–Watson tests on the residuals, sorting on the predictor that may be problematic. (*Note* that traditionally Durbin–Watson tests sort on *time* to test for temporal autocorrelation. This idea is revisited in Chap. 9.) A discernible result indicates that residuals take similar values at similar values of the input—a sign that the predictor needs to be respecified. The lmtest library (users will need to install with install.packages the first time) provides commands for several diagnostic tests, including the Durbin–Watson test. Sorting the residuals on the rigor of evolution standards (**phase1**), we run the test:

```
install.packages("lmtest")
library(lmtest)
dwtest(mod.hours, order.by=evolution$phase1)
```

This yields a statistic of $d = 1.8519$ with an approximate p-value of $p = 0.01368$, indicating that the residuals are similar based on the value of the covariate. Therefore, we might proceed to respecify our functional form by adding polynomial terms for **phase1**:

```
mod.cubic<-lm(hrs_allev~phase1*senior_c+phase1*notest_p+
    female+biocred3+degr3+evol_course+certified+idsci_trans+
    confident+I(phase1^2)*senior_c+I(phase1^3)*senior_c+
    I(phase1^2)*notest_p+I(phase1^3)*notest_p,data=evolution)
```

As with the RESET test itself, our new model (mod.cubic) illustrates how we can use additional features of the lm command. Again, by using the I function, we can perform algebra on any input variable within the model command. As before, the caret (^) raises a variable to a power, allowing our polynomial function. Again, for interaction terms, simply multiplying two variables with an asterisk (*) ensures that the main effects and product terms of all variables in the interaction are included. Hence, we allow seniority and whether there is no assessment test each to interact with the full polynomial form of evolution standards.

6.2.2 Heteroscedasticity

When the error variance in the residuals is not uniform across all observations, a model has heteroscedastic error variance, the estimates are inefficient, and the standard errors are biased to be too small. The first tool we use to assess whether the error variance is homoscedastic (or constant for all observations) versus heteroscedastic is a simple scatterplot of the residuals. Figure 6.1 offered us the plot of our residuals against the fitted values, and Fig. 6.2 offers an example plot of the residuals against a predictor. Besides studying the running mean to evaluate functional form, we also assess the spread of residuals. If the dispersion of the residuals is a constant band around zero, then we may use this as a visual confirmation of homoscedasticity. However, in the two panels of Fig. 6.2, we can see that the preponderance of residuals is more narrowly concentrated close to zero for teachers who are less inclined to self-identify as a scientist, while the residuals are more spread-out among those who are more inclined to identify as a scientist. (The extreme residuals are about the same for all values of X, making this somewhat tougher to spot, but the spread of concentrated data points in the middle expands at higher values.) All of this suggests that self-identification as a scientist corresponds with heteroscedasticity for this model.

Besides visual methods, we also have the option of using a test statistic in a Breusch–Pagan test. Using the `lmtest` library (which we loaded earlier), the syntax is as follows:

```
bptest(mod.hours, studentize=FALSE)
```

The default of `bptest` is to use Koenker's studentized version of this test. Hence, the `studentize=FALSE` option gives the user the choice of using the original version of the Breusch–Pagan test. The null hypothesis in this chi-squared test is homoscedasticity. In this case, our test statistic is $\chi^2_{12df} = 51.7389$ ($p < 0.0001$). Hence, we reject the null hypothesis and conclude that the residuals are not homoscedastic.

Without homoscedasticity, our results are not efficient, so how might we correct for this? Perhaps the most common solution to this issue is to use Huber–White robust standard errors, or sandwich standard errors (Huber 1967; White 1980). The downside of this method is that it ignores the inefficiency of the OLS estimates and continues to report these as the parameter estimates. The upside, however, is that although OLS estimates are inefficient under heteroscedasticity, they are unbiased. Since the standard errors are biased, correcting them fixes the biggest problem heteroscedasticity presents us. Computing Huber–White standard errors can be accomplished using the `sandwich` (needing a first-time install) and `lmtest` libraries:

```
install.packages("sandwich")
library(sandwich)
coeftest(mod.hours,vcov=vcovHC)
```

The lmtest library makes the coeftest command available, and the sandwich library makes the variance-covariance matrix vcovHC available within this. (Both libraries require installation on first use.) The coeftest command will now present the results of mod.hours again, with the same OLS estimates as before, the new Huber–White standard errors, and values of *t* and *p* that correspond to the new standard errors.

Finally, we also have the option to reestimate our model using WLS. To do this, the analyst must construct a model of the squared residuals as a way of forecasting the heteroscedastic error variance for each observation. While there are a few ways to do this effectively, here is the code for one plan. First, we save the squared residuals and fit an auxiliary model of the logarithm of these squared residuals:

```
evolution$resid2<-mod.hours$residuals^2
weight.reg<-lm(log(resid2)~phase1*senior_c+phase1*notest_p+
    female+biocred3+degr3+evol_course+certified+idsci_trans+
    confident, data=evolution)
```

A key caveat of WLS is that all weights must be nonnegative. To guarantee this, the code here models the logarithm of the squared residuals; therefore, the exponential of the fitted values from this auxiliary regression serve as positive predictions of the squared residuals. (Other solutions to this issue exist as well.) The auxiliary regression simply includes all of the predictors from the original regression in their linear form, but the user is not tied to this assumption. In fact, WLS offers the BLUE under heteroscedasticity, but only if the researcher properly models the error variance. Hence, proper specification of the auxiliary regression is essential. In WLS, we essentially want to highly weight values with a low error variance and give little weight to those with a high error variance. Hence, for our final WLS regression, the weights command takes the reciprocal of the predicted values (exponentiated to be on the original scale of the squared residuals):

```
wls.mod<-lm(hrs_allev~phase1*senior_c+phase1*notest_p+
    female+biocred3+degr3+evol_course+certified+idsci_trans+
    confident,data=evolution,
    weights=I(1/exp(weight.reg$fitted.values)))
summary(wls.mod)
```

This presents us with a set of estimates that accounts for heteroscedasticity in the residuals.

6.2.3 Normality

While not part of the Gauss–Markov theorem, an important assumption that we make with linear regression models is that the disturbances are normally distributed. If this assumption is not true, then OLS actually is still BLUE. The normality assumption is, however, essential for our usual inferential statistics to be accurate. Hence, we test this assumption by examining the empirical distribution of the

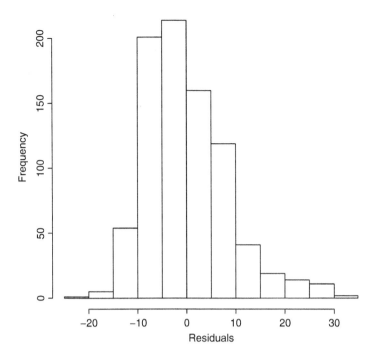

Fig. 6.3 Histogram of residuals from model of hours teaching evolution

predicted residuals. An easy first place to start is to examine a histogram of the residuals.

```
hist(mod.hours$residuals,xlab="Residuals",main="")
```

This histogram is reported in Fig. 6.3. Generally, we would like a symmetric bell curve that is neither excessively flat nor peaked. If both *skew* (referring to whether the distribution is symmetric or if the tails are even) and *kurtosis* (referring to the distribution's peakedness) are similar to a normal distribution, we may use this figure in favor of our assumption. In this case, the residuals appear to be right-skewed, suggesting that normality is not a safe assumption in this case.

A slightly more complex figure (albeit potentially more informative) is called a quantile–quantile plot. In this figure, the quantiles of the empirical values of the residuals are plotted against the quantiles of a theoretical normal distribution. The less these quantities correspond, the less reasonable it is to assume the residuals are distributed normally. Such a figure is constructed in R as follows:

```
qqnorm(mod.hours$residuals)
qqline(mod.hours$residuals,col="red")
```

The first line of code (qqnorm) actually creates the quantile–quantile plot. The second line (qqline) adds a guide line to the existing plot. The complete graph is located in Fig. 6.4. As can be seen, at lower and higher quantiles, the sample values

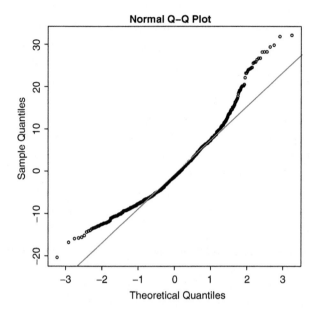

Fig. 6.4 Normal quantile–quantile plot for residuals from model of hours of teaching evolution

deviate substantially from the theoretical values. Again, the assumption of normality is questioned by this figure.

Besides these substantively focused assessments of the empirical distribution, researchers also can use test statistics. The most commonly used test statistic in this case is the Jarque–Bera test, which is based on the skew and kurtosis of the residuals' empirical distribution. This test uses the null hypothesis that the residuals are normally distributed and the alternative hypothesis that they are not.[7] The `tseries` library can calculate this statistic, which we install on first use:

```
install.packages("tseries")
library(tseries)
jarque.bera.test(mod.hours$residuals)
```

In our case, $\chi^2 = 191.5709$, so we reject the null hypothesis and conclude that the residuals are not normally distributed. Like diagnostics for heteroscedasticity, we would prefer a null result since we prefer not to reject the assumption.

All three diagnostics indicate a violation of the normality assumption, so how might we respond to this violation? In many cases, the best answer probably lies in the next chapter on Generalized Linear Models (GLMs). Under this framework, we can assume a wider range of distributions for the outcome variable, and we also can transform the outcome variable through a link function. Another somewhat

---

[7]In other words, if we fail to reject the null hypothesis for a Jarque–Bera test, then we conclude that there is not significant evidence of non-normality. Note that this is different from concluding that we do have normality. However, this is the strongest conclusion we can draw with this test statistic.

similar option would be to transform the dependent variable somehow. In the case of our running example on hours spent on evolution, our outcome variable cannot be negative, so we might add 1 to each teacher's response and take the logarithm of our dependent variable. Bear in mind, though, that this has a bigger impact on the model's *functional form* (see Gujarati and Porter 2009, pp. 162–164), and we have to assume that the disturbances of the model with a logged dependent variable are normally distributed for inferential purposes.

6.2.4 Multicollinearity

Although it is not a statistical assumption of the linear model, we now turn to diagnosing the presence of multicollinearity among predictors. Multicollinearity means that a predictor is a function of one or more other predictors. If a predictor is an exact function of other predictors, then there is perfect multicollinearity in the set of regressors. Under perfect multicollinearity, the model cannot be estimated as is and must be respecified. For example, if a researcher included both "year of birth" and "age" of a survey respondent in a cross-sectional analysis, one variable would be a perfect function of the other and therefore the model would not be estimable.

A common situation is for a predictor to have high, but not perfect, multi-collinearity. The issue that emerges is that standard errors for regression coefficients will start to become large. Importantly, though, OLS is still BLUE in the case of high but imperfect multicollinearity. In other words, the large standard errors are accurate and still reflective of the most efficient estimator that is possible. Nevertheless, it is often a good idea to get a sense of whether multicollinearity is present in a regression model.

The general approach for assessing multicollinearity relies on auxiliary regressions of predictors. Among the summary measures of these results is the variance inflation factor (VIF). For each predictor, the VIF gives us some idea of the degree to which common variance among predictors increases the standard error of the predictor's coefficient. VIFs can take any non-negative value, and smaller values are more desirable. A common rule of thumb is that whenever a VIF exceeds 10, it can be concluded that multicollinearity is shaping the results.[8]

In R, VIFs can be computed for all coefficients using the car library, installed in Chap. 2:

```
library(car)
vif(mod.hours)
```

---

[8] A VIF of 10 means that 90 % of the variance in a predictor can be explained by the other predictors, which in most contexts can be regarded as a large degree of common variance. Unlike other diagnostic tests, though, this rule of thumb should not be regarded as a test statistic. Ultimately the researcher must draw a substantive conclusion from the results.

Table 6.2 Variance inflation factors for predictors of hours spent teaching evolution

Predictor	VIF
Standards index 2007	1.53
Seniority (centered)	1.12
Standards × seniority	1.10
Believes there is no test	1.12
Standards × believes no test	1.63
Teacher is female	1.08
Credits earned in biology (0–2)	1.15
Science degrees (0–2)	1.11
Completed evolution class	1.17
Has normal certification	1.03
Identifies as scientist	1.12
Self-rated expertise (−1 to +2)	1.20

The VIFs calculated in this way are presented in Table 6.2. As can be seen in the table, all of the VIFs are small, implying that multicollinearity is not a major issue in this model. In situations where multicollinearity does emerge, though, sometimes the best advice is to do nothing. For a discussion of how to decide whether doing nothing is the best approach or another solution would work better, see Gujarati and Porter (2009, pp. 342–346).

6.2.5   Outliers, Leverage, and Influential Data Points

As a final diagnostic, it is a good idea to determine whether any observations are exerting excessive influence on the results of a linear model. If one or two observations drive an entire result that otherwise would not emerge, then a model including these observations may be misleading. We consider three types of problematic data points: outliers (for which the residual is exceedingly large), leverage points (which take a value of a predictor that is disproportionately distant from other values), and influence points (outliers with a lot of leverage). The most problematic of these are influence points because they have the greatest ability to distort partial regression coefficients.

A simple diagnostic for these features of observations again is to simply examine scatterplots of residuals, such as those reported in Figs. 6.1 and 6.2. If an observation stands out on the predictor's scale then it has leverage. If it stands out on the residual scale then it is an outlier. If it stands out on both dimensions, then it is an influence point. Neither of the figures for this model show any warning signs in this respect. Another option for assessing these attributes for observations is to calculate the quantities of Studentized residuals to detect outliers, hat values to detect leverage points, and Cook's distances to detect influential data points. The car library again offers a simple way to view these quantities for all observations.

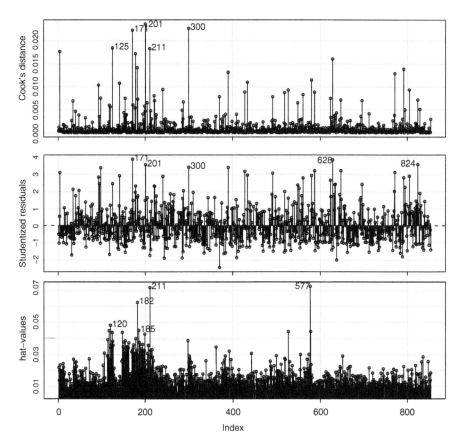

Fig. 6.5 Cook's distances, Studentized residuals, and hat values from model of hours teaching evolution

```
influenceIndexPlot(mod.hours,
     vars=c("Cook","Studentized","hat"),id.n=5)
```

The values of these three quantities are reported in Fig. 6.5, which shows Cook's distances, Studentized residuals, and hat values, respectively. In any of these plots, an extreme value relative to the others indicates that an observation may be particularly problematic. In this figure, none of the observations stand out particularly, and none of the values of Cook's distance are remotely close to 1 (which is a common rule-of-thumb threshold for this quantity). Hence, none of the observations appear to be particularly problematic for this model. In an instance where some observations do appear to exert influence on the results, the researcher must decide whether it is reasonable to keep the observations in the analysis or if any of them ought to be removed. Removing data from a linear model can easily be accomplished with the `subset` option of `lm`.

We now have considered how to fit linear models in R and how to conduct several diagnostics to determine whether OLS presents us with the BLUE. While this is a common model in Political Science, researchers frequently need to model limited dependent variables in the study of politics. To address dependent variables of this nature, we turn in the next chapter to GLMs. These models build on the linear model framework but allow outcome variables that are bounded or categorical in nature.

6.3 Practice Problems

This set of practice problems will draw from Owsiak's (2013) work on democratization, in which he shows that states that settle all of their international borders tend to become more democratic. Please load the foreign library and then download a subset of Owsiak's data, saved in the Stata-formatted file owsiakJOP2013.dta. This file can be downloaded from the Dataverse linked on page vii or the chapter content linked on page 79. These are *panel data* that include observations for 200 countries from 1918 to 2007, with a total of 10,434 country-years forming the data. The countries in these data change over time (just as they changed in your history book) making this what we call an unbalanced panel. Hence, our subsequent model includes lagged values of several variables, or values from the previous year. See Chap. 8 for more about nested data, and Chap. 9 for more about temporal data. For this exercise, our standard OLS tools will work well.

1. Start by using the na.omit command, described on page 81, to eliminate missing observations from these data. Then compute the descriptive statistics for the variables in this data set.
2. To replicate Model 2 from Owsiak (2013), estimate a linear regression with OLS using the following specification (with variable names in parentheses): The dependent variable is. Polity score (**polity2**), and the predictors are an indicator for having all borders settled (**allsettle**), lagged GDP (**laggdpam**), lagged change in GDP (**laggdpchg**), lagged trade openness (**lagtradeopen**), lagged military personnel (**lagmilper**), lagged urban population (**lagupop**), lagged pervious non-democratic movement (**lagsumdown**), and lagged Polity score (**lagpolity**).
3. Plot the residuals against the fitted values.
4. Is there heteroscedasticity in the residuals? Based on scatterplots and a Breusch–Pagan test, what do you conclude?

   a. Estimate Huber–White standard errors for this model with the sandwich library and coeftest command.
   b. For <u>bonus</u> credit, you can reproduce Owsiak's (2013) results exactly by computing *clustered standard errors*, clustering on country (variable name: **ccode**). You can do this in three steps: First, install the multiwayvcov library. Second, define an error variance-covariance matrix using the cluster.vcov command. Third, use that error variance-covariance matrix as an argument in the coeftest command from the lmtest library.

5. Determine whether multicollinearity is a concern by calculating the VIFs for the predictors in this model.
6. Are the residuals of this model normally distributed? Use any of the discussed methods to draw a conclusion.
7. For <u>bonus</u> credit, you can evaluate whether there is autocorrelation in the residuals, as will be discussed further in Chap. 9. To to this, first install the `plm` library. Second, refit your model using the `plm` command. (Be sure to specify `model="pooling"` as an option in the command to estimate with OLS.) Third, use the `pbgtest` to conduct a panel Breusch–Godfrey test to evaluate whether there is serial correlation in the residuals. What conclusion do you draw?

Chapter 7
Generalized Linear Models

While the linear regression model is common to Political Science, many of the outcome measures researchers wish to study are binary, ordinal, nominal, or count variables. When we study these limited dependent variables, we turn to techniques such as logistic regression, probit regression, ordered logit (and probit) regression, multinomial logit (and probit) regression, Poisson regression, and negative binomial regression. A review of these and several other methods can be seen in volumes such as King (1989) and Long (1997).

In fact, all of these techniques can be thought of as special cases of the *generalized linear model*, or GLM (Gill 2001). The GLM approach in brief is to transform the mean of our outcome in some way so that we can apply the usual logic of linear regression modeling to the transformed mean. This way, we can model a broad class of dependent variables for which the distribution of the disturbance terms violates the normality assumption from the Gauss–Markov theorem. Further, in many cases, the outcome is bounded, so the *link function* we use to transform the mean of the outcome may reflect a more realistic functional form (Gill 2001, pp. 31–32).

The glm command in R is flexible enough to allow the user to specify many of the most commonly used GLMs, such as logistic and Poisson regression. A handful of models that get somewhat regular usage, such as ordered logit and negative binomial regression, actually require unique commands that we also will cover. In general, though, the glm command is a good place to look first when a researcher has a limited dependent variable. In fact, the glm command takes an argument called family that allows the user to specify what kind of model he or she wishes to estimate. By typing ?family into the R console, the user can get a quick overview of which models the glm command can estimate.

Electronic supplementary material: The online version of this chapter (doi: 10.1007/978-3-319-23446-5_7) contains supplementary material, which is available to authorized users.

This chapter proceeds by illustrating examples with binary outcomes, ordinal outcomes, and count outcomes. Each of these sections uses a different example data set in order to consider dependent variables of each type. Each section will introduce its example data in turn.

7.1 Binary Outcomes

We first consider binary outcome variables, or variables that take only two possible values. Usually these outcomes are coded 0 or 1 for simplicity of interpretation. As our example in this section, we use survey data from the Comparative Study of Electoral Systems (CSES). Singh (2014a) studies a subset of these data that consists of 44,897 survey respondents from 30 elections. These elections occurred between the years of 1996–2006 in the countries of Canada, the Czech Republic, Denmark, Finland, Germany, Hungary, Iceland, Ireland, Israel, Italy, the Netherlands, New Zealand, Norway, Poland, Portugal, Slovenia, Spain, Sweden, Switzerland, and the United Kingdom.

Singh uses these data to assess how ideological distance shapes individuals' vote choice and willingness to vote in the first place. Building on the spatial model of politics advanced by Hotelling (1929), Black (1948), Downs (1957), and others, the article shows that linear differences in ideology do a better job of explaining voter behavior than squared differences. The variables in the data set are as follows:

voted: Indicator coded 1 if the respondent voted, 0 if not.
votedinc: Indicator coded 1 if the respondent voted for the incumbent party, 0 if he or she voted for another party. (Non-voters are missing.)
cntryyear: A character variable listing the country and year of the election.
cntryyearnum: A numeric index identifying the country-year of the election.
distanceinc: Distance between the survey respondent and the incumbent party on a 0–10 ideology scale.
distanceincsq: Squared distance between the voter and incumbent party.
distanceweighted: Distance between the survey respondent and the most similar political party on a 0–10 ideology scale, weighted by the competitiveness of the election.
distancesqweighted: Squared weighted distance between the voter and most similar ideological party.

The data are saved in Stata format, so we will need to load the `foreign` library. Download the file `SinghJTP.dta` from the Dataverse linked on page vii or the chapter content linked on page 97. Then open the data as follows:

```
library(foreign)
voting<-read.dta("SinghJTP.dta",convert.factors=FALSE)
```

A good immediate step here would be to use commands such as `summary` as well as graphs to get a feel for the descriptive attributes of the data. This is left for the reader.

7.1.1 Logit Models

As a first model from these data, we will model the probability that a respondent voted for the incumbent party, rather than another party. We will use only one predictor in this case, and that is the distance between the voter and the incumbent party. We craft this as a *logistic regression* model. The syntax for this model is:

```
inc.linear<-glm(votedinc~distanceinc,
    family=binomial(link="logit"),data=voting)
```

The syntax of glm (**g**eneralized **l**inear **m**odel) is nearly identical to lm: We still start with a functional specification that puts the dependent variable to the left of the tilde (~) and predictors on the right separated with plus signs. Again, we reference our dataset with the data option. Now, however, we *must* use the family option to specify which GLM we want to estimate. By specifying binomial(link="logit"), we declare a binary outcome and that we are estimating a logit, rather than probit, model. After estimation, by typing summary(inc.linear) we get the output from our logistic regression model, which is as follows:

```
Call:
glm(formula = votedinc ~ distanceinc, family = binomial
  (link = "logit"),
    data = voting)

Deviance Residuals:
    Min       1Q   Median       3Q      Max
-1.2608  -0.8632  -0.5570   1.0962   2.7519

Coefficients:
            Estimate Std. Error z value Pr(>|z|)
(Intercept)  0.19396    0.01880   10.32   <2e-16 ***
distanceinc -0.49469    0.00847  -58.41   <2e-16 ***
---
Signif. codes:  0  ***  0.001  **  0.01  *  0.05 . 0.1
  1

(Dispersion parameter for binomial family taken to be 1)

    Null deviance: 47335  on 38210  degrees of freedom
Residual deviance: 42910  on 38209  degrees of freedom
  (6686 observations deleted due to missingness)
AIC: 42914

Number of Fisher Scoring iterations: 4
```

Table 7.1 Logit model of probability of voting for incumbent party, 30 cross-national elections

Predictor	Estimate	Std. error	z value	$\Pr(> |z|)$
Intercept	0.1940	0.0188	10.32	0.0000
Distance	−0.4947	0.0085	−58.41	0.0000

Notes: $N = 38{,}211$. AIC $= 42{,}914$. 69 % correctly predicted. Data from Singh (2014a)

The printout looks similar to the printout of the linear model we estimated in Chap. 6.[1] A more formal presentation of our results can be found in Table 7.1.[2] Comparing these results to the linear model, however, a few differences are important to note. First, the coefficient estimates themselves are not as meaningful as those of the linear model. A logit model transforms our outcome of interest, the probability of voting for the incumbent party, because it is bounded between 0 and 1. The logit transform is worthwhile because it allows us to use a linear prediction framework, but it calls for an added step of effort for interpretation. (See Sect. 7.1.3 for more on this.) A second difference in the output is that it reports z ratios instead of t ratios: Just as before, these are computed around the null hypothesis that the coefficient is zero, and the formula for the ratio uses the estimate and standard error in the same way. Yet, we now need to assume these statistics follow a normal distribution, rather than a t distribution.[3] Third, different fit statistics are presented: deviance scores and the Akaike information criterion (AIC).[4]

In Table 7.1, we report the coefficients, standard errors, and inferential information. We also report the AIC, which is a good fit index and has the feature of penalizing for the number of parameters. Unlike R^2 in linear regression, though, the AIC has no natural metric that gives an absolute sense of model fit. Rather, it works better as a means of comparing models, with *lower* values indicating a better penalized fit. To include a measure of fit that does have a natural scale to it, we also report what percentage of responses our model correctly predicts. To compute this, all we need to do is determine whether the model would predict a vote for the incumbent party and compare this to how the respondent actually voted. In R, we can roll our own computation:

---

[1]In this case, the coefficient estimates we obtain are similar to those reported by Singh (2014a). However, our standard errors are smaller (and hence z and p values are bigger) because Singh clusters the standard errors. This is a useful idea because the respondents are nested within elections, though multilevel models (which Singh also reports) address this issue as well—see Sect. 8.1.

[2]LaTeX users can create a table similar to this quickly by typing: `library(xtable); xtable(inc.linear)`.

[3]An explanation of how the inferential properties of this model are derived can be found in Eliason (1993, pp. 26–27).

[4]Deviance is calculated as -2 times the logged ratio of the fitted likelihood to the saturated likelihood. Formally, $-2 \log \frac{L_1}{L_2}$, where L_1 is the fitted likelihood and L_2 is the saturated likelihood. R reports two quantities: the null deviance computes this for an intercept-only model that always predicts the modal value, and the residual deviance calculates this for the reported model.

```
predicted<-as.numeric(
    predict.glm(inc.linear,type="response")>.5)
true<-voting$votedinc[voting$voted==1]
correct<-as.numeric(predicted==true)
100*table(correct)/sum(table(correct))
```

On the first line, we create a vector of the predictions from the model. The
code uses the predict.glm command, which usefully can forecast from any
model estimated with the glm command. By specifying type="response" we
clarify that we want our predictions to be on the probability scale (instead of the
default scale of latent utility). We then ask if each probability is greater than 0.5.
By wrapping all of this in the as.numeric command, we count all probabilities
above 0.5 as predicted values of 1 (for the incumbent) and all that are less than 0.5
as predicted values of 0 (against the incumbent). On the second line, we simply
subset the original vector of the outcome from the original data to those that voted
and hence were included in the model. This subsetting step is essential because the
glm command automatically deletes missing data from estimation. Hence, without
subsetting, our predicted and true values would not properly link together. On the
third line, we create a vector coded 1 if the predicted value matches the true value,
and on the fourth line we create a table of this vector. The printout is:

```
correct
        0         1
30.99108 69.00892
```

Hence, we know that the model correctly predicts 69 % of the outcome values,
which we report in Table 7.1.

As one more example of logistic regression, Singh (2014a) compares a model
with linear ideological distances to one with squared ideological distances. To fit
this alternative model, we type:

```
inc.squared<-glm(votedinc~distanceincsq,
    family=binomial(link="logit"),data=voting)
summary(inc.squared)
```

The output of the summary command on the second line is:

```
Call:
glm(formula = votedinc ~ distanceincsq, family = binomi
 al(link = "logit"),
    data = voting)

Deviance Residuals:
    Min       1Q    Median       3Q      Max
-1.1020  -0.9407  -0.5519   1.2547   3.6552

Coefficients:
               Estimate Std. Error z value Pr(>|z|)
(Intercept)   -0.179971   0.014803  -12.16   <2e-16 ***
```

```
distanceincsq -0.101549   0.002075   -48.94   <2e-16 ***
---
Signif. codes:  0  ***  0.001  **  0.01  *  0.05  .
  0.1  1
```

(Dispersion parameter for binomial family taken to be 1)

```
    Null deviance: 47335  on 38210  degrees of freedom
Residual deviance: 43087  on 38209  degrees of freedom
  (6686 observations deleted due to missingness)
AIC: 43091
```

Number of Fisher Scoring iterations:}5

With this second model we can see how the AIC can be useful: With a higher value of 43,091 in the quadratic model, we conclude that the model with linear ideological distance fits better with an AIC of 42,914. This corresponds to the original article's conclusion that the linear form of the variable fits better.

7.1.2 Probit Models

Logit models have gained traction over the years for the sake of simplicity in computation and interpretation. (For instance, logit models can be interpreted with *odds ratios*.) However, a key assumption of logit models is that the error term in the latent variable model (or the latent utility) has a logistic distribution. We may be more content to assume that the error term of our model is normally distributed, given the prevalence of this distribution in nature and in asymptotic results.[5] *Probit regression* allows us to fit a model with a binary outcome variable with a normally distributed error term in the latent variable model.

To show how this alternative model of a binary outcome works, we turn to a model of the probability a survey respondent voted at all. Singh (2014a) models this as a function of the ideological proximity to the nearest party weighted by the competitiveness of the election. The theory here is that individuals with a relatively proximate alternative in a competitive election are more likely to find it worthwhile to vote. We fit this model as follows:

```
turnout.linear<-glm(voted~distanceweighted,
    family=binomial(link="probit"),data=voting)
summary(turnout.linear)
```

---

[5]Additionally, in advanced settings for which we need to develop a multivariate distribution for multiple outcome variables, the normal distribution is relatively easy to work with.

The output of our summary command is:

```
Call:
glm(formula = voted ~ distanceweighted, family = binomi
 al(link = "probit"),
    data = voting)

Deviance Residuals:
    Min       1Q    Median        3Q       Max
-1.9732   0.5550   0.5550   0.5776   0.6644

Coefficients:
                     Estimate Std. Error z value Pr(>|z|)
(Intercept)          1.068134   0.009293 114.942  < 2e-16
  ***
distanceweighted -0.055074   0.011724  -4.698 2.63e-06
  ***
---
Signif. codes:  0  ***  0.001  **  0.01  *  0.05  .
0.1  1

(Dispersion parameter for binomial family taken to
  be 1)

    Null deviance: 37788  on 44896  degrees of freedom
Residual deviance: 37766  on 44895  degrees of freedom
AIC: 37770

Number of Fisher Scoring iterations: 4
```

The layout of these probit model results look similar to the results of the logit model.
Note, though, that changing the distribution of the latent error term to a normal
distribution changes the scale of the coefficients, so the values will be different
between logit and probit models. The substantive implications typically are similar
between the models, so the user must decide which model works best in terms of
assumptions and interpretation for the data at hand.

7.1.3 Interpreting Logit and Probit Results

An important feature of GLMs is that the use of a link function makes the
coefficients more difficult to interpret. With a linear regression model, as estimated
in Chap. 6, we could simply interpret the coefficient in terms of change in the
expected value of the outcome itself, holding the other variables equal. With a GLM,
though, the mean of the outcome has been transformed, and the coefficient speaks
to change in the transformed mean. Hence, for analyses like logit and probit models,

we need to take additional steps in order to interpret the effect an input has on the outcome of interest.

For a logistic regression model, the analyst can quickly calculate the *odds ratio* for each coefficient simply by taking the exponential of the coefficient.[6] Recall that the *odds* of an event is the ratio of the probability the event occurs to the probability it does not occur: $\frac{p}{1-p}$. The odds ratio tells us the multiplicative factor by which the odds will change for a unit increase in the predictor. Within R, if we want the odds ratio for our distance coefficient in Table 7.1, we simply type:

```
exp(inc.linear$coefficients[-1])
```

This syntax will take the exponential of every coefficient estimate from our model, no matter the number of covariates. The [-1] omits the intercept, for which an odds ratio would be meaningless. Having only one predictor, the printout in this case is:

```
distanceinc
   0.6097611
```

We need to be careful when interpreting the meaning of odds ratios. In this case, for a one point increase in distance from the incumbent party on the ideology scale, the odds that a respondent will vote for the incumbent party diminish by a factor of 0.61. (With multiple predictors, we would need to add the *ceteris paribus* caveat.) If, instead of interpreting as a multiplicative factor, the analyst preferred to discuss change in percentage terms, type:

```
100*(exp(inc.linear$coefficients[-1])-1)
```

In this case a value of -39.02389 is returned. Hence, we can say: for a one point increase in distance from the incumbent party on the ideology scale, the odds that a respondent will vote for the incumbent party diminish by 39 %. Remember, though, that all of these statements relate specifically to *odds*, so in this case we are referring to a 39 % decrease in the ratio of the probability of voting for the incumbent to the probability of voting for any other party.

An alternative interpretation that often is easier to explain in text is to report *predicted probabilities* from a model. For a logistic regression model, inputting the predictions from the linear function (the latent utilities) into the logistic cumulative distribution function produces the predicted probability that the outcome takes a value of 1. A simple approach to intuitively illustrate the effect of a predictor is to plot the predicted probabilities at every value that a predictor can take, which shows how the probability changes in a nonlinear way as the predictor changes. We proceed first by creating our predicted probabilities:

```
distances<-seq(0,10,by=.1)
inputs<-cbind(1,distances)
colnames(inputs)<-c("constant","distanceinc")
inputs<-as.data.frame(inputs)
```

---

[6]This is because the logit link function is the log-odds, or logarithm of the odds of the event.

```
forecast.linear<-predict(inc.linear,newdata=inputs,
     type="response")
```

On the first line, we create a **seq**uence of possible distances from the incumbent party, ranging from the minimum (0) to the maximum (10) in small increments (0.1). We then create a matrix named `inputs` that stores predictor values of interest for all predictors in our model (using the **c**olumn **bind**, `cbind`, command to combine two vectors as columns in a matrix). Subsequently, we name the columns to match our variable names and recategorize this matrix **as** a **data frame**. On the final line, we use the `predict` command, which saves the predicted probabilities to a vector. Observe the use of the `newdata` option to specify our data frame of predictor values and the `type` option to specify that we want our predicted values on the `response` scale. By setting this to the response scale, the command returns predicted probabilities of voting for the incumbent party at each hypothetical distance.

As an alternative to the model in which voting for the incumbent is a function of the linear ideological distance between the voter and the party, we also fitted a model using the squared distance. We easily can compute the predicted probability from this alternative model against the value of distance on its original scale. Again, the predicted probabilities are computed by typing:

```
inputs2<-cbind(1,distances^2)
colnames(inputs2)<-c("constant","distanceincsq")
inputs2<-as.data.frame(inputs2)
forecast.squared<-predict(inc.squared,newdata=inputs2,
     type="response")
```

In this case, we use the original vector `distances` that captured hypothetical predictor values, and square them. By using these squared values, we save our predicted probabilities from the alternative model into the vector `forecast.squared`.

To plot the predicted probabilities from each model on the same space, we type:

```
plot(y=forecast.linear,x=distances,ylim=c(0,.6),type="l",
     lwd=2,xlab="",ylab="")
lines(y=forecast.squared,x=distances,lty=2,col="blue",lwd=2)
legend(x=6,y=.5,legend=c("linear","squared"),lty=c(1,2),
     col=c("black","blue"),lwd=2)
mtext("Ideological Distance",side=1,line=2.75,cex=1.2)
mtext("Probability of Voting for Incumbent",side=2,
     line=2.5,cex=1.2)
```

On the first line, we plot the predicted probabilities from the model with linear distance. On the vertical axis (`y`) are the probabilities, and on the horizontal axis (`x`) are the values of distance. We bound the probabilities between 0 and 0.6 for a closer look at the changes, set `type="l"` to produce a line plot, and use the option `lwd=2` to increase the line thickness. We also set the x- and y-axis labels to be empty (`xlab=""`,`ylab=""`) so that we can fill in the labels later with a more precise command. On the second line, we add another line to the open figure of the

Fig. 7.1 Predicted
probability of voting for the
incumbent party as a function
of ideological distance from
the incumbents, based on a
linear and a quadratic
functional form

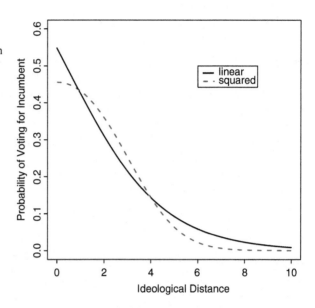

predicted probabilities from the model with squared distance. This time, we color
the line blue and make it dashed (`lty=2`) to distinguish it from the other model's
predicted probabilities. On the third line, we add a legend to the plot, located at the
coordinates where `x=6` and `y=0.5`, that distinguishes the lines based on the linear
and squared distances. Finally, on the last two lines we add axis labels using the
`mtext` command: The `side` option lets us declare which axis we are writing on,
the `line` command determines how far away from the axis the label is printed, and
the `cex` command allows us to expand the font size (to 120% in this case). The
full results are presented in Fig. 7.1. As the figure shows, the model with squared
distance is more responsive at middle values, with a flatter response at extremes.
Hence, Singh's (2014a) conclusion that linear distance fits better has substantive
implications for voter behavior.

As one final example of reporting predicted probabilities, we turn to an example
from the probit model we estimated of turnout. Predicted probabilities are computed
in a similar way for probit models, except that the linear predictions (or utilities) are
now input into a normal cumulative distribution function. In this example, we will
add to our presentation of predicted probabilities by including confidence intervals
around our predictions, which convey to the reader the level of uncertainty in our
forecast. We begin as we did in the last example, by creating a data frame of
hypothetical data values and producing predicted probabilities with them:

```
wght.dist<-seq(0,4,by=.1)
inputs.3<-cbind(1,wght.dist)
colnames(inputs.3)<-c("constant","distanceweighted")
inputs.3<-as.data.frame(inputs.3)
forecast.probit<-predict(turnout.linear,newdata=inputs.3,
    type="link",se.fit=TRUE)
```

In this case, weighted ideological distance from the nearest ideological party is our one predictor. This predictor ranges from approximately 0–4, so we create a vector spanning those values. On the last line of the above code, we have changed two features: First, we have specified `type="link"`. This means that our predictions are now linear predictions of the latent utility, and not the probabilities in which we are interested. (This will be corrected in a moment.) Second, we have added the option `se.fit=TRUE`, which provides us with a standard error of each linear prediction. Our output object, `forecast.probit` now contains both the linear forecasts and the standard errors.

The reason we saved the linear utilities instead of the probabilities is that doing so will make it easier for us to compute confidence intervals that stay within the probability limits of 0 and 1. To do this, we first compute the confidence intervals of the linear predictions. For the 95 % confidence level, we type:

```
lower.ci<-forecast.probit$fit-1.95996399*forecast.probit$se.fit
upper.ci<-forecast.probit$fit+1.95996399*forecast.probit$se.fit
```

Notice that by calling `forecast.probit$fit` we obtain the linear predictions of utilities, and by calling `forecast.probit$se.fit` we call the standard errors of our forecast. 1.95996399 is the two-tailed 95 % critical value from a normal distribution. Now that we have vectors of the lower and upper bounds of the confidence interval, we can insert these into the normal cumulative distribution function to put the bounds on the predicted probability scale.

We can now plot the predicted probabilities with confidence intervals as follows:

```
plot(y=pnorm(forecast.probit$fit),x=wght.dist,ylim=c(.7,.9),
     type="l",lwd=2,xlab="Weighted Ideological Distance",
     ylab="Probability of Turnout")
lines(y=pnorm(lower.ci),x=wght.dist,lty=3,col="red",lwd=2)
lines(y=pnorm(upper.ci),x=wght.dist,lty=3,col="red",lwd=2)
```

In the first line, we plot the predicted probabilities themselves. To obtain the probabilities for the vertical axis, we type `y=pnorm(forecast.probit$fit)`. The `pnorm` function is the normal cumulative distribution function, so this converts our linear utility predictions into actual probabilities. Meanwhile, `x=wght.dist` places the possible values of weighted distance to the nearest party on the horizontal axis. On the second line, we plot the lower bound of the 95 % confidence interval of predicted probabilities. Here, `pnorm(lower.ci)` converts the confidence interval forecast onto the probability scale. Finally, we repeat the process on line three to plot the upper bound of the confidence interval. The full output can be seen in Fig. 7.2. A noteworthy feature of this plot is that the confidence interval becomes noticeably wide for the larger values of weighted distance. This is because the mean of the variable is low and there are few observations at these higher values.

The predicted probabilities in both of these cases were simple because they included only one predictor. For any GLM, including a logit or probit model, predicted probabilities and their level of responsiveness depend on the value of all covariates. Whenever a researcher has multiple predictors in a GLM model,

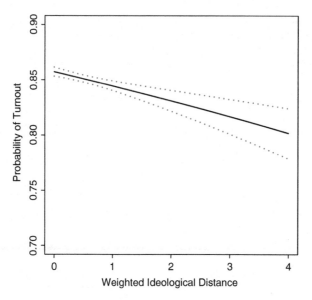

Fig. 7.2 Predicted probability of turning out to vote as a function of weighted ideological distance from the nearest party, with 95 % confidence intervals

reasonable values of the control variables must be included in the forecasts. See Sect. 7.3.3 for an example of using the `predict` function for a GLM that includes multiple predictors.

7.2 Ordinal Outcomes

We now turn to ordinal outcome measures. Ordinal variables have multiple categories as responses that can be ranked from lowest to highest, but other than the rankings the numeric values have no inherent meaning. As an example of an ordinal outcome variable, we again use survey data from the CSES, this time from Singh's (2014b) study of satisfaction with democracy. Relative to the previous example, these data have a wider scope, including 66,908 respondents from 62 elections. The variables in this data set are as follows:

satisfaction: Respondent's level of satisfaction with democracy. Ordinal scale coded 1 (not at all satisfied), 2 (not very satisfied), 3 (fairly satisfied), or 4 (very satisfied).

cntryyear: A character variable listing the country and year of the election.

cntryyearnum: A numeric index identifying the country-year of the election.

freedom: Freedom House scores for a country's level of freedom. Scores range from −5.5 (least free) to −1 (most free).

gdpgrowth: Percentage growth in Gross Domestic Product (GDP).

gdppercapPPP: GDP per capita, computed using purchasing price parity (PPP), chained to 2000 international dollars, in thousands of dollars.

CPI: Corruption Perceptions Index. Scores range from 0 (least corrupt) to 7.6 (most corrupt).

efficacy: Respondent thinks that voting can make a difference. Ordinal scale from 1 (disagree) to 5 (agree).

educ: Indicator coded 1 if the respondent graduated from college, 0 if not.

abstained: Indicator coded 1 if the respondent abstained from voting, 0 if the respondent voted.

prez: Indicator coded 1 if the country has a presidential system, 0 if not.

majoritarian_prez: Indicator coded 1 if the country has a majoritarian system, 0 if not.

winner: Indicator coded 1 if the respondent voted for the winning party, 0 if not.

voted_ID: Indicator coded 1 if the respondent voted for the party he or she identifies with, 0 if not.

voted_affect: Indicator coded 1 if the respondent voted for the party he or she rated highest, 0 if not.

voted_ideo: Indicator coded 1 if the respondent voted for the most similar party on ideology, 0 if not.

optimality: Vote optimality scale ranging from 0 to 3, coded by adding **voted_ID**, **voted_affect**, and **voted_ideo**.

winnerXvoted_ID: Interaction term between voting for the winner and voting by party identification.

winnerXvoted_affect: Interaction term between voting for the winner and voting for the highest-rated party.

winnerXvoted_ideo: Interaction term between voting for the winner and voting by ideological similarity.

winnerXoptimality: Interaction term between voting for the winner and the vote optimality scale.

These data are also in Stata format, so if the `foreign` library is not already loaded, it will need to be called. To load our data, download the file `SinghEJPR.dta` from the Dataverse linked on page vii or the chapter content linked on page 97. Then type:

```
library(foreign)
satisfaction<-read.dta("SinghEJPR.dta")
```

In this example, we wish to model each respondent's level of satisfaction with democracy. This variable takes on the values 1, 2, 3, and 4, and we can only make statements about which values reflect higher levels of satisfaction. In other words, we can say that a value of 4 ("very satisfied") reflects higher satisfaction than a value of 3 ("fairly satisfied"), a value of 3 is more than 2 ("not very satisfied"), and therefore a value of 4 is higher than a value of 2. We cannot, however, say *how much* more satisfaction one value reflects relative to another, as the numbers have no inherent meaning other than providing a rank order of satisfaction. To do so would require us to quantify adjectives such as "very" and "fairly." Hence, an ordered logit or ordered probit model is going to be appropriate for this analysis.

As our first example, Singh (2014b, Table SM2) fits a model in which satisfaction in democracy is based on whether the respondent voted for the candidate most ideologically proximate, whether the candidate voted for the winner, and the interaction between these two variables.[7] The most important of these terms is the interaction, as it tests the hypothesis that individuals who were on the winning side *and* voted for the most similar party ideologically will express the greatest satisfaction.

Turning to specifics, for ordinal regression models we actually must use the special command `polr` (short for **p**roportional **o**dds **l**ogistic **r**egression), which is part of the MASS package. Most R distributions automatically install MASS, though we still need to load it with the `library` command.[8] In order to load the MASS package and then estimate an *ordered logit* model with these data, we would type:

```
library(MASS)
satisfaction$satisfaction<-ordered(as.factor(
    satisfaction$satisfaction))
ideol.satisfaction<-polr(satisfaction~voted_ideo*winner+
    abstained+educ+efficacy+majoritarian_prez+
    freedom+gdppercapPPP+gdpgrowth+CPI+prez,
    method="logistic",data=satisfaction)
summary(ideol.satisfaction)
```

Observe that we recode our dependent variable, `satisfaction`, using the `as.factor` command that was introduced in Sect. 2.4.2. We further embed this within the `ordered` command to convey that the factor can be ordered numerically. We had to recode in this way because the model command `polr` requires the outcome to be saved as a vector of class `factor`. Meanwhile, the right-hand side of the model resembles all other models we have estimated so far by separating variable names by plus signs. Notice that we use interactive notation with `voted_ideo*winner`, in order to include both terms plus the product.[9] All together, we have modeled satisfaction as a function of whether the voter voted for the most ideologically similar party, voted for the winner, an interaction term between the two, and several other individual-level and country-level control variables. Within the command, the option `method="logistic"` specifies that we wish to estimate an ordered *logit* model rather than use another link function. At the end of the line, we specify our `data` option as usual to point to our data set of interest.

---

[7]This and the next example do not exactly replicate the original results, which also include random effects by country-year. Also, the next example illustrates ordered probit regression, instead of the ordered logistic model from the original article. Both of the examples are based on models found in the online supporting material at the *European Journal of Political Research* website.

[8]If a user does need to install the package, `install.packages("MASS")` will do the job.

[9]An equivalent specification would have been to include `voted_ideo+winner+ winnerXvoted_ideo` as three separate terms from the data.

After estimating this model, we type `summary(ideol.satisfaction)` into the console. The output looks like this:

```
Call:
polr(formula=satisfaction~voted_ideo*winner+abstained+
    educ+efficacy+majoritarian_prez+freedom+gdppercap
    PPP+
    gdpgrowth+CPI+prez,data=satisfaction,method=
    "logistic")

Coefficients:
                        Value Std. Error   t value
voted_ideo           -0.02170   0.023596   -0.9198
winner                0.21813   0.020638   10.5694
abstained            -0.25425   0.020868  -12.1838
educ                  0.08238   0.020180    4.0824
efficacy              0.16246   0.006211   26.1569
majoritarian_prez     0.05705   0.018049    3.1609
freedom               0.04770   0.014087    3.3863
gdppercapPPP          0.01975   0.001385   14.2578
gdpgrowth             0.06653   0.003188   20.8673
CPI                  -0.23153   0.005810  -39.8537
prez                 -0.11503   0.026185   -4.3930
voted_ideo:winner     0.19004   0.037294    5.0957

Intercepts:
     Value   Std. Error t value
1|2  -2.0501   0.0584   -35.1284
2|3  -0.0588   0.0575    -1.0228
3|4   2.7315   0.0586    46.6423

Residual Deviance: 146397.33
AIC: 146427.33
```

The output shows the estimate of each coefficient, the standard error, and the z value. (Though R calls it a t value, maximum likelihood methods typically call for z ratios, as mentioned previously.) After the coefficient presentation, three *cut points* are presented under the label of `Intercepts`. These cut points identify the model by finding where on a latent utility scale the cutoff is between a respondent's choosing 1 versus 2 as a response, 2 versus 3, and 3 versus 4. Although the cut points often are often not of substantive interest, they are important for the sake of forecasting predicted outcomes. The default fit statistics in the output are the residual deviance and the AIC.

The results are presented more formally in Table 7.2. Although R's base output omits the p value, the user can easily draw inferences based on the available information: Either through computing confidence intervals, comparing the z value to a critical value, or computing p values oneself. For instance, the key hypothesis

Table 7.2 Ordered logit model of satisfaction with democracy, 62 cross-national elections

Predictor	Estimate	Std. error	z value	$\Pr(> \lvert z \rvert)$
Voted for proximate party	−0.0217	0.0236	−0.9198	0.3577
Voted for winner	0.2181	0.0206	10.5694	0.0000
Voted proximate×winner	0.1900	0.0373	5.0957	0.0000
Abstained	−0.2542	0.0209	−12.1838	0.0000
College graduate	0.0824	0.0202	4.0824	0.0000
Efficacy	0.1625	0.0062	26.1569	0.0000
Majoritarian system	0.0571	0.0180	3.1609	0.0016
Freedom	0.0477	0.0141	3.3863	0.0007
Economic development	0.0197	0.0014	14.2578	0.0000
Economic growth	0.0665	0.0032	20.8673	0.0000
Corruption	−0.2315	0.0058	−39.8537	0.0000
Presidential system	−0.1150	0.0262	−4.3930	0.0000
τ_1	−2.0501	0.0584	−35.1284	0.0000
τ_2	−0.0588	0.0575	−1.0228	0.3064
τ_3	2.7315	0.0586	46.6423	0.0000

Notes: $N = 66,908$. AIC $= 146,427$. Data from Singh (2014b)

here is for the interaction term to be positive. Hence, we can obtain our one-tailed p value by typing:

```
1-pnorm(5.0957)
```

R prints out `1.737275e-07`, which in scientific notation means $p = 0.00000017$. Therefore, we will conclude with 99.9 % confidence that the coefficient on the interaction term is discernibly greater than zero. In Table 7.2, we have opted to report the two-tailed p values.[10]

A nice feature of using the logit link function, is that the results can be interpreted in terms of odds ratios. Odds ratios need to be computed and interpreted a bit differently for an ordinal model, though. See Long (1997, pp. 138–140) for a full explanation. For ordered logit models, we must exponentiate the *negative* value of a coefficient and interpret the odds of being in lower groups relative to higher groups. By way of example, the odds ratios for our coefficients from Table 7.2, along with the percentage changes in odds, can be produced at once:

---

[10]Unfortunately the `xtable` command does not produce ready-made LATEX tables for results from `polr`. By creating a matrix with the relevant results, though, LATEX users can produce a table faster than hand coding, though some revisions of the final product are necessary. Try the following:
```
coef<-c(ideol.satisfaction$coefficients,ideol.satisfaction$zeta)
se<-sqrt(diag(vcov(ideol.satisfaction)))
z<-coef/se
p<-2*(1-pnorm(abs(z)))
xtable(cbind(coef,se,z,p),digits=4)
```

```
exp(-ideol.satisfaction$coefficients)
100*(exp(-ideol.satisfaction$coefficients)-1)
```

The resulting printout from the second line is:

```
       voted_ideo              winner            abstained
          2.194186          -19.597657           28.949139
              educ            efficacy  majoritarian_prez
         -7.908003          -14.994659           -5.545347
           freedom        gdppercapPPP            gdpgrowth
         -4.658313           -1.955471           -6.436961
               CPI                prez  voted_ideo:winner
         26.053177           12.190773          -17.307376
```

If we wanted to interpret the effect of efficacy, then, we could say for a one point increase on a five-point efficacy scale, the odds a respondent will report that they are "not at all satisfied" with democracy relative to any of the three higher categories decrease by 15 %, *ceteris paribus*. Also, the odds that a respondent will report "not at all satisfied" or "not very satisfied" relative to the two higher categories also decrease by 15 %, all else equal. Further still, the odds that a respondent will report one of the bottom three satisfaction levels relative to the highest category of "very satisfied" diminish by 15 %, holding the other predictors constant. In general, then, we can interpret an odds ratio for an ordered logit as shaping the odds of all options below a threshold relative to all options above a threshold.

As a second example, we turn now to a model of voter satisfaction that focuses not on the role of ideological proximity in vote choice, but instead on which party the voter evaluated the most highly when asked to rate the parties. Again, the interaction between voting for the highest-rated party and also voting for the winning party is the primary coefficient of interest. This time, we will also try a different link function and estimate an *ordered probit* model instead of an ordered logit model. In this case we will type:

```
affect.satisfaction<-polr(satisfaction~voted_affect*winner+
    abstained+educ+efficacy+majoritarian_prez+
    freedom+gdppercapPPP+gdpgrowth+CPI+prez,
    method="probit",data=satisfaction)
```

Besides changing one of the interacted variables, the only difference between this code and the prior command for the ordered logit command is the specification of `method="probit"`. This changes the scale of our coefficients somewhat, but the substantive implications of results are generally similar regardless of this choice. By typing `summary(affect.satisfaction)`, we obtain the output:

```
Call:
polr(formula = satisfaction ~ voted_affect * winner +
  abstained +
    educ + efficacy + majoritarian_prez + freedom +
    gdppercapPPP +
```

```
gdpgrowth + CPI + prez, data = satisfaction, method
  = "probit")
```

Coefficients:
```
                       Value Std. Error t value
voted_affect         0.03543  0.0158421   2.237
winner               0.04531  0.0245471   1.846
abstained           -0.11307  0.0170080  -6.648
educ                 0.05168  0.0115189   4.487
efficacy             0.09014  0.0035177  25.625
majoritarian_prez    0.03359  0.0101787   3.300
freedom              0.03648  0.0082013   4.448
gdppercapPPP         0.01071  0.0007906  13.546
gdpgrowth            0.04007  0.0018376  21.803
CPI                 -0.12897  0.0033005 -39.075
prez                -0.03751  0.0147650  -2.540
voted_affect:winner  0.14278  0.0267728   5.333
```

Intercepts:
```
     Value    Std. Error t value
1|2  -1.1559    0.0342   -33.7515
2|3  -0.0326    0.0340    -0.9586
3|4   1.6041    0.0344    46.6565
```

```
Residual Deviance: 146698.25
AIC: 146728.25
```

Once again, our hypothesis of interest is supported by the results, with a positive and discernible effect on the interaction between voting for the winning party and voting for the highest-rated party.

7.3 Event Counts

As a third type of GLM, we turn to models of event counts. Whenever our dependent variable is the number of events that occurs within a defined period of time, the variable will have the feature that it can never be negative and must take on a discrete value (e.g., 0,1,2,3,4, ...). Count outcomes therefore tend to have a strong right skew and a discrete probability distribution such as the Poisson or negative binomial distribution.

As an example of count data, we now return to Peake and Eshbaugh-Soha's (2008) data that were previously discussed in Chap. 3. Recall that the outcome variable in this case is the number of television news stories related to energy policy in a given month. (See Chap. 3 for additional details on the data.) The number of news stories in a month certainly is an event count. However, note that because these are monthly data, they are *time dependent*, which is a feature we ignore at this time. In Chap. 9 we revisit this issue and consider models that account for time. For now, though, this illustrates how we usually fit count models in R.

First, we load the data again:[11]

```
pres.energy<-read.csv("PESenergy.csv")
```

After viewing the descriptive statistics on our variables and visualizing the data as we did in Chap. 3, we can now turn to fitting a model.

7.3.1 Poisson Regression

The simplest count model we can fit is a Poisson model. If we were to type:

```
energy.poisson<-glm(Energy~rmn1173+grf0175+grf575+jec477+
    jec1177+jec479+embargo+hostages+oilc+Approval+Unemploy,
    family=poisson(link=log),data=pres.energy)
```

This will fit a Poisson regression model in which TV coverage of energy policy is a function of six terms for presidential speeches, an indicator for the Arab oil embargo, an indicator for the Iran hostage crisis, the price of oil, presidential approval, and the unemployment rate.[12] Notice that this time, we set `family=poisson(link=log)`, declaring the distribution of the outcome as Poisson and specifying our log link function. If we type `summary(energy.poisson)` into the console, R returns the following output:

```
Call:
glm(formula = Energy ~ rmn1173 + grf0175 + grf575 +
 jec477 +
    jec1177 + jec479 + embargo + hostages + oilc +
      Approval +
    Unemploy, family = poisson(link = log), data = pres.
      energy)

Deviance Residuals:
   Min      1Q  Median      3Q     Max
-8.383  -2.994  -1.054   1.536  11.399

Coefficients:
            Estimate Std. Error z value Pr(>|z|)
(Intercept) 13.250093   0.329121  40.259  < 2e-16   ***
rmn1173      0.694714   0.077009   9.021  < 2e-16   ***
```

---

[11]The footnote should read: "For users who do not have the file handy from Chapter 3, please download the file from the Dataverse linked on page vii or the chapter content linked on page 97.

[12]Note that the presidential speech terms are coded 1 only in the month of the speech, and 0 in all other months. The terms for the oil embargo and hostage crisis were coded 1 while these events were ongoing and 0 otherwise.

```
grf0175            0.468294    0.096169     4.870    1.12e-06    ***
grf575            -0.130568    0.162191    -0.805    0.420806
jec477             1.108520    0.122211     9.071    < 2e-16     ***
jec1177            0.576779    0.155511     3.709    0.000208    ***
jec479             1.076455    0.095066    11.323    < 2e-16     ***
embargo            0.937796    0.051110    18.349    < 2e-16     ***
hostages          -0.094507    0.046166    -2.047    0.040647    *
oilc              -0.213498    0.008052   -26.515    < 2e-16     ***
Approval          -0.034096    0.001386   -24.599    < 2e-16     ***
Unemploy          -0.090204    0.009678    -9.321    < 2e-16     ***
---
Signif. codes:  0  ***    0.001  **   0.01  *    0.05  .  0.1   1
```

(Dispersion parameter for poisson family taken to be 1)

```
    Null deviance: 6009.0  on 179  degrees of freedom
Residual deviance: 2598.8  on 168  degrees of freedom
AIC: 3488.3
```

Number of Fisher Scoring iterations: 5

The format of the output—coefficient estimates, standard errors, z, and p—should be very familiar by now, as are the deviance and AIC scores. In this case the link function is simply a logarithm, so although the coefficients themselves are not very meaningful, interpretation is still simple. As one option, if we take the exponential of a coefficient, this offers us a *count ratio*, which allows us to deduce the percentage change in the expected count for a change in the input variable. For instance, if we wanted to interpret the effect of presidential approval, we could type:

```
exp(-.034096)
```

Here, we simply inserted the estimated coefficient from the printed output. The result gives us a count ratio of 0.9664787. We could interpret this as meaning for a percentage point increase in the president's approval rating, coverage of energy policy diminishes by 3.4 % on average and holding all other predictors equal. As a quick way to get the count ratio and percentage change for every coefficient, we could type:

```
exp(energy.poisson$coefficients[-1])
100*(exp(energy.poisson$coefficients[-1])-1)
```

In both lines the [-1] index for the coefficient vector throws away the intercept term, for which we do not want a count ratio. The printout from the second line reads:

```
    rmn1173      grf0175      grf575      jec477      jec1177
100.313518   59.726654  -12.240295  202.987027    78.029428
      jec479      embargo     hostages        oilc     Approval
193.425875  155.434606   -9.017887  -19.224639   -3.352127
    Unemploy
 -8.625516
```

From this list, we can simply read-off the percentage changes for a one-unit increase in the input, holding the other inputs equal. For a graphical means of interpretation, see Sect. 7.3.3.

7.3.2 Negative Binomial Regression

An intriguing feature of the Poisson distribution is that the variance is the same as the mean. Hence, when we model the logarithm of the mean, our model is simultaneously modeling the variance. Often, however, we find that the variance of our count variable is wider than we would expect given the covariates—a phenomenon called *overdispersion*. Negative binomial regression offers a solution to this problem by estimating an extra dispersion parameter that allows the conditional variance to differ from the conditional mean.

In R, **n**egative **b**inomial regression models actually require a special command from the MASS library called glm.nb. If the MASS library is not loaded, be sure to type library(MASS) first. Then, we can fit the negative binomial model by typing:

```
energy.nb<-glm.nb(Energy~rmn1173+grf0175+grf575+jec477+
    jec1177+jec479+embargo+hostages+oilc+Approval+Unemploy,
    data=pres.energy)
```

Notice that the syntax is similar to the glm command, but there is no family option since the command itself specifies that. By typing summary(energy.nb) the following results print:

```
Call:
glm.nb(formula = Energy ~ rmn1173 + grf0175 + grf575 +
   jec477 +
    jec1177 + jec479 + embargo + hostages + oilc +
      Approval +
    Unemploy, data = pres.energy, init.theta =
      2.149960724, link = log)

Deviance Residuals:
    Min       1Q    Median       3Q       Max
 -2.7702  -0.9635  -0.2624   0.3569    2.2034

Coefficients:
             Estimate Std. Error z value Pr(>|z|)
(Intercept) 15.299318   1.291013  11.851  < 2e-16 ***
rmn1173      0.722292   0.752005   0.960  0.33681
grf0175      0.288242   0.700429   0.412  0.68069
grf575      -0.227584   0.707969  -0.321  0.74786
jec477       0.965964   0.703611   1.373  0.16979
```

```
jec1177          0.573210    0.702534    0.816   0.41455
jec479           1.141528    0.694927    1.643   0.10045
embargo          1.140854    0.350077    3.259   0.00112 **
hostages         0.089438    0.197520    0.453   0.65069
oilc            -0.276592    0.030104   -9.188   < 2e-16 ***
Approval        -0.032082    0.005796   -5.536   3.1e-08 ***
Unemploy        -0.077013    0.037630   -2.047   0.04070 *
---
Signif. codes:  0  ***  0.001  **  0.01  *  0.05  .  0.1  1

(Dispersion parameter for Negative Binomial(2.15) family
   taken
to be 1)

    Null deviance: 393.02   on 179   degrees of freedom
Residual deviance: 194.74   on 168   degrees of freedom
AIC: 1526.4

Number of Fisher Scoring iterations: 1


           Theta:   2.150
       Std. Err.:   0.242

 2 x log-likelihood:   -1500.427
```

The coefficients reported in this output can be interpreted in the same way that coefficients from a Poisson model are interpreted because both model the logarithm of the mean. The key addition, reported at the end of the printout, is the dispersion parameter θ. In this case, our estimate is $\hat{\theta} = 2.15$, and with a standard error of 0.242 the result is discernible. This indicates that overdispersion is present in this model. In fact, many of the inferences drawn vary between the Poisson and negative binomial models. The two models are presented side by side in Table 7.3. As the results show, many of the discernible results from the Poisson model are not discernible in the negative binomial model. Further, the AIC is substantially lower for the negative binomial model, indicating a better fit even when penalizing for the extra overdispersion parameter.

7.3.3 Plotting Predicted Counts

While count ratios are certainly a simple way to interpret coefficients from count models, we have the option of graphing our results as well. In this case, we model the logarithm of our mean parameter, so we must exponentiate our linear prediction to predict the expected count given our covariates. As with logit and probit models, for count outcomes the `predict` command makes forecasting easy.

Suppose we wanted to plot the effect of presidential approval on the number of TV news stories on energy, based on the two models of Table 7.3. This situation contrasts a bit from the graphs we created in Sect. 7.1.3. In all of the logit and probit examples, we only had one predictor. By contrast, in this case we have several other predictors, so we have to set those to plausible alternative values. For this example, we will set the value of all dummy variable predictors to their modal value of zero, while the price of oil and unemployment are set to their mean. If we fail to insert reasonable values for the covariates, the predicted counts will not resemble the actual mean and the size of the effect will not be reasonable.[13] In this example, the way in which we use the `predict` command to forecast average counts with multiple predictors can be used in exactly the same way for a logit or probit model to forecast predicted probabilities with multiple predictors.

Table 7.3 Two count models of monthly TV new stories on energy policy, 1969–1983

Parameter	Poisson			Negative binomial		
	Estimate	Std. error	$\Pr(> |z|)$	Estimate	Std. error	$\Pr(> |z|)$
Intercept	13.2501	0.3291	0.0000	15.2993	1.2910	0.0000
Nixon 11/73	0.6947	0.0770	0.0000	0.7223	0.7520	0.3368
Ford 1/75	0.4683	0.0962	0.0000	0.2882	0.7004	0.6807
Ford 5/75	−0.1306	0.1622	0.4208	−0.2276	0.7080	0.7479
Carter 4/77	1.1085	0.1222	0.0000	0.9660	0.7036	0.1698
Carter 11/77	0.5768	0.1555	0.0002	0.5732	0.7025	0.4145
Carter 4/79	1.0765	0.0951	0.0000	1.1415	0.6949	0.1005
Arab oil embargo	0.9378	0.0511	0.0000	1.1409	0.3501	0.0011
Iran hostage crisis	−0.0945	0.0462	0.0406	0.0894	0.1975	0.6507
Price of oil	−0.2135	0.0081	0.0000	−0.2766	0.0301	0.0000
Presidential approval	−0.0341	0.0014	0.0000	−0.0321	0.0058	0.0000
Unemployment	−0.0902	0.0097	0.0000	−0.0770	0.0376	0.0407
θ	—			2.1500	0.2419	0.0000
AIC	3488.2830			1526.4272		

Notes: $N = 180$. Data from Peake and Eshbaugh-Soha (2008)

---

[13]Besides this approach of making predictions using central values of control variables, Hanmer and Kalkan (2013) make the case that forecasting outcomes based on the observed values of control variables in the data set is preferable. Readers are encouraged to consult their article for further advice on this issue.

Turning to specifics, in our data the variable `approve` ranges from 24% approval to 72.3%. Thus, we construct a vector that includes the full range of approval as well as plausible values of all of the other predictors:

```
approval<-seq(24,72.3,by=.1)
inputs.4<-cbind(1,0,0,0,0,0,0,0,0,mean(pres.energy$oilc),
    approval,mean(pres.energy$Unemploy))
colnames(inputs.4)<-c("constant","rmn1173","grf0175",
    "grf575","jec477","jec1177","jec479","embargo","hostages",
    "oilc","Approval","Unemploy")
inputs.4<-as.data.frame(inputs.4)
```

The first line above creates the vector of hypothetical values of our predictor of interest. The second line creates a matrix of hypothetical data values—setting the indicator variables to zero, the continuous variables to their means, and approval to its range of hypothetical values. The third line names the columns of the matrix after the variables in our model. On the last line, the matrix of predictor values is converted to a data frame.

Once we have the data frame of predictors in place, we can use the `predict` command to forecast the expected counts for the Poisson and negative binomial models:

```
forecast.poisson<-predict(energy.poisson,newdata=inputs.4,
    type="response")
forecast.nb<-predict(energy.nb,newdata=inputs.4,type="response")
```

These two lines only differ in the model from which they draw coefficient estimates for the forecast.[14] In both cases, we specify `type="response"` to obtain predictions on the count scale.

To graph our forecasts from each model, we can type:

```
plot(y=forecast.poisson,x=approval,type="l",lwd=2,
    ylim=c(0,60),xlab="Presidential Approval",
    ylab="Predicted Count of Energy Policy Stories")
lines(y=forecast.nb,x=approval,lty=2,col="blue",lwd=2)
legend(x=50,y=50,legend=c("Poisson","Negative Binomial"),
    lty=c(1,2),col=c("black","blue"),lwd=2)
```

The first line plots the Poisson predictions as a line with the `type="l"` option. The second line adds the negative binomial predictions, coloring the line blue and dashing it with `lty=2`. Finally, the `legend` command allows us to quickly distinguish which line represents which model. The full output is presented in Fig. 7.3. The predictions from the two models are similar and show a similar negative effect of approval. The negative binomial model has a slightly lower forecast at low values of approval and a slightly shallower effect of approval, such that the predicted counts overlap at high values of approval.

---

[14] As a side note, by using R's matrix algebra commands, described further in Chap. 10, the user can compute predicted counts easily with alternate syntax. For instance, for the negative binomial model, we could have typed: `forecast.nb<-exp(as.matrix(inputs.4)%*%energy.nb$coefficients)`.

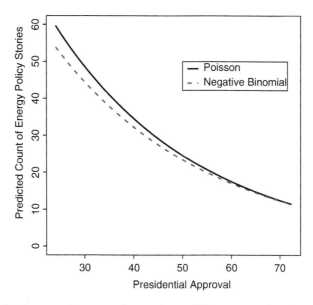

Fig. 7.3 Predicted count of energy policy stories on TV news as a function of presidential approval, holding continuous predictors at their mean and nominal predictors at their mode. Predictions based on Poisson and negative binomial model results

After the first seven chapters of this volume, users should now be able to perform most of the basic tasks that statistical software is designed to do: manage data, compute simple statistics, and estimate common models. In the remaining four chapters of this book, we now turn to the unique features of R that allow the user greater flexibility to apply advanced methods with packages developed by other users and tools for programming in R.

7.4   Practice Problems

1. Logistic regression: Load the `foreign` library, and download a subset of Singh's (2015) cross-national survey data on voter turnout, the file `stdSingh.dta`, available from the Dataverse listed on page vii or the chapter content listed on page 97. The outcome variable is whether the survey respondent voted (**voted**). A key predictor, with which several variables are interacted, is the degree to which a citizen is subject to mandatory voting rules. This is measured with a scale of how severe the compulsory voting rules are (**severity**). Five predictors should be interacted with **severity**: age (**age**), political knowledge (**polinfrel**), income (**income**), efficacy (**efficacy**), and partisanship (**partyID**). Five more predictors should be included only for additive effects: district magnitude (**dist_magnitude**), number of parties (**enep**), victory margin

(**vicmarg_dist**), parliamentary system (**parliamentary**), and per capita GDP (**development**). All of the predictor variables have been standardized.

   a. Estimate a logistic regression model with these data, including the five interaction terms.
   b. What is the odds ratio for number of parties? How would you interpret this term?
   c. Plot the effect of per capita GDP on the probability of turning out. Hold all predictors other than development at their mean. *Hint:* Build on the code starting on page 107. If you used R's interaction notation (e.g., if age*severity is a term in the model), then when you create a new dataset of predictor values, you need only define your values for the original variables, and not for the products. In other words, you would need a column for **age**, for **severity**, and for any other predictors, but not for **age** × **severity**.
   d. <u>Bonus:</u> Plot the effect of age on probability of turnout for three circumstances: When severity of compulsory voting rules is at its minimum, at its mean, and at its maximum. Hold all other predictors besides age and severity at their mean. Your final result should show three different predicted probability lines.

2. Ordered logit: The practice problems from Chapter 2 introduced Hanmer and Kalkan's (2013) subset of the 2004 American National Election Study. If you do not have these data already, the file hanmerKalkanANES.dta can be downloaded from the Dataverse linked on page vii or from the chapter content linked on page 97. Load the foreign library and open these data. (Again, be sure to specify the convert.factors=F option.) Consider two outcome variables: retrospective economic evaluations (**retecon**, taking on ordinal values coded −1, −0.5, 0, 0.5, and 1) and assessment of George W. Bush's handling of the war in Iraq (**bushiraq**, taking on ordinal values coded 0, 0.33, 0.67, and 1). There are seven predictor variables: partisanship on a seven-point scale (**partyid**), ideology on a seven-point scale (**ideol7b**), an indicator of whether the respondent is white (**white**), an indicator of whether the respondent is female (**female**), age of the respondent (**age**), level of education on a seven-point scale (**educ1_7**), and income on a 23-point scale (**income**).

   a. Estimate an ordered logistic model of retrospective economic evaluations as a function of the seven predictors.
   b. What is the odds ratio on the coefficient for female? How would you interpret this term?
   c. Estimate an ordered logistic model of evaluation of Bush's handling of the war in Iraq as a function of the seven predictors.
   d. What is the odds ratio on the coefficient for the seven-point partisanship scale? How would you interpret this term?
   e. <u>Bonus:</u> The results of a model are biased if there is *reciprocal causation*, meaning that one of the independent variables not only influences the dependent variable, but also the dependent variable influences the independent

variable. Suppose you were worried about reciprocal causation bias in the model of retrospective economic evaluations. Which independent variable or variables would be most suspect to this criticism?

3. Count model: In the practice problems from Chapters 3 and 4, we introduced Peake and Eshbaugh-Soha's (2008) analysis of drug policy coverage. If you do not have their data from before, download `drugCoverage.csv` from the Dataverse linked on page vii or the chapter content linked on page 97. The outcome variable is news coverage of drugs (**drugsmedia**), and the four inputs are an indicator for a speech on drugs that Ronald Reagan gave in September 1986 (**rwr86**), an indicator for a speech George H.W. Bush gave in September 1989 (**ghwb89**), the president's approval rating (**approval**), and the unemployment rate (**unemploy**).[15]

   a. Estimate a Poisson regression model of drug policy coverage as a function of the four predictors.
   b. Estimate a negative binomial regression model of drug policy coverage as a function of the four predictors. Based on your models' results, which model is more appropriate, Poisson or negative binomial? Why?
   c. Compute the count ratio for the presidential approval predictor for each model. How would you interpret each quantity?
   d. Plot the predicted counts from each model contingent on the unemployment level, ranging from the minimum to maximum observed values. Hold the two presidential speech variables at zero, and hold presidential approval at its mean. Based on this figure, what can you say about the effect of unemployment in each model?

---

[15] Just as in the example from the chapter, these are time series data, so methods from Chap. 9 are more appropriate.

Chapter 8
Using Packages to Apply Advanced Models

In the first seven chapters of this book, we have treated R like a traditional statistical software program and reviewed how it can perform data management, report simple statistics, and estimate a variety of regression models. In the remainder of this book, though, we turn to the added flexibility that R offers—both in terms of programming capacity that is available for the user as well as providing additional applied tools through *packages*. In this chapter, we focus on how loading additional batches of code from user-written packages can add functionality that many software programs will not allow. Although we have used packages for a variety of purposes in the previous seven chapters (including car, gmodels, and lattice, to name a few), here we will highlight packages that enable unique methods. While the CRAN website lists numerous packages that users may install at any given time, we will focus on four particular packages to illustrate the kinds of functionality that can be added.

The first package we will discuss, lme4, allows users to estimate multilevel models, thereby offering an extension to the regression models discussed in Chaps. 6 and 7 (Bates et al. 2014). The other three were all developed specifically by Political Scientists to address data analytic problems that they encountered in their research: MCMCpack allows users to estimate a variety of models in a Bayesian framework using Markov chain Monte Carlo (MCMC) (Martin et al. 2011). cem allows the user to conduct coarsened exact matching—a method for causal inference with field data (Iacus et al. 2009, 2011). Lastly, wnominate allows the user to scale choice data, such as legislative roll call data, to estimate ideological ideal points of legislators or respondents (Poole and Rosenthal 1997; Poole et al. 2011). The following four sections will consider each package separately, so each section will introduce its data example in turn. These sections are designed to offer a brief overview of the

Electronic supplementary material: The online version of this chapter (doi: 10.1007/978-3-319-23446-5_8) contains supplementary material, which is available to authorized users.

kinds of capacities R packages offer, though some readers may be unfamiliar with
the background behind some of these methods. The interested reader is encouraged
to consult with some of the cited resources to learn more about the theory behind
these methods.

8.1 Multilevel Models with `lme4`

Having discussed linear models in Chap. 6 and several examples of generalized
linear models in Chap. 7, we now turn to an extension of these kinds of models:
multilevel models. Multilevel models, or hierarchical models, are appropriate
whenever data of interest have either a nested or longitudinal structure. A nested
structure occurs when observations can be thought of as being within or part of
an upper-level unit: A common policy example is to study learning outcomes for
students, but the students are nested within classrooms. In such a case, the researcher
would need to account for the fact that the students in the sample are not independent
of each other, but are likely to be similar if in the same classroom. Similarly,
whenever a researcher studies individuals that have repeated observations over time,
it is reasonable to think of the time-referenced observations as being embedded
within the individual's observations. For example, in the LaLonde (1986) data first
introduced in Chap. 4, the income of participants in his study are observed in 1974,
1975, and 1978. Some policy analyses might opt to consider the three temporal
observations for each individual as being nested within each individual's case.[1]
More comprehensive explanations of multilevel models can be found in Scott et al.
(2013) and Gelman and Hill (2007). We proceed by extending two of our prior
examples to illustrate a multilevel linear model and a multilevel logit model.

8.1.1 Multilevel Linear Regression

In this example, we return to our example from Chap. 6 on the number of hours
teachers spend in the classroom teaching evolution. Originally, we fitted a linear
model using ordinary least squares (OLS) as our estimator. However, Berkman and
Plutzer (2010) make the point that teachers in the same state are likely to share
similar features. These features could be similarities in training, in the local culture,
or in state law. To account for these unobserved similarities, we can think of teachers
as being *nested* within states. For this reason, we will add a *random effect* for each
state. Random effects account for *intraclass correlation*, or error correlation among

---

[1]Note that this multilevel approach to panel data is most sensible for short panels such as these
where there are many individuals relative to the number of time points. For long panels in which
there are many time points relative to the number of individuals, more appropriate models are
described as pooled time series cross-section methods. For more on the study of short panels, see
Monogan (2011) and Fitzmaurice et al. (2004).

observations within the same group. In the presence of intraclass correlation, OLS estimates are inefficient because the disturbance terms are not independent, so a random effects model accounts for this problem.

First, we reload the data from the National Survey of High School Biology Teachers as follows:[2]

```
rm(list=ls())
library(foreign)
evolution<-read.dta("BPchap7.dta")
evolution$female[evolution$female==9]<-NA
evolution<-subset(evolution,!is.na(female))
```

Recall that we had a handful of observations of female that needed to be recoded as missing. As before, we subset our data to omit these missing observations.

In order to fit a multilevel model, there are actually a few commands available. We will opt to use a command from the lme4 (**l**inear **m**ixed **e**ffect) library.[3] On our first use, we will install the package, and then on every use we will load the library:

```
install.packages("lme4")
library(lme4)
```

Once we have loaded the library, we fit our multilevel linear model using the lmer (**l**inear **m**ixed **e**ffects **r**egression) command:

```
hours.ml<-lmer(hrs_allev~phase1+senior_c+ph_senior+notest_p+
    ph_notest_p+female+biocred3+degr3+evol_course+certified+
    idsci_trans+confident+(1|st_fip),data=evolution)
```

The syntax to the lmer command is nearly identical to the code we used when fitting a model with OLS using lm. In fact, the only attribute we added is the additional term (1|st_fip) on the right-hand side of the model. This adds a random intercept by state. On any occasion for which we wish to include a random effect, in parentheses we place the term for which to include the effect followed by a vertical pipe and the variable that identifies the upper-level units. So in this case we wanted a random intercept (hence the use of 1), and we wanted these to be assigned by state (hence the use of st_fip).

We obtain our results by typing:

```
summary(hours.ml)
```

In our result output, R prints the correlation between all of the *fixed effects*, or estimated regression parameters. This part of the printout is omitted below:

```
Linear mixed model fit by REML ['lmerMod']
Formula:
hrs_allev~phase1+senior_c+ph_senior+notest_p+ph_notest
   _p+
```

---

[2]If you do not have these data from before, you can download the file BPchap7.dta from the Dataverse on page vii or the chapter content on page 125.

[3]See also the nlme library, which was a predecessor to lme4.

```
    female+biocred3+degr3+evol_course+certified+idsci_
       trans+
    confident+(1|st_fip)
   Data: evolution
```

REML criterion at convergence: 5940

Scaled residuals:
```
    Min       1Q   Median      3Q      Max
-2.3478  -0.7142  -0.1754  0.5566  3.8846
```

Random effects:
```
 Groups    Name            Variance  Std.Dev.
 st_fip    (Intercept)     3.089     1.758
 Residual                  67.873    8.239
Number of obs: 841, groups:  st_fip, 49
```

Fixed effects:
```
              Estimate  Std. Error  t value
(Intercept)   10.5676       1.2138    8.706
phase1         0.7577       0.4431    1.710
senior_c      -0.5291       0.3098   -1.708
ph_senior     -0.5273       0.2699   -1.953
notest_p       0.1134       0.7490    0.151
ph_notest_p   -0.5274       0.6598   -0.799
female        -0.9702       0.6032   -1.608
biocred3       0.5157       0.5044    1.022
degr3         -0.4434       0.3887   -1.141
evol_course    2.3894       0.6270    3.811
certified     -0.5335       0.7188   -0.742
idsci_trans    1.7277       1.1161    1.548
confident      2.6739       0.4468    5.984
```

The output first prints a variety of fit statistics: AIC, BIC, log-likelihood, deviance, and restricted maximum likelihood deviance. Second, it prints the variance and standard deviation of the random effects. In this case, the variance for the st_fip term is the variance of our state-level random effects. The residual variance corresponds to the error variance of regression that we would normally compute for our residuals. Last, the fixed effects that are reported are synonymous with linear regression coefficients that we normally are interested in, albeit now our estimates have accounted for the intraclass correlation among teachers within the same state. Table 8.1 compares our OLS and multilevel estimates side-by-side. As can be seen, the multilevel model now divides the unexplained variance into two components (state and individual-level), and coefficient estimates have changed somewhat.

Table 8.1 Two models of hours of class time spent teaching evolution by high school biology teachers

Parameter	OLS			Multilevel		
	Estimate	Std. error	Pr(> |z|)	Estimate	Std. error	Pr(> |z|)
Intercept	10.2313	1.1905	0.0000	10.5675	1.2138	0.0000
Standards index 2007	0.6285	0.3331	0.0596	0.7576	0.4431	0.0873
Seniority (centered)	−0.5813	0.3130	0.0636	−0.5291	0.3098	0.0876
Standards × seniority	−0.5112	0.2717	0.0603	−0.5273	0.2699	0.0508
Believes there is no test	0.4852	0.7222	0.5019	0.1135	0.7490	0.8795
Standards × believes no test	−0.5362	0.6233	0.3899	−0.5273	0.6598	0.4241
Teacher is female	−1.3546	0.6016	0.0246	−0.9703	0.6032	0.1077
Credits earned in biology (0–2)	0.5559	0.5072	0.2734	0.5157	0.5044	0.3067
Science degrees (0–2)	−0.4003	0.3922	0.3077	−0.4434	0.3887	0.2540
Completed evolution class	2.5108	0.6300	0.0001	2.3894	0.6270	0.0001
Has normal certification	−0.4446	0.7212	0.5377	−0.5335	0.7188	0.4580
Identifies as scientist	1.8549	1.1255	0.0997	1.7277	1.1161	0.1216
Self- rated expertise (−1 to +2)	2.6262	0.4501	0.0000	2.6738	0.4468	0.0000
State-level variance	—			3.0892		
Individual-level variance	69.5046			67.8732		

Notes: $N = 841$. Data from Berkman and Plutzer (2010)

8.1.2 Multilevel Logistic Regression

While somewhat more complex, the logic of multilevel modeling can also be applied when studying limited dependent variables. There are two broad approaches to extending GLMs into a multilevel framework: marginal models, which have a population-averaged interpretation, and generalized linear mixed models (GLMMs), which have an individual-level interpretation (Laird and Fitzmaurice 2013, pp. 149–156). While readers are encouraged to read further on the kinds of models available, their estimation, and their interpretation, for now we focus on the process of estimating a GLMM.

In this example, we return to our example from Sect. 7.1.1 from the last chapter, on whether a survey respondent reported voting for the incumbent party as a function of the ideological distance from the party. As Singh (2014a) observes, voters making their choice in the same country-year are going to face many features of the choice that are unique to that election. Hence, intraclass correlation among voters within the same election is likely. Further, the effect of ideology itself may be stronger in some elections than it is in others: Multilevel methods including GLMMs allow us to evaluate whether there is variation in the effect of a predictor across groups, which is a feature that we will use.

Turning to the specifics of code, if the `lme4` library is not loaded, we need that again. Also, if the data from are not loaded, then we need to load the `foreign` library and the data set itself. All of this is accomplished as follows:[4]

```
library(lme4)
library(foreign)
voting<-read.dta("SinghJTP.dta")
```

Building on the model from Table 7.1, we first simply add a random intercept to our model. The syntax for estimating the model and printing the results is:

```
inc.linear.ml<-glmer(votedinc~distanceinc+(1|cntryyear),
     family=binomial(link="logit"),data=voting)
summary(inc.linear.ml)
```

Notice that we now use the `glmer` command (**g**eneralized **l**inear **m**ixed **e**ffects **r**egression). By using the `family` option, we can use any of the common link functions available for the `glm` command. A glance at the output shows that, in addition to the traditional fixed effects that reflect logistic regression coefficients, we also are presented with the variance of the random intercept for country and year of the election:

```
Generalized linear mixed model fit by the Laplace
  approximation
Formula: votedinc ~ distanceinc + (1 | cntryyear)
   Data: voting
      AIC       BIC    logLik deviance
 41998.96 42024.62 -20996.48 41992.96
Random effects:
 Groups    Name          Variance Std.Dev.
 cntryyear (Intercept) 0.20663  0.45457
Number of obs: 38211, groups: cntryyear, 30

Fixed effects:
               Estimate    Std. Error   z value Pr(>|z|)
(Intercept)  0.161788717  0.085578393   1.89053 0.058687 .
distanceinc -0.501250136  0.008875997 -56.47254  < 2e-16  ***
---
Signif. codes:  0  ***  0.001  **  0.01  *  0.05  .  0.1  1

Correlation of Fixed Effects:
            (Intr)
distanceinc -0.185
```

To replicate a model more in line with Singh's (2014a) results, we now fit a model that includes a random intercept and a random coefficient on ideological distance, both contingent on the country and year of the election. The syntax for estimating this model and printing the output is:

---

[4]If you do not have these data from before, you can download the file `SinghJTP.dta` from the Dataverse on page vii or the chapter content on page 125.

```
inc.linear.ml.2<-glmer(votedinc~distanceinc+
    (distanceinc|cntryyear),family=binomial(link="logit"),
    data=voting)
summary(inc.linear.ml.2)
```

Notice that we now have conditioned the variable `distanceinc` by `cntryyear`. This adds a random coefficient for ideological distance. Also, by default, adding this random effect also adds a random intercept as well. Our output in this case is:

```
Generalized linear mixed model fit by the Laplace
  approximation
Formula: votedinc ~ distanceinc + (distanceinc |
  cntryyear)
  Data: voting
  AIC    BIC  logLik deviance
 41074  41117  -20532    41064
Random effects:
 Groups     Name         Variance Std.Dev. Corr
 cntryyear  (Intercept)  0.616658 0.78528
            distanceinc  0.098081 0.31318  -0.808
Number of obs: 38211, groups: cntryyear, 30

Fixed effects:
            Estimate Std. Error z value Pr(>|z|)
(Intercept)  0.26223   0.14531    1.805   0.0711 .
distanceinc -0.53061   0.05816   -9.124   <2e-16 ***
---
Signif. codes: 0 *** 0.001 ** 0.01 * 0.05 . 0.1 1

Correlation of Fixed Effects:
            (Intr)
distanceinc -0.808
```

Under random effects, we first see the variance for the election-referenced random intercept, and then variance for the election-referenced coefficient for ideological distance. The fixed effects for the logistic regression coefficients are also presented in the usual way. The AIC indicates that this version of the model fits better than either the model with only a random intercept or the model from Table 7.1 that included no random effects, as the score of 41,074 is lower than the AIC of either of those models. In sum, this discussion should offer a sense of the kinds of hierarchical models that R can estimate using lme4 (Bates et al. 2014).

8.2   Bayesian Methods Using `MCMCpack`

The `MCMCpack` package allows users to perform Bayesian inference on a variety
of common regression models and measurement models. The package even has
a command, `MCMCmetrop1R`, that will construct a MCMC sample from a user-
defined distribution using a Metropolis algorithm. Readers who wish to learn more
about Bayesian methods are encouraged to consult resources such as: Carlin and
Louis (2009), Gelman et al. (2004), Gill (2008), and Robert (2001).

  As a simple illustration of how the package functions, we focus in this section
on some of the common regression models that are programmed into the package.
This is powerful for the R user in that researchers who prefer to report Bayesian
models can easily do so if their model specification conforms to a common structure.
In illustrating these techniques, we will revisit one more time the linear model of
evolution hours by Berkman and Plutzer (2010) and the logistic regression model of
incumbent party support by Singh (2014a).

8.2.1   Bayesian Linear Regression

To estimate our Bayesian linear regression model, we must reload the data from the
National Survey of High School Biology Teachers, if they are not already loaded:

```
rm(list=ls())
library(foreign)
evolution<-read.dta("BPchap7.dta")
evolution$female[evolution$female==9]<-NA
evolution<-subset(evolution,!is.na(female))
```

With the data loaded, we must install `MCMCpack` if this is the first use of the
package on the computer. Once the program is installed, we then must load the
library:

```
install.packages("MCMCpack")
library(MCMCpack)
```

Now we can use **MCMC** to fit our Bayesian linear **regress**ion model with the
`MCMCregress` command:

```
mcmc.hours<-MCMCregress(hrs_allev~phase1+senior_c+ph_senior+
    notest_p+ph_notest_p+female+biocred3+degr3+
    evol_course+certified+idsci_trans+confident,data=evolution)
```

Be prepared that estimation with MCMC usually takes a longer time computation-
ally, though simple models such as this one usually finish fairly quickly. Also,
because MCMC is a simulation-based technique, it is normal for summaries of
the results to differ slightly across replications. To this end, if you find differences
between your results and those printed here after using the same code, you need not
worry unless the results are markedly different.

While the above code relies on the defaults of the MCMCregress command, a few of this command's options are essential to highlight: A central feature of Bayesian methods is that the user must specify *priors* for all of the parameters that are estimated. The defaults for MCMCregress are vague conjugate priors for the coefficients and the variance of the disturbances. However, the user has the option of specifying his or her own priors on these quantities.[5] Users are encouraged to review these options and other resources about how to set priors (Carlin and Louis 2009; Gelman et al. 2004; Gill 2008; Robert 2001). Users also have the option to change the number of iterations in the MCMC sample with the mcmc option and the burn-in period (i.e., number of starting iterations that are discarded) with the burnin option. Users should always assess model *convergence* after estimating a model with MCMC (to be discussed shortly) and consider if either the burn-in or number of iterations should be changed if there is evidence of nonconvergence.

After estimating the model, typing summary(mcmc.hours) will offer a quick summary of the *posterior* sample:

```
Iterations = 1001:11000
Thinning interval = 1
Number of chains = 1
Sample size per chain = 10000


1. Empirical mean and standard deviation for each
   variable, plus standard error of the mean:
```

	Mean	SD	Naive SE	Time-series SE
(Intercept)	10.2353	1.1922	0.011922	0.011922
phase1	0.6346	0.3382	0.003382	0.003382
senior_c	-0.5894	0.3203	0.003203	0.003266
ph_senior	-0.5121	0.2713	0.002713	0.002713
notest_p	0.4828	0.7214	0.007214	0.007214
ph_notest_p	-0.5483	0.6182	0.006182	0.006182
female	-1.3613	0.5997	0.005997	0.006354
biocred3	0.5612	0.5100	0.005100	0.005100
degr3	-0.4071	0.3973	0.003973	0.003973
evol_course	2.5014	0.6299	0.006299	0.005870
certified	-0.4525	0.7194	0.007194	0.007194
idsci_trans	1.8658	1.1230	0.011230	0.010938
confident	2.6302	0.4523	0.004523	0.004590
sigma2	70.6874	3.5029	0.035029	0.035619

---

[5]For priors on the coefficients, the option b0 sets the vector of means of a multivariate Gaussian prior, and B0 sets the variance-covariance matrix of the multivariate Gaussian prior. The prior distribution of the error variance of regression is inverse Gamma, and this distribution can be manipulated by setting its shape parameter with option c0 and scale parameter with option d0. Alternatively, the inverse Gamma distribution can be manipulated by changing its mean with the option sigma.mu and its variance with the option sigma.var.

2. Quantiles for each variable:

```
                 2.5%        25%       50%       75%      97.5%
(Intercept)    7.92359   9.438567  10.2273  11.03072  12.59214
phase1        -0.02787   0.405026   0.6384   0.86569   1.30085
senior_c      -1.22527  -0.808038  -0.5885  -0.37351   0.04247
ph_senior     -1.04393  -0.694228  -0.5105  -0.32981   0.03152
notest_p      -0.92717  -0.006441   0.4863   0.97734   1.88868
ph_notest_p   -1.75051  -0.972112  -0.5462  -0.13138   0.63228
female        -2.52310  -1.771210  -1.3595  -0.96109  -0.18044
biocred3      -0.42823   0.212168   0.5558   0.90768   1.55887
degr3         -1.19563  -0.671725  -0.4048  -0.14536   0.38277
evol_course    1.26171   2.073478   2.5064   2.92601   3.73503
certified     -1.84830  -0.942671  -0.4477   0.03113   0.95064
idsci_trans   -0.33203   1.107771   1.8667   2.63507   4.09024
confident      1.73568   2.324713   2.6338   2.94032   3.48944
sigma2        64.12749  68.277726  70.5889  72.95921  77.84095
```

Since MCMC produces a sample of simulated parameter values, all of the reported information is based on simple descriptive statistics of the simulated output (which is 10,000 sets of parameters, in this case). Part 1 of the summary above shows the mean of the sample for each parameter, standard deviation of each parameter's sample, and two versions of the standard error of the mean. Part 2 of the summary shows percentiles of each parameter's sample. Table 8.2 shows one common format for presenting results from a model like this: reporting the mean and standard

Table 8.2 Linear model of hours of class time spent teaching evolution by high school biology teachers (MCMC Estimates)

Predictor	Mean	Std. Dev.	[95 % Cred. Int.]	
Intercept	10.2353	1.1922	[7.9236:	12.5921]
Standards index 2007	0.6346	0.3382	[−0.0279:	1.3008]
Seniority (centered)	−0.5894	0.3203	[−1.2253:	0.0425]
Standards × seniority	−0.5121	0.2713	[−1.0439:	0.0315]
Believes there is no test	0.4828	0.7214	[−0.9272:	1.8887]
Standards × believes no test	−0.5483	0.6182	[−1.7505:	0.6323]
Teacher is female	−1.3613	0.5997	[−2.5231:	−0.1804]
Credits earned in biology (0–2)	0.5612	0.5100	[−0.4282:	1.5589]
Science degrees (0–2)	−0.4071	0.3973	[−1.1956:	0.3828]
Completed evolution class	2.5014	0.6299	[1.2617:	3.7350]
Has normal certification	−0.4525	0.7194	[−1.8483:	0.9506]
Identifies as scientist	1.8658	1.1230	[−0.3320:	4.0902]
Self-rated expertise (−1 to +2)	2.6302	0.4523	[1.7357:	3.4894]
Error variance of regression	70.6874	3.5029	[64.1275:	77.8410]

Notes: $N = 841$. Data from Berkman and Plutzer (2010)

deviation of each parameter's marginal posterior distribution, and a 95 % *credible interval* based on the percentiles.[6]

When a user loads MCMCpack in R, the coda library will also load.[7] coda is particularly useful because it allows the user to assess convergence of models estimated with MCMC and report additional quantities of interest. As was mentioned earlier, whenever a researcher estimates a model using MCMC, he or she should assess whether there is any evidence of nonconvergence. In the event that the Markov chains have not converged, the model should be sampled for more iterations. MCMCregress estimates the model using a single chain. Hence, for our model of the number of hours of evolution taught in high school classrooms, we can assess convergence using **Geweke**'s convergence **diag**nostic, which simply asks whether the means of the first and last parts of the chain are the same. To compute this diagnostic, we type:

```
geweke.diag(mcmc.hours, frac1=0.1, frac2=0.5)
```

Here we have specified that we want to compare the mean of the first 10 % of the chain (frac1=0.1) to the mean of the last 50 % of the chain (frac2=0.5). The resulting output presents a *z*-ratio for this difference of means test for each parameter:

```
Fraction in 1st window = 0.1
Fraction in 2nd window = 0.5
```

(Intercept)	phase1	senior_c	ph_senior	notest_p
-1.34891	-1.29015	-1.10934	-0.16417	0.95397
ph_notest_p	female	biocred3	degr3	evol_course
1.13720	-0.57006	0.52718	1.25779	0.62082
certified	idsci_trans	confident	sigma2	
1.51121	-0.87436	-0.54549	-0.06741	

In this case, none of the test statistics surpass any common significance thresholds for a normally distributed test statistic, so we find no evidence of nonconvergence. Based on this, we may be content with our original MCMC sample of 10,000.

One more thing we may wish to do with our MCMC output is **plot** the overall estimated **dens**ity function of our marginal posterior distributions. We can plot these one at a time using the densplot function, though the analyst will need to reference the parameter of interest based on its numeric order of appearance in the summary table. For example, if we wanted to plot the coefficient for the indicator of whether a teacher completed an evolution class (**evol_course**), that is the tenth

---

[6]To write out a similar table to Table 8.2 in LaTeX, load the xtable library in R and type the following into the console:
```
xtable(cbind(summary(mcmc.hours)$statistics[,1:2],
summary(mcmc.hours)$quantiles[,c(1,5)]),digits=4)
```
[7]This frequently occurs when one package depends on code from another.

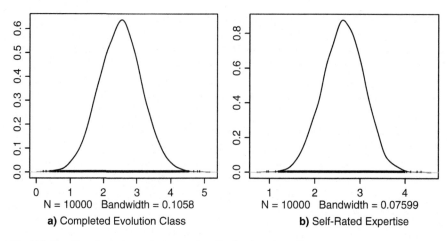

Fig. 8.1 Density plots of marginal posterior distribution of coefficients for whether the teacher completed an evolution class and the teacher's self-rated expertise. Based on an MCMC sample of 10,000 iterations (1000 iteration burn-in). (**a**) Completed evolution class; (**b**) Self-rated expertise

parameter estimate reported in the table. Similarly, if we wanted to report the density plot for the coefficient of the teacher's self-rated expertise (**confident**), that is the thirteenth parameter reported in the summary table. Hence we could plot each of these by typing:

```
densplot(mcmc.hours[,10])
densplot(mcmc.hours[,13])
```

The resulting density plots are presented in Fig. 8.1. As the figures show, both of these marginal posterior distributions have an approximate normal distribution, and the mode is located near the mean and median reported in our summary output.

8.2.2 Bayesian Logistic Regression

As one additional illustration that MCMCpack estimates a variety of models, we illustrate Bayesian logistic regression, using Singh's (2014a) data on voting for incumbent parties one last time. If you do not have these data or the library loaded, be sure to do so:

```
library(MCMCpack)
library(foreign)
voting<-read.dta("SinghJTP.dta")
```

To estimate the Bayesian **logit** model using **MCMC**, we type:

```
inc.linear.mcmc<-MCMClogit(votedinc~distanceinc,data=voting)
```

Just as with the MCMCregress command, we have chosen to use the defaults in this case, but users are encouraged to consider setting their own priors to suit their needs. As a matter of fact, this is one case where we will need to raise the number of iterations in our model. We can check convergence of our model using the Geweke diagnostic:

```
geweke.diag(inc.linear.mcmc, frac1=0.1, frac2=0.5)
```

Our output in this case actually shows a significant difference between the means at the beginning and end of the chain for each parameter:

```
Fraction in 1st window = 0.1
Fraction in 2nd window = 0.5


(Intercept) distanceinc
      2.680        -1.717
```

The absolute value of both z-ratios exceeds 1.645, so we can say the mean is significantly different for each parameter at the 90 % confidence level, which is evidence of nonconvergence.

As a response, we can double both our burn-in period and number of iterations to 2,000 and 20,000, respectively. The code is:

```
inc.linear.mcmc.v2<-MCMClogit(votedinc~distanceinc,
    data=voting,burnin=2000,mcmc=20000)
```

We can now check for the convergence of this new sample by typing:

```
geweke.diag(inc.linear.mcmc.v2, frac1=0.1, frac2=0.5)
```

Our output now shows nonsignificant z-ratios for each parameter, indicating that there is no longer evidence of nonconvergence:

```
Fraction in 1st window = 0.1
Fraction in 2nd window = 0.5


(Intercept) distanceinc
   -1.0975        0.2128
```

Proceeding with this sample of 20,000, then, if we type
summary(inc.linear.mcmc.v2) into the console, the output is:

```
Iterations = 2001:22000
Thinning interval = 1
Number of chains = 1
Sample size per chain = 20000

1. Empirical mean and standard deviation for each
   variable, plus standard error of the mean:
```

```
              Mean        SD  Naive SE  Time-series SE
(Intercept)  0.1940  0.01846  1.305e-04       0.0003857
distanceinc -0.4946  0.00829  5.862e-05       0.0001715
```

2. Quantiles for each variable:

```
              2.5%      25%      50%      75%     97.5%
(Intercept)  0.1573   0.1817   0.1944   0.2063   0.2298
distanceinc -0.5105  -0.5003  -0.4946  -0.4890  -0.4783
```

These results are similar to those that we reported last chapter in Table 7.1, though now we have the opportunity to interpret the findings as a Bayesian. As with Bayesian linear regression, if we wished to report density plots of each parameter, we could apply the densplot command just as before. Overall, this brief illustration should show researchers how easy it is to use Bayesian methods in R with MCMCpack. Readers who wish to use more advanced Bayesian methods are encouraged to consult the MCMCpack reference manual and Martin et al. (2011).

8.3   Causal Inference with cem

A prominent innovation in political methodology has been the development of several new matching methods. In brief, matching is a technique designed to select a subset of field data to make for a fair comparison of individuals who receive a treatment to control individuals who did not receive the treatment. With matching, some observations are thrown away so that the remaining control and treatment observations are similar on all covariates that are known to shape the outcome of interest. In the absence of experimental data, matching methods serve to allow the researcher to isolate how the treatment variable affects responses (see Rubin 2006 for a thorough treatment of causal inference with matching).

Political Scientists have developed several new matching methods (Imai and van Dyk 2004; Sekhon and Grieve 2012). As an illustration of one of these, and how the novel technique is implemented in R, we turn to the method developed by Iacus et al. (2009, 2011, 2012), Coarsened Exact Matching (CEM). In short, CEM proceeds by temporarily recoding each covariate into an ordered variable that lumps similar values of the covariate together. The data are then sorted into strata based on their profiles of the coarsened variables, and any observations in a stratum that does not contain at least one treatment and one control unit are thrown away. The resulting sample should show much more balance in the control variables between the treated and control observations. In R, this technique is implemented with the cem command within the cem package.

8.3.1 Covariate Imbalance, Implementing CEM, and the ATT

As our example data, we return to LaLonde's (1986) study of the National
Supported Work Demonstration that we previously examined in Chaps. 4 and 5. Our
treatment variable (**treated**) indicates if the individual received the treatment from
the National Supported Work Demonstration, meaning the person was placed in a
private sector job for a year with public funds covering the labor costs. We would
like to know the causal effect of this treatment on the individual's earnings in
1978, after the treatment was completed (**re78**). In Sect. 5.1.1 we did a naïve test
of this hypothesis by simply using a difference of means test between the treated
individuals and the control group without controlling for any of the other variables
that are likely to affect annual income. In our naïve test, we found that income was
higher for the treated group, but now we can ask what the estimated effect is when
we account for other important covariates.

As was noted in earlier chapters, LaLonde's data are already included in the cem
package, so we can load these data easily if we have already loaded the cem library.
The following lines of code clean up, install cem (in case you have not already),
opens cem, and loads LaLonde's data (named LL):[8]

```
rm(list=ls())
install.packages("cem")
library(cem)
data(LL)
```

An important task when using matching methods is assessing the degree to which
the data are *balanced*, or the degree to which treated cases have a similar distribution
of covariate values relative to the control group. We can assess the degree to which
our treatment and control groups have differing distributions with the imbalance
command. In the code below, we first increase the penalty for scientific notation
(an option if you prefer decimal notation). Then, we create a vector naming the
variables we do not want to assess balance for—the treatment variable (**treated**)
and the outcome of interest (**re78**). All other variables in the dataset are covariates
that we believe can shape income in 1978, so we would like to have balance on
them. In the last line, we actually call the imbalance command.

```
options(scipen=8)
todrop <- c("treated","re78")
imbalance(group=LL$treated, data=LL, drop=todrop)
```

Within the imbalance command, the group argument is our treatment variable
that defines the two groups for which we want to compare the covariate distributions.
The data argument names the dataset we are using, and the drop option allows us
omit certain variables from the dataset when assessing covariate balance. Our output
from this command is as follows:

---

[8]LaLonde's data is also available in the file LL.csv, available in the Dataverse (see page vii) or
the chapter content (see page 125).

```
Multivariate Imbalance Measure: L1=0.735
Percentage of local common support: LCS=12.4%
```

Univariate Imbalance Measures:

	statistic	type	L1	min	25%
age	0.179203803	(diff)	4.705882e-03	0	1
education	0.192236086	(diff)	9.811844e-02	1	0
black	0.001346801	(diff)	1.346801e-03	0	0
married	0.010703110	(diff)	1.070311e-02	0	0
nodegree	-0.083477916	(diff)	8.347792e-02	0	-1
re74	-101.486184085	(diff)	5.551115e-17	0	0
re75	39.415450601	(diff)	5.551115e-17	0	0
hispanic	-0.018665082	(diff)	1.866508e-02	0	0
u74	-0.020099030	(diff)	2.009903e-02	0	0
u75	-0.045086156	(diff)	4.508616e-02	0	0

	50%	75%	max
age	0.00000	-1.0000	-6.0000
education	1.00000	1.0000	2.0000
black	0.00000	0.0000	0.0000
married	0.00000	0.0000	0.0000
nodegree	0.00000	0.0000	0.0000
re74	69.73096	584.9160	-2139.0195
re75	294.18457	660.6865	490.3945
hispanic	0.00000	0.0000	0.0000
u74	0.00000	0.0000	0.0000
u75	0.00000	0.0000	0.0000

The first line of our output reports $\mathcal{L}_1$, which is a measure of multivariate imbalance created by Iacus et al. (2011). A fuller explanation is available in that article, but in general this statistic ranges from 0 to 1, with lower values indicating better balance. When $\mathcal{L}_1 = 0$ the two distributions perfectly overlap, and when $\mathcal{L}_1 = 1$ the two distributions do not overlap at all. Turning to the table, each row shows several balance statistics for an individual covariate. For all of these statistics, values closer to zero are better. The column labeled statistic shows the difference in means between the variables, and the column labeled L1 computes $\mathcal{L}_1^j$, which is the same measure as $\mathcal{L}_1$ but only calculated for the individual covariate. The remaining columns show quantile differences between the two groups (e.g., the difference in the two groups' respective minima, the difference between the groups' respective 25th percentiles, etc.).

Next, we will actually use the cem command to perform Coarsened Exact Matching on our data. Within the cem command, we list our treatment variable with the treatment argument, our dataset with the data argument, and any variables we do not want to match on with the drop argument. The drop argument should always include our outcome variable, if it is in the same data set, as well as any data indices or irrelevant variables. We could use a vector to list all of the variables we want to be ignored, as we did with the `imbalance` command before, but in this case, only the outcome `re78` needs to be skipped. We type:

```
cem.match.1 <- cem(treatment="treated", data=LL, drop="re78")
cem.match.1
```

Our immediate output from this is simply the following:

```
          G0  G1
All       425 297
Matched   222 163
Unmatched 203 134
```

This tells us that our original data had 425 control observations and 297 treated observations. CEM included 222 of the control and 163 of the treated observations in the matched sample, and the rest are pruned away. To be clear: All observations are still contained in the original LL dataset, but now the object `cem.match.1` itemizes which observations are matched or not.

Since CEM proceeds by grouping similar values of covariates into strata, an important feature of this is how we set the ordered intervals of each predictor in coarsening. The `cem` command has reasonable defaults if the user does not set these intervals, but it is important to record what the intervals are. To see what our intervals were for the values of our predictors, we could type: `cem.match.1$breaks`. This would give us the following output:

```
$age
 [1]  17.0 20.8 24.6 28.4 32.2 36.0 39.8 43.6 47.4 51.2 55.0

$education
 [1]   3.0  4.3  5.6  6.9  8.2  9.5 10.8 12.1 13.4 14.7 16.0

$black
 [1] 0.0 0.1 0.2 0.3 0.4 0.5 0.6 0.7 0.8 0.9 1.0

$married
 [1] 0.0 0.1 0.2 0.3 0.4 0.5 0.6 0.7 0.8 0.9 1.0

$nodegree
 [1] 0.0 0.1 0.2 0.3 0.4 0.5 0.6 0.7 0.8 0.9 1.0

$re74
 [1]     0.000  3957.068  7914.136 11871.204 15828.272 19785.340
 [7] 23742.408 27699.476 31656.544 35613.612 39570.680

$re75
 [1]     0.000  3743.166  7486.332 11229.498 14972.664 18715.830
 [7] 22458.996 26202.162 29945.328 33688.494 37431.660

$hispanic
 [1] 0.0 0.1 0.2 0.3 0.4 0.5 0.6 0.7 0.8 0.9 1.0
```

```
$u74
 [1]  0.0  0.1  0.2  0.3  0.4  0.5  0.6  0.7  0.8  0.9  1.0

$u75
 [1]  0.0  0.1  0.2  0.3  0.4  0.5  0.6  0.7  0.8  0.9  1.0
```

To illustrate what this means, consider age. The lowest category of coarsened age lumps together everyone aged 17–20.8, the second category lumps everyone aged 20.8–24.6, and so forth. Variables like black, married, nodegree, hispanic, u74, and u75 are actually binary, so most of the categories being created are unnecessary, though empty bins will not hurt our analysis. Of course, users are not required to use software defaults, and Iacus et al. urge researchers to use substantive knowledge of each variable's measurement to set the ranges of the coarsening bins (2012, p. 9). Section 8.3.2 offers details on doing this.

Now we can assess imbalance in the new matched sample by typing:

```
imbalance(LL$treated[cem.match.1$matched],
      LL[cem.match.1$matched,], drop=todrop)
```

Our output from this is as follows:

```
Multivariate Imbalance Measure: L1=0.592
Percentage of local common support: LCS=25.2%

Univariate Imbalance Measures:
```

	statistic	type	L1	min	25%	50%
age	-0.42486044	(diff)	0.00000000	0	-1	-2.0000
education	-0.10855027	(diff)	0.10902006	0	0	-1.0000
black	-0.01771403	(diff)	0.01771403	0	0	0.0000
married	-0.01630465	(diff)	0.01630465	0	0	0.0000
nodegree	0.09022827	(diff)	0.09022827	0	0	0.0000
re74	-119.33548135	(diff)	0.00000000	0	0	0.0000
re75	-50.01527694	(diff)	0.00000000	0	0	-49.3559
hispanic	0.01561377	(diff)	0.01561377	0	0	0.0000
u74	0.01619411	(diff)	0.01619411	0	0	0.0000
u75	0.02310286	(diff)	0.02310286	0	0	0.0000

	75%	max
age	0.00	1.000
education	0.00	0.000
black	0.00	0.000
married	0.00	0.000
nodegree	0.00	0.000
re74	-492.95	416.416
re75	-136.45	-852.252
hispanic	0.00	0.000
u74	0.00	0.000
u75	0.00	0.000

Compare this to the original data. We now have $\mathcal{L}_1 = 0.592$, which is less than our score of 0.735 for the raw data, indicating that multivariate balance is better in the matched sample. Turning to the individual covariates, you can see something of a mixed bag, but overall the balance looks better. For instance, with age the difference in means is actually a bit larger in absolute value with the matched sample (0.42) than the raw data (0.18). However, $\mathscr{L}_1^{\mathrm{age}}$ is now minuscule in the matched sample, and less than the 0.0047 value for the raw data. This is likely on account of the fact that the raw data has a larger discrepancy at the high end than the matched sample has. The user now must decide whether the treated and control cases are sufficiently balanced or whether to try other coarsenings to improve balance.

If the user is satisfied with the level of balance, he or she can proceed to estimate the **A**verage **T**reatment effect on the **T**reated (ATT) using the command `att`. This quantity represents the causal effect on the kind of individual who received the treatment. In this command we specify what our matched sample is using the `obj` argument, the outcome variable (**re78**) and treatment (**treated**) using the `formula` argument, and our data using the `data` argument. This gives us:

```
est.att.1 <- att(obj=cem.match.1, formula=re78~treated, data=LL)
est.att.1
```

Our output from this is:

```
            G0   G1
All        425  297
Matched    222  163
Unmatched  203  134

Linear regression model on CEM matched data:

SATT point estimate: 550.962564 (p.value=0.368242)
95% conf. interval: [-647.777701, 1749.702830]
```

The output recaps the features of our matched sample and then reports our estimate of the sample average treatment effect on the treated (SATT): We estimate in our sample that individuals receiving the treatment earned $551 more on average than those who did not receive the treatment. However, this effect is not statistically discernible from zero ($p = 0.368$). This is a markedly different conclusion from the one we drew in Chap. 5, when we observed a $886 difference that was statistically significant. This illustrates the importance of statistical control.

8.3.2 Exploring Different CEM Solutions

As a final point, if a researcher is not happy with the level of balance or the sample size in the matched sample, then a tool for finding better balance is the `cemspace` command. This command randomly produces several different coarsenings for the control variables (250 different coarsenings by default). The command then plots the level of balance against the number of treated observations included in the matched sample. The following code calls this command:

```
cem.explore<-cemspace(treatment="treated",data=LL,drop="re78")
```

The syntax of `cemspace` is similar to `cem`, though two more options are important: `minimal` and `maximal`. These establish what the minimum and maximum allowed number of coarsened intervals is for the variables. The command above uses the defaults of 1 and 5, which means that no more than five intervals may be included for a variable. Hence, all matched samples from this command will be coarser than what we used in Sect. 8.3.1, and therefore less balanced. The user could, however, increase `maximal` to 12 or even a higher number to create finer intervals and potentially improve the balance over our prior result.

Our output from `cemspace` is shown in Fig. 8.2. *On account of the random element in choosing coarsenings, your results will not exactly match this figure.* Figure 8.2a shows the interactive figure that opens up. The horizontal axis of this figure shows the number of matched treatment units in descending order, while the vertical axis shows the level of imbalance. In general, a matched sample at the bottom-left corner of the graph would be ideal as that would indicate the best balance (reducing bias) and the largest sample (increasing efficiency). Normally, though, we have to make a choice on this tradeoff, generally putting a bit more weight on minimizing imbalance. By clicking on different points on the graph, the second window that `cemspace` creates, shown in Fig. 8.2b will show the intervals used in that particular coarsening. The user can copy the vectors of the interval cutpoints and paste them into his or her own code. *Note:* R will not proceed with new commands until these two windows are closed.

In Fig. 8.2a, one of the potential coarsenings has been chosen, and it is highlighted and yellow. If we want to implement this coarsening, we can copy the vectors shown in the second window illustrated in Fig. 8.2b. Pasting these into our own R script produces the following code:

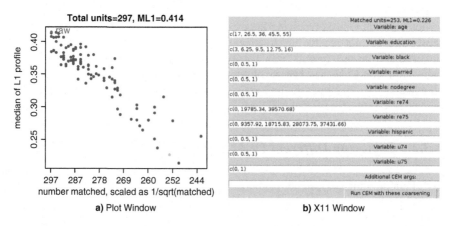

a) Plot Window   **b)** X11 Window

Fig. 8.2 Plot of balance statistics for 250 matched samples from random coarsenings against number of treated observations included in the respective matched sample. (**a**) Plot window; (**b**) X11 window

```
age.cut<-c(17, 26.5, 36, 45.5, 55)
education.cut<-c(3, 6.25, 9.5, 12.75, 16)
black.cut<-c(0, 0.5, 1)
married.cut<-c(0, 0.5, 1)
nodegree.cut<-c(0, 0.5, 1)
re74.cut<-c(0, 19785.34, 39570.68)
re75.cut<-c(0, 9357.92, 18715.83, 28073.75, 37431.66)
hispanic.cut<-c(0, 0.5, 1)
u74.cut<-c(0, 0.5, 1)
u75.cut<-c(0, 1)
new.cuts<-list(age=age.cut, education=education.cut,
     black=black.cut, married=married.cut,
     nodegree=nodegree.cut, re74=re74.cut, re75=re75.cut,
     hispanic=hispanic.cut, u74=u74.cut, u75=u75.cut)
```

We end this code by creating a *list* of all of these vectors. While our vectors here have been created using a coarsening created by cemspace, this is the procedure a programmer would use to create his or her own cutpoints for the intervals. By substituting the vectors above with user-created cutpoint vectors, a researcher can use his or her own knowledge of the variables' measurement to coarsen.

Once we have defined our own cutpoints, either by using cemspace or substantive knowledge, we can now apply CEM with the following code:

```
cem.match.2 <- cem(treatment="treated", data=LL, drop="re78",
     cutpoints=new.cuts)
```

Our key addition here is the use of the cutpoints option, where we input our list of intervals. Just as in Sect. 8.3.1, we can now assess the qualities of the matched sample, imbalance levels, and compute the ATT if we wish:

```
cem.match.2
imbalance(LL$treated[cem.match.2$matched],
     LL[cem.match.2$matched,], drop=todrop)
est.att.2 <- att(obj=cem.match.2, formula=re78~treated, data=LL)
est.att.2
```

In this case, in part because of the coarser bins we are using, the balance is worse that what we found in the previous section. Hence, we would be better off in this case sticking with our first result. The reader is encouraged to try to find a coarsening that produces better balance than the software defaults.

8.4 Legislative Roll Call Analysis with wnominate

Methodologists in Political Science and other disciplines have developed a wide array of measurement models, several of which are available for user implementation in R. Without a doubt, one of the most prominent measurement models in the discipline is NOMINATE, short for **nomina**l **t**hree-step **e**stimation (McCarty et al. 1997; Poole and Rosenthal 1997; Poole et al. 2011). The NOMINATE model analyzes roll call data from legislative votes, placing legislators, and policy alternatives they vote on in ideological space. The model is particularly prominent because Poole, Rosenthal, and colleagues make DW-NOMINATE scores available for both the US House of Representatives and Senate for every term of Congress. Countless authors have used these data, typically interpreting the first dimension score as a scale of liberal-conservative ideology.

In brief, the basic logic of the model draws from the spatial proximity model of politics, which essentially states that both individuals' ideological preferences and available policy alternatives can be represented in geometric space of one or more dimensions. An individual generally will vote for the policy choice that is closest in space to his or her own ideological ideal point (Black 1958; Downs 1957; Hotelling 1929). The NOMINATE model is based on these assumptions, and places legislators and policy options in ideological space based on how legislators' votes divide over the course of many roll call votes and when legislators behave unpredictably (producing errors in the model). For example, in the US Congress, liberal members typically vote differently from conservative members, and the extreme ideologues are the most likely to be in a small minority whenever there is wide consensus on an issue. Before applying the NOMINATE method to your own data—and even before downloading pre-measured DW-NOMINATE data to include in a model you estimate—be sure to read more about the method and its assumptions because thoroughly understanding how a method works is essential before using it. In particular, Chap. 2 and Appendix A from Poole and Rosenthal (1997) and Appendix A from McCarty et al. (1997) offer detailed, yet intuitive, descriptions of how the method works.

In R, the wnominate package implements W-NOMINATE, which is a version of the NOMINATE algorithm that is intended only to be applied to a single legislature. W-NOMINATE scores are internally valid, so it is fair to compare legislators' scores within a single dataset. However, the scores cannot be externally compared to scores when W-NOMINATE is applied to a different term of the legislature or a different body of actors altogether. Hence, it is a good method for trying to make cross-sectional comparisons among legislators of the same body.

While the most common application for W-NOMINATE has been the US Congress, the method could be applied to any legislative body. To that end, the working example in this section focuses on roll call votes cast in the United Nations. This UN dataset is available in the wnominate package, and it pools 237 roll call votes cast in the first three sessions of the UN (1946–1949) by 59 member nations. The variables are labeled **V1** to **V239**. **V1** is the name of the member nation, and **V2** is a categorical variable either coded as "WP" for a member of the Warsaw Pact, or "Other" for all other nations. The remaining variables sequentially identify roll call votes.

To begin, we clean up, install the wnominate package the first time we use it, load the library, and load the UN data:[9]

```
rm(list=ls())
install.packages("wnominate")
library(wnominate)
data(UN)
```

[9]The UN data is also available in the file UN.csv, available in the Dataverse (see page vii) or the chapter content (see page 125)

Once the data are loaded, they can be viewed with the standard commands such as fix, but for a quick view of what the data look like, we could simply type: head(UN[,1:15]). This will show the structure of the data through the first 13 roll call votes.

Before we can apply W-NOMINATE, we have to reformat the data to an object of class rollcall. To do this, we first need to redefine our UN dataset as a matrix, and split the names of the countries, whether the country was in the Warsaw Pact, and the set of roll calls into three separate parts:

```
UN<-as.matrix(UN)
UN.2<-UN[,-c(1,2)]
UNnames<-UN[,1]
legData<-matrix(UN[,2],length(UN[,2]),1)
```

The first line turned the UN data frame into a matrix. (For more on matrix commands in R, see Chap. 10.) The second line created a new matrix, which we have named UN.2, which has eliminated the first two columns (country name and member of Warsaw Pact) to leave only the roll calls. The third line exported the names of the nations into the vector UNnames. (In many other settings, this would instead be the name of the legislator or an identification variable.) Lastly, our variable of whether a nation was in the Warsaw Pact has been saved as a one-column matrix named legData. (In many other settings, this would be a legislator's political party.) Once we have these components together, we can use the rollcall command to define a rollcall-class object that we name rc as follows:

```
rc<-rollcall(data=UN.2,yea=c(1,2,3),nay=c(4,5,6),
     missing=c(7,8,9),notInLegis=0,legis.names=UNnames,
     legis.data=legData,desc="UN Votes",source="voteview.com")
```

We specify our matrix of roll call votes with the data argument. Based on how the data in the roll call matrix are coded, we use the yea, nay, and missing arguments to translate numeric codes into their substantive meaning. Additionally, notInLegis allows us to specify a code that specifically means that the legislator was not a member at the time of the vote (e.g., a legislator died or resigned). We have no such case in these data, but the default value is notInLegis=9, and 9 means something else to us, so we need to specify an unused code of 0. With legis.names we specify the names of the voters, and with legis.data we specify additional variables about our voters. Lastly, desc and source allow us to record additional information about our data.

With our data formatted properly, we can now apply the W-NOMINATE model. the command is simply called wnominate:

```
result<-wnominate(rcObject=rc,polarity=c(1,1))
```

With the rcObject argument, we simply name our properly formatted data. The polarity argument, by contrast, requires substantive input from the researcher: The user should specify a vector that lists which observation should clearly fall on the positive side of each dimension estimated. Given the politics of the Cold

War, we use observation #1, the USA, as the anchor on both dimensions we estimate. By default, wnominate places voters in two-dimensional ideological space (though this could be changed by specifying the dims option).

To view the results of our estimation, we can start by typing: summary(result). This prints the following output.

```
SUMMARY OF W-NOMINATE OBJECT
----------------------------


Number of Legislators:    59 (0 legislators deleted)
Number of Votes:    219 (18 votes deleted)
Number of Dimensions:    2
Predicted Yeas:    4693 of 5039 (93.1%) predictions
 correct
Predicted Nays:    4125 of 4488 (91.9%) predictions
 correct
Correct Classification:    89.5% 92.56%
APRE:    0.574 0.698
GMP:    0.783 0.841



The first 10 legislator estimates are:
                coord1D coord2D
United States    0.939    0.344
Canada           0.932    0.362
Cuba             0.520   -0.385
Haiti            0.362   -0.131
Dominican Rep    0.796   -0.223
Mexico           0.459    0.027
Guatemala        0.382    0.364
Honduras         0.588   -0.266
El Salvador      0.888   -0.460
Nicaragua        0.876   -0.301
```

The output begins by recapping several descriptive features of our data and then turns to fit indices. It lists, for instance the correct prediction of yeas and nays, and then under "Correct Classification" lists the percent correctly predicted by the first dimension alone and then both dimensions together. At 89.5 %, the first dimension can explain a lot by itself. The output ends by listing the estimates for our first 10 observations. As can be seen, the USA does take a positive value on both dimensions, per our specification in the model.

We can obtain additional output by typing: plot(result). The result of this command is presented in Fig. 8.3. The top-left panel visualizes the W-NOMINATE scores for the 59 voting nations. The horizontal axis is the first dimension of the score, the vertical axis is the second dimension, and each point represents a nation's position. Hence, in the two-dimensional ideological space defined internally to UN

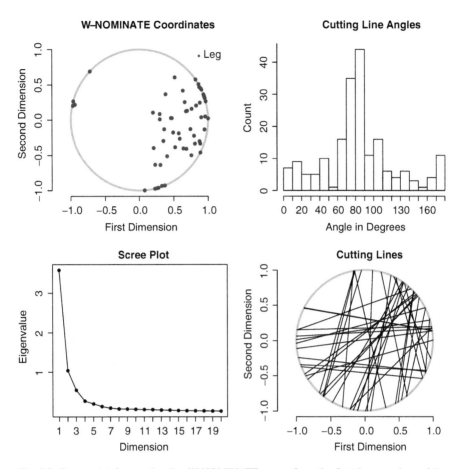

Fig. 8.3 Output plot from estimating W-NOMINATE scores from the first three sessions of the United Nations

proceedings, this is where each nation falls. The bottom-left panel shows a scree plot, which lists the eigenvalue associated with each dimension. Larger eigenvalues indicate that a dimension has more explanatory power. As in all scree plots, each additional dimension has lower explanatory value than the previous one.[10] The top-right panel shows the distribution of the angles of the cutting lines. The cutting lines divide yea from nay votes on a given issue. The fact that so many cutting lines are near the 90° mark indicates that the first dimension is important for many of the

---

[10]When choosing how many dimensions to include in a measurement model, many scholars use the "elbow rule," meaning they do not include any dimensions past a visual elbow in the scree plot. In this case, a scholar certainly would not include more than three dimensions, and may be content with two. Another common cutoff is to include any dimension for which the eigenvalue exceeds 1, which would have us stop at two dimensions.

votes. Finally, the bottom-right panel shows the Coombs Mesh from this model—a visualization of how all of the cutting lines on the 237 votes come together in a single space.

If the user is satisfied with the results of this measurement model, then it is straightforward to write the scores into a useable data format. Within our wnominate output named `result` we can call the attribute named `legislators`, which saves our ideal points for all countries, any non-roll call variables we specified (e.g., Warsaw Pact or not), and a variety of other measures. We save this as a new data frame named `scores` and then write that to a CSV file:

```
scores<-result$legislators
write.csv(scores,"UNscores.csv")
```

Just remember to use the `setwd` command to specify the folder in which you wish to save the output file.

Once we have our W-NOMINATE ideal points in a separate data frame, we can do anything we normally would with data in R, such as draw our own graphs. Suppose we wanted to reproduce our own graph of the ideal points, but we wanted to mark which nations were members of the Warsaw Pact versus those that were not. We could easily do this using our `scores` data. The easiest way to do this might be to use the `subset` command to create separate data frames of our two groups:

```
wp.scores<-subset(scores, V1=="WP")
other.scores<-subset(scores, V1=="Other")
```

Once we have these subsets in hand, we can create the relevant graph in three lines of code.

```
plot(x=other.scores$coord1D, y=other.scores$coord2D,
     xlab="First Dimension", ylab="Second Dimension",
     xlim=c(-1,1), ylim=c(-1,1), asp=1)
points(x=wp.scores$coord1D, y=wp.scores$coord2D,
     pch=3,col='red')
legend(x=-1,y=-.75,legend=c("Other","Warsaw Pact"),
     col=c("black","red"),pch=c(1,3))
```

In the call to `plot`, we graph the 53 nations that were not members of the Warsaw Pact, putting the first dimension on the horizontal axis, and the second on the vertical axis. We label our axes appropriately using `xlab` and `ylab`. We also set the bounds of our graph as running from −1 to 1 on both dimensions, as scores are constrained to fall in these ranges. Importantly, we guarantee that the scale of the two dimensions is the same, as we generally should for this kind of measurement model, by setting the **asp**ect ratio to 1 (`asp=1`). On the second line of code, we use the `points` command to add the six observations that were in the Warsaw Pact, coloring these observations red and using a different plotting character. Lastly, we add a legend.

Figure 8.4 presents the output from our code. This graph immediately conveys that the first dimension is capturing the Cold War cleavage between the USA and its allies versus the Soviet Union and its allies. We specified that the USA would take positive coordinates on both dimensions, so we can see that the Soviet allies

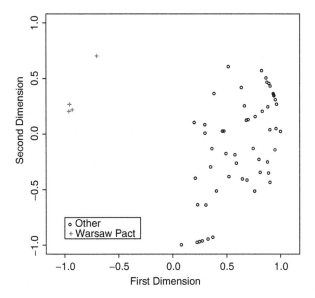

Fig. 8.4 Plot of first and second dimensions of W-NOMINATE scores from the first three sessions of the United Nations. A *red cross* indicates a member of the Warsaw Pact, and a *black circle* indicates all other UN members (Color figure online)

(represented with red crosses) are at the extremes of negative values on the first dimension.

To recap, this chapter has illustrated four examples of how to use R packages to implement advanced methods. The fact that these packages are freely available makes cutting-edge work in political methodology and from a variety of disciplines readily available to any R user. No book could possibly showcase all of the researcher-contributed packages that are available, not least because new packages are being made available on a regular basis. The next time you find yourself facing a taxing methodological problem, you may want to check the CRAN servers to see if someone has already written a program that provides what you need.

8.5   Practice Problems

This set of practice problems considers each of the example libraries in turn, and then suggests you try using a brand new package that has not been discussed in this chapter. Each question calls for a unique data set.

1. Multilevel Logistic Regression: Revisit Singh's (2015) data on voter turnout as a function of compulsory voting rules and several other predictors. If you do not have the file stdSingh.dta, please download it from the Dataverse (see page vii) or the chapter content (see page 125). (These data were first introduced in

Sect. 7.4.) Refit this logistic regression model using the `glmer` command, and include a random intercept by country-year (**cntryyear**). Recall that the outcome is turnout (**voted**). The severity of compulsory voting rules (**severity**) is interacted with the first five predictors: age (**age**), political knowledge (**polinfrel**), income (**income**), efficacy (**efficacy**), and partisanship (**partyID**). Five more predictors should be included only for additive effects: district magnitude (**dist_magnitude**), number of parties (**enep**), victory margin (**vicmarg_dist**), parliamentary system (**parliamentary**), and per capita GDP (**development**). Again, all of the predictor variables have been standardized. What do you learn from this multilevel logistic regression model estimated with `glmer` that you do not learn from a pooled logistic regression model estimated with `glm`?

2. Bayesian Poisson model with MCMC: Determine how to estimate a Poisson model with MCMC using `MCMCpack`. Reload Peake and Eshbaugh-Soha's (2008) data on energy policy news coverage, last discussed in Sect. 7.3. If you do not have the file `PESenergy.csv`, you may download it from the Dataverse (see page vii) or the chapter content (see page 125). Estimate a Bayesian Poisson model in which the outcome is energy coverage (**Energy**), and the inputs are six indicators for presidential speeches (**rmn1173**, **grf0175**, **grf575**, **jec477**, **jec1177**, and **jec479**), an indicator for the Arab oil embargo (**embargo**), an indicator for the Iran hostage crisis (**hostages**), the price of oil (**oilc**), presidential approval (**Approval**), and the unemployment rate (**Unemploy**). Use a Geweke test to determine whether there is any evidence of nonconvergence. How should you change your code in R if nonconvergence is an issue? Summarize your results in a table, and show a density plot of the partial coefficient on Richard Nixon's November 1973 speech (**rmn1173**).

3. Coarsened Exact Matching: In Chap. 5, the practice problems introduced Alvarez et al.'s (2013) data from a field experiment in Salta, Argentina in which some voters cast ballots through e-voting, and others voted in the traditional setting. Load the `foreign` library and open the data in Stata format. If you do not have the file `alpl2013.dta`, you may download it from the Dataverse (see page vii) or the chapter content (see page 125). In this example, the treatment variable is whether the voter used e-voting or traditional voting (**EV**). The covariates are age group (**age_group**), education (**educ**), white collar worker (**white_collar**), not a full-time worker (**not_full_time**), male (**male**), a count variable for number of six possible technological devices used (**tech**), and an ordinal scale for political knowledge (**pol_info**). Use the `cem` library to answer the following:

   a. How balanced are the treatment and control observations in the raw data?
   b. Conduct coarsened exact matching with the `cem` command. How much has the balance improved as a result?
   c. Consider three possible response variables: whether the voter evaluated the voting experience positively (**eval_voting**), whether the voter evaluated the speed of voting as quick (**speed**), and whether the voter is sure his or her vote is being counted (**sure_counted**). What is the average treatment effect on the treated (ATT) on your matched dataset for each of these three responses?

d. How do your estimates of the average treatment effects on the treated differ from simple difference-of-means tests?

4. W-NOMINATE: Back in Sect. 2.1, we introduced Lewis and Poole's roll call data for the 113th US Senate. Consult the code there to read these data, which are in fixed width format. The file name is `sen113kh.ord`, and it is available from the Dataverse (see page vii) and the chapter content (see page 125).

   a. Format the data as a matrix and create the following: a separate matrix just of the 657 roll calls, a vector of the ICPSR identification numbers, and a matrix of the non-roll call variables. Use all of these to create a `rollcall`-class object. The roll call votes are coded as follows: 1 = Yea, 6 = Nay, 7 & 9 = missing, and 0 = not a member.
   b. Estimate a two-dimensional W-NOMINATE model for this roll call object. From the summary of your results, report the following: How many legislators were deleted? How many votes were deleted? Was was the overall correct classification?
   c. Examine the output plot of your estimated model, including the W-NOMINATE coordinates and the scree plot. Based on the scree plot, how many dimensions do you believe are sufficient to characterize voting behavior in the 113th Senate? Why?

5. Bonus: Try learning how to use a package you have never used before. Install the `Amelia` package, which conducts multiple imputation for missing data. Have a look at Honaker et al.'s (2011) article in the *Journal of Statistical Software* to get a feel for the logic of multiple imputation and to learn how to do this in R. Fit a linear model on imputed datasets using the `freetrade` data from the `Amelia` library. What do you find?

Chapter 9
Time Series Analysis

Most of the methods described so far in this book are oriented primarily at cross-sectional analysis, or the study of a sample of data taken at the same point in time. In this chapter, we turn to methods for modeling a time series, or a variable that is observed sequentially at regular intervals over time (e.g., daily, weekly, monthly, quarterly, or annually). Time series data frequently have trends and complex error processes, so failing to account for these features can produce spurious results (Granger and Newbold 1974). Several approaches for time series analysis have emerged to address these problems and prevent false inferences. Within Political Science, scholars of public opinion, political economy, international conflict, and several other subjects regularly work with time-referenced data, so adequate tools for time series analysis are important in political analysis.

Many researchers do not think of R as a program for time series analysis, instead using specialty software such as Autobox, EViews, or RATS. Even SAS and Stata tend to get more attention for time series analysis than R does. However, R actually has a wide array of commands for time series models, particularly through the TSA and vars packages. In this chapter, we will illustrate three approaches to time series analysis in R: the Box–Jenkins approach, extensions to linear models estimated with least squares, and vector autoregression. This is not an exhaustive list of the tools available for studying time series, but is just meant to introduce a few prominent methods. See Sect. 9.4 for some further reading on time series.

Both the Box–Jenkins approach and extensions to linear models are examples of single equation time series models. Both approaches treat one time series as an outcome variable and fit a model of that outcome that can be stated in one equation, much like the regression models of previous chapters can be stated in a single equation. Since both approaches fall into this broad category, the working

Electronic supplementary material: The online version of this chapter (doi: 10.1007/978-3-319-23446-5_9) contains supplementary material, which is available to authorized users.

dataset we use for both the Box–Jenkins approach and extensions to linear models
will be Peake and Eshbaugh-Soha's (2008) monthly data on television coverage of
energy policy that was first introduced in Chap. 3. By contrast, vector autoregression
is a multiple equation time series model (for further details on this distinction, see
Brandt and Williams 2007 or Lütkepohl 2005). With a vector autoregression model,
two or more time series are considered endogenous, so multiple equations are
required to fully specify the model. This is important because endogenous variables
may affect each other, and to interpret an input variable's effect, the broader context
of the full system must be considered. Since multiple equation models have such a
different specification, when discussing vector autoregression the working example
will be Brandt and Freeman's (2006) analysis of weekly political actions in the
Israeli–Palestinian conflict; more details will be raised once we get to that section.

9.1   The Box–Jenkins Method

The Box–Jenkins approach to time series relies on autoregressive integrated moving
average (ARIMA) models to capture the error process in the data. For a comprehensive explanation of this approach, see Box et al. (2008). The basic logic of this
approach is that a time series should be filtered, or *prewhitened*, of any trends
and error processes before attempting to fit an inferential model. Once a model
of the *noise*, or error, has been specified, then the researcher can proceed to test
hypotheses.[1] On account of nonlinear functional forms that often emerge in ARIMA
and transfer function models, these usually are estimated with maximum likelihood.
    To illustrate the process from identifying an error model to testing a hypothesis,
we revisit Peake and Eshbaugh-Soha's (2008) monthly time series on energy policy
coverage. We start by reloading our data:[2]

```
pres.energy<-read.csv("PESenergy.csv")
```

Our outcome variable is the number of energy-related stories on nightly television
news by month (**Energy**). A good first step is to plot the series being studied to see
if any trends or other features are immediately apparent. Look back at Fig. 3.6 for
the example code we used to plot our outcome variable (**Energy**) and the price of
oil, which is one of the predictors (**oilc**). As a first look at the news coverage series,
the data appear to be *stationary*, meaning that they hover around a mean without
trending in one direction or showing an *integrated* pattern.
    As a substantively important point about time series in general, the distinction
between *stationary* and *nonstationary* series is important. Many time series methods

---

[1]Many use ARIMA models for forecasting future values of a series. ARIMA models themselves are
atheoretical, but often can be effective for prediction. Since most Political Science work involves
testing theoretically motivated hypotheses, this section focuses more on the role ARIMA models
can serve to set up inferential models.

[2]If you do not have the data file PESenergy.csv already, you can download it from the
Dataverse (see page vii) or the online chapter content (see page 155).

are designed specifically for modeling stationary series, so applying them to a nonstationary series can be problematic. A *stationary* series is one for which the mean and variance do not change conditional on time, and the series does not trend in one direction. If a stationary series is disturbed, or moved to a higher or lower value, it eventually returns back to an equilibrium level. The two kinds of *nonstationary* series are trending series and integrated series. With a *trending* series, as its name implies, the conditional average changes over time, typically rising or falling consistently. For example, nominal prices of consumer goods may rise or fall from one quarter to the next, but the average value tends to rise over time. An *integrated series*, also called a unit root series, does not have an equilibrium value and has the feature of "long memory." This means that if something changes the value of a series, then future values of the series will be affected by that change long into the future. For instance, suppose the Dow Jones Industrial Average dropped 300 points in 1 day, from 18,200 to 17,900. In such a case, future values of the Dow will be based on the new value of 17,900 plus however much the value rose or fell each subsequent day, and the Dow will not tend to revert back to earlier values. Importantly, by *differencing* the current value of a series from its previous value, or measuring how much a series changed from one time to the next, trending or integrated series can be made stationary. Hence, many models for stationary series can be applied to the difference of a nonstationary series. Whenever doing applied time series work always look at the graph of the series, such as Fig. 3.6 in this case, as well as the diagnostics to be described to determine whether you are studying a stationary, trending, or unit root series.[3]

As a second step, we turn to diagnostic measures and look at the **a**uto**c**orrelation **f**unction (ACF) and **p**artial **a**uto**c**orrelation **f**unction (PACF). The autocorrelation function shows how much current values of a series correlate with previous values at a certain *lag*. *Lags* are important for time series modeling, as will be seen later in the chapter, and they act by changing the index of a series to shift time back and form a new series. For example, a first-order lag is a new series where each observation is the value that occurred one time period previously. A second-order lag is a new series where each observation is the value from two time periods previously, and so forth. This is important when using the autocorrelation function because, if we are studying a series y with time index t, ACF(1) would give us the correlation between y_t and y_{t-1}. (For energy coverage, then, ACF(1) tells us the correlation between current months' coverage with prior months' coverage.) Subsequently, ACF(2) would be the autocorrelation between y_t and y_{t-2}, and more generally ACF(p) is the autocorrelation between y_t and y_{t-p}. The PACF provides the autocorrelation between current and lagged values *that is not accounted for by all prior lags*. So for the first lag, ACF(1)=PACF(1), but for all subsequent lags only the autocorrelation unique to that lag shows up in the PACF. If we wanted to know the ACF and PACF of our energy policy series, we would type:

---

[3]In addition to examining the original series or the autocorrelation function, an Augmented Dickey–Fuller test also serves to diagnose whether a time series has a unit root. By loading the `tseries` package, the command `adf.test` will conduct this test in R.

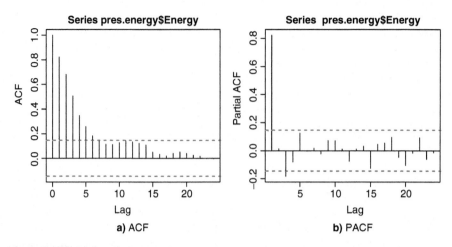

Fig. 9.1 Autocorrelation function and partial autocorrelation function of monthly TV coverage of energy policy through 24 lags. (**a**) ACF. (**b**) PACF

```
acf(pres.energy$Energy,lag.max=24)
pacf(pres.energy$Energy,lag.max=24)
```

The acf and pacf functions are available without loading a package, though the code changes slightly if users load the TSA package.[4] Notice that within the acf and pacf functions, we first list the series we are diagnosing. Second, we designate lag.max, which is the number of lags of autocorrelation we wish to consider. Since these are monthly data, 24 lags gives us 2 years' worth of lags. In some series, *seasonality* will emerge, in which we see evidence of similar values at the same time each year. This would be seen with significant lags around 12 and 24 with monthly data (or around 4, 8, and 12, by contrast, with quarterly data). No such evidence appears in this case.

The graphs of our ACF and PACF are shown in Fig. 9.1. In each of these figures, the horizontal axis represents the lag length, and the vertical axis represents the correlation (or partial correlation) value. At each lag, the autocorrelation for that lag is shown with a solid histogram-like line from zero to the value of the correlation. The blue dashed lines represent the threshold for a significant correlation. Specifically, the blue bands represent the 95 % confidence interval based on an uncorrelated series.[5] All of this means that if the histogram-like line does not

---

[4]The primary noticeable change is that the default version of acf graphs the zero-lag correlation, ACF(0), which is always 1.0. The TSA version eliminates this and starts with the first lag autocorrelation, ACF(1).

[5]The formula for these error bands is: $0 \pm 1.96 \times se_r$. The standard error for a correlation coefficient is: $se_r = \sqrt{\frac{1-r^2}{n-2}}$. So in this case, we set $r = 0$ under the null hypothesis, and n is the sample size (or series length).

cross the dashed line, the level of autocorrelation is not discernibly different from zero, but correlation spikes outside of the error band are statistically significant.

The ACF, in Fig. 9.1a starts by showing the zero-lag autocorrelation, which is just how much current values correlate with themselves—always exactly 1.0. Afterward, we see the more informative values of autocorrelation at each lag. At one lag out, for instance, the serial correlation is 0.823. For two lags, it drops to 0.682. The sixth lag is the last lag to show discernible autocorrelation, so we can say that the ACF decays rapidly. The PACF, in Fig. 9.1b, skips the zero lag and starts with first-order serial correlation. As expected, this is 0.823, just like the ACF showed. However, once we account for first-order serial correlation, the partial autocorrelation terms at later lags are not statistically discernible.[6]

At this point, we determine which ARIMA error process would leave an empirical footprint such as the one this ACF and PACF show. For more details on common footprints, see Enders (2009, p. 68). Notationally, we call the error process ARIMA(p,d,q), where p is the number of autoregressive terms, d is how many times the series needs to be differenced, and q is the number of moving average terms. Functionally, a general *ARMA* model, which includes autoregressive and moving average components, is written as follows:

$$y_t = \alpha_0 + \sum_{i=1}^{p} \alpha_i y_{t-i} + \sum_{i=1}^{q} \beta_i \epsilon_{t-i} + \epsilon_t \tag{9.1}$$

Here, y_t is our series of interest, and this ARMA model becomes an ARIMA model when we decide whether we need to difference y_t or not. Notice that y_t is lagged p times for the autoregressive terms, and the disturbance term (ϵ_t) is lagged q times for the moving average terms. In the case of energy policy coverage, the ACF shows a rapid decay and we see one significant spike in the PACF, so we can say we are dealing with a first-order autoregressive process, denoted AR(1) or ARIMA(1,0,0).

Once we have identified our **a**uto**r**egressive **i**ntegrated **m**oving **a**verage model, we can estimate it using the `arima` function:

```
ar1.mod<-arima(pres.energy$Energy,order=c(1,0,0))
```

The first input is the series we are modeling, and the `order` option allows us to specify p, d, and q (in order) for our ARIMA(p,d,q) process. By typing `ar1.mod`, we see the output of our results:

```
Call:
arima(x = pres.energy$Energy, order = c(1, 0, 0))

Coefficients:
          ar1    intercept
       0.8235      32.9020
s.e.   0.0416       9.2403
```

---

[6]Technically, PACF at the third lag is negative and significant, but the common patterns of error processes suggest that this is unlikely to be a critical part of the ARIMA process.

```
sigma^2 estimated as 502.7: log likelihood=-815.77,
 aic=1637.55
```

Pretty simply, this shows us the estimate and standard error of the autoregressive coefficient (ar1) and intercept, as well as the residual variance, log likelihood, and AIC.

The next step in the Box–Jenkins modeling process is to diagnose whether the estimated model sufficiently filters the data.[7] We do this in two ways: First, by studying the ACF and PACF for the residuals from the ARIMA model. The code is:

```
acf(ar1.mod$residuals,lag.max=24)
pacf(ar1.mod$residuals,lag.max=24)
```

As with many other models, we can call our residuals using the model name and a dollar sign (ar1.mod$residuals). The resulting graphs are presented in Fig. 9.2. As the ACF and PACF both show, the second and fourth lags barely cross the significance threshold, but there is no clear pattern or evidence of an overlooked feature of the error process. Most (but not all) analysts would be content with this pattern in these figures.

As a second step of diagnosing whether we have sufficiently filtered the data, we compute the Ljung–**Box** Q-**test**. This is a joint test across several lags of whether there is evidence of serial correlation in any of the lags. The null hypothesis is that

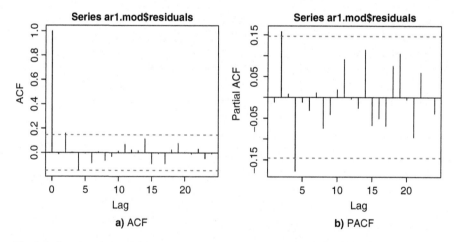

Fig. 9.2 Autocorrelation function and partial autocorrelation function for residuals of AR(1) model through 24 lags. *Blue dashed lines* represent a 95 % confidence interval for an uncorrelated series. (**a**) ACF. (**b**) PACF (Color figure online)

---

[7]Here we show in the main text how to gather one diagnostic at a time, but the reader also may want to try typing tsdiag(ar1.mod,24) to gather graphical representations of a few diagnostics all at once.

the data are independent, so a significant result serves as evidence of a problem. The syntax for this test is:

```
Box.test(ar1.mod$residuals,lag=24,type="Ljung-Box")
```

We first specify the series of interest, then with the `lag` option state how many lags should go into the test, and lastly with `type` specify `Ljung-Box` (as opposed to the Box–Pierce test, which does not perform as well). Our results from this test are:

```
        Box-Ljung test

data:  ar1.mod$residuals
X-squared = 20.1121, df = 24, p-value =
0.6904
```

Our test statistic is not significant ($p = 0.6904$), so this test shows no evidence of serial correlation over 2 years' lags. If we are satisfied that AR(1) characterizes our error process, we can proceed to actual modeling in the next section.

9.1.1   Transfer Functions Versus Static Models

To estimate a theoretically motivated model, we need to draw an important distinction between two types of functional forms: On one hand, a *static* functional form assumes that current values of predictors affect current values of outcomes. For example, we may believe that the price of oil in a given month affects coverage of energy issues on television in the same month, while next month's oil prices will affect next month's energy coverage. If we think that this is the only process going on, then we want a static functional form. On the other hand, we may use a *dynamic* functional form. In the case of oil prices, this would mean that this month's oil prices affect this month's energy coverage, and also coverage in the next month to a lesser degree, the month after to a lesser degree still, and so on. Essentially, a dynamic functional form allows spillover effects from each observation of an input.

Estimating a static regression model with an ARIMA error process only requires two steps in R. First, all of the predictor variables must be placed in a matrix. Second, we can simply add one option to our `arima` function:

```
predictors<-as.matrix(subset(pres.energy,select=c(rmn1173,
    grf0175,grf575,jec477,jec1177,jec479,embargo,hostages,
    oilc,Approval,Unemploy)))
static.mod<-arima(pres.energy$Energy, order=c(1,0,0),
    xreg=predictors)
```

In this code, we first subset our original dataset and treat the subset **as** a **matrix** named `predictors`. Second, we use the same `arima` function as we used to estimate our AR(1) noise model, but add the option `xreg=predictors`. This now estimates a model in which temporal error process is corrected for, but we also include theoretically motivated predictors of interest. If we type `static.mod`, the output is:

```
Call:
arima(x=pres.energy$Energy,order=c(1,0,0),xreg=
  predictors)
```

```
Coefficients:
          ar1   intercept   rmn1173   grf0175   grf575
       0.8222      5.8822   91.3265   31.8761  -8.2280
s.e.   0.0481     52.9008   15.0884   15.4643  15.2025
        jec477    jec1177    jec479   embargo  hostages
       29.6446    -6.6967  -20.1624   35.3247 -16.5001
s.e.   15.0831    15.0844   15.2238   15.1200  13.7619
          oilc   Approval  Unemploy
        0.8855    -0.2479    1.0080
s.e.    1.0192     0.2816    3.8909
```

```
sigma^2 estimated as 379.3: log likelihood=-790.42,
  aic=1608.84
```

This now shows us the estimate and standard error not only for the autoregressive coefficient and intercept, but also for the partial regression coefficient of every other predictor in the model. Again, the three fit measures are reported at the end of the printout.

If we would like to include one or more predictors that have a dynamic effect, then we turn to the method of *transfer functions*, which specify that a predictor has a spillover effect on subsequent observations. A special case of this is called *intervention analysis*, wherein a treatment is coded with an indicator (Box and Tiao 1975). With intervention analysis, a variety of functional forms can emerge, depending largely on whether the indicator variable is coded a *pulse* (taking a value of 1 only at the treatment time, and 0 otherwise) or a *step* (taking on a value of 0 before the treatment and 1 at all subsequent times). It is advisable to try both codings and to read further into the functional form of each (Enders 2009, Sect. 5.1).

As an illustration, we fit a transfer function for a pulse intervention for Richard Nixon's speech in November 1973. To estimate this model, we now need to load the TSA package to access the arimax function (**ARIMA** with **x** predictors). Remember that you may need to use install.packages to download TSA:

```
install.packages("TSA")
library(TSA)
dynamic.mod<-arimax(pres.energy$Energy,order=c(1,0,0),
    xreg=predictors[,-1],xtransf=predictors[,1],
    transfer=list(c(1,0)))
```

The syntax to arimax is similar to arima, but we are now allowed a few more options for transfer functions. Notice in this case that we use the code xreg=predictors[-1] to remove the indicator for Nixon's November 1973 speech from the static predictors. We instead place this predictor with the xtransf option. The last thing we need to do is specify the order of our transfer function, which we do with the option transfer. The transfer option accepts a list of vectors, one vector per transfer function predictor. For our one transfer function, we specify `c(1,0)`: The first term refers to the order of the dynamic decay term (so a 0 here actually reverts back to a static model), and the second term refers to the lag length of the predictor's effect (so if we expected an effect to *grow*, we might put a higher number than 0 here). With these settings, we say that Nixon's speech had an effect in the month he gave it, and then the effect spilled over to subsequent months at a decaying rate.

By typing `dynamic.mod`, we get our output:

```
Call:
arimax(x=pres.energy$Energy,order=c(1,0,0),
 xreg=predictors[,-1],
    xtransf = predictors[, 1], transfer = list(c(1, 0)))

Coefficients:
          ar1   intercept   grf0175    grf575    jec477
       0.8262    20.2787    31.5282   -7.9725   29.9820
s.e.   0.0476    46.6870    13.8530   13.6104   13.5013
       jec1177     jec479    embargo  hostages      oilc
       -6.3304   -19.8179    25.9388  -16.9015    0.5927
s.e.   13.5011    13.6345    13.2305   12.4422    0.9205
       Approval   Unemploy    T1-AR1     T1-MA0
       -0.2074     0.1660     0.6087   160.6241
s.e.    0.2495     3.5472     0.0230    17.0388

sigma^2 estimated as 305.1: log likelihood=-770.83,
 aic=1569.66
```

The output is similar to that from the static ARIMA regression model, but now there are two terms for the effect of Nixon's speech. The first, `T1-AR1`, gives the decay term. The closer this term is to 1, the more persistent the variable's effect is. The second term, `T1-MA0`, is the initial effect of the speech on energy coverage in the month it was given.[8] In terms of model fit, notice that the output of every ARIMA or transfer function model we have estimated reports the Akaike information criterion (AIC). With this measure, lower scores indicate a better penalized fit. With a score of 1569.66, this dynamic transfer function model has the lowest AIC of any model

---

[8] In this case, we have a pulse input, so we can say that in November 1973, the effect of the speech was an expected 161 increase in news stories, holding all else equal. In December 1973, the carryover effect is that we expect 98 more stories, holding all else equal because $161 \times 0.61 \approx 98$. In January 1974, the effect of the intervention is we expect 60 more stories, *ceteris paribus* because $161 \times 0.61 \times 0.61 \approx 60$. The effect of the intervention continues forward in a similar decaying pattern. By contrast, *if* we had gotten these results with a *step* intervention instead of a *pulse* intervention, then these effects would accumulate rather than decay. Under this hypothetical, the effects would be 161 in November 1973, 259 in December 1973 (because 161+98=259), and 319 in January 1974 (because 161+98+60=319).

we have fitted to these data. Hence, the dynamic model has a better fit than the static
model or the atheoretical AR(1) model with no predictors.

To get a real sense of the effect of an intervention analysis, though, an analyst
should always try to draw the effect that they modeled. (Again, it is key to study
the functional form behind the chosen intervention specification, as described by
Enders 2009, Sect. 5.1.) To draw the effect of our intervention for Nixon's 1973
speech, we type:

```
months<-c(1:180)
y.pred<-dynamic.mod$coef[2:12]%*%c(1,predictors[58,-1])+
    160.6241*predictors[,1]+
    160.6241*(.6087^(months-59))*as.numeric(months>59)
plot(y=pres.energy$Energy,x=months,xlab="Month",
    ylab="Energy Policy Stories",type="l",axes=F)
axis(1,at=c(1,37,73,109,145),labels=c("Jan. 1969",
    "Jan. 1972","Jan. 1975","Jan. 1978","Jan. 1981"))
axis(2)
box()
lines(y=y.pred,x=months,lty=2,col="blue",lwd=2)
```

On the first line, we simply create a time index for the 180 months in the study. In
the second line, we create predicted values for the effect of the intervention holding
everything else equal. A critical assumption that we make is that we hold all other
predictors equal by setting them to their values from October 1973, the 58th month
of the series (hence, `predictors[58,-1]`). So considering the components of
this second line, the first term multiplies the coefficients for the static predictors by
their last values before the intervention, the second term captures the effect of the
intervention in the month of the speech, and the third term captures the spillover
effect of the intervention based on the number of months since the speech. The next
four lines simply draw a plot of our original series' values and manage some of the
graph's features. Lastly, we add a dashed line showing the effect of the intervention
holding all else constant. The result is shown in Fig. 9.3. As the figure shows, the
result of this intervention is a large and positive jump in the expected number of
news stories, that carries over for a few months but eventually decays back to
pre-intervention levels. This kind of graph is essential for understanding how the
dynamic intervention actually affects the model.

As a final graph to supplement our view of the dynamic intervention effect, we
could draw a plot that shows how well predictions from the full model align with
true values from the series. We could do this with the following code:

```
months<-c(1:180)
full.pred<-pres.energy$Energy-dynamic.mod$residuals
plot(y=full.pred,x=months,xlab="Month",
    ylab="Energy Policy Stories",type="l",
    ylim=c(0,225),axes=F)
points(y=pres.energy$Energy,x=months,pch=20)
legend(x=0,y=200,legend=c("Predicted","True"),
    pch=c(NA,20),lty=c(1,NA))
axis(1,at=c(1,37,73,109,145),labels=c("Jan. 1969",
    "Jan. 1972","Jan. 1975","Jan. 1978","Jan. 1981"))
axis(2)
box()
```

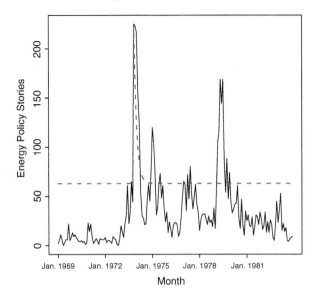

Fig. 9.3 The *dashed line* shows the dynamic effect of Nixon's Nov. 1973 speech, holding all else equal. The *solid line* shows observed values of the series

Again, we start by creating a time index, months. In the second line, we create our predicted values by subtracting the residuals from the true values. In the third line of code, we draw a line graph of the predicted values from the model. In the fourth line, we add points showing the true values from the observed series. The remaining lines complete the graph formatting. The resulting graph is shown in Fig. 9.4. As can be seen, the in-sample fit is good, with the predicted values tracking the true values closely.

As a final point here, the reader is encouraged to consult the code in Sect. 9.5 for alternative syntax for producing Figs. 9.3 and 9.4. The tradeoff of the alternative way of drawing these figures is that it requires more lines of code on the one hand, but on the other hand, it is more generalizable and easier to apply to your own research. Plus, the alternative code introduces how the ts command lets analysts convert a variable to a *time series object*. Seeing both approaches is worthwhile for illustrating that, in general, many tasks can be performed in many ways in R.

9.2   Extensions to Least Squares Linear Regression Models

A second approach to time series analysis draws more from the econometric literature and looks for ways to extend linear regression models to account for the unique issues associated with time-referenced data. Since we already discussed visualization with these data extensively in Sect. 9.1, we will not revisit graphing issues here. As with Box–Jenkins type models, though, the analyst should always

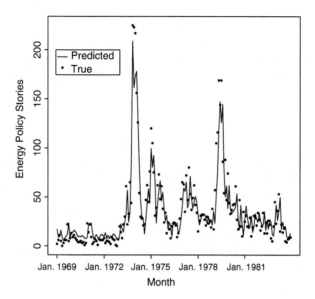

Fig. 9.4 Predicted values from a full transfer function model on a line, with actual observed values as points

begin by drawing a line plot of the series of interest, and ideally a few key predictors as well. Even diagnostic plots such as the ACF and PACF would be appropriate, in addition to residual diagnostics such as we will discuss shortly.

When modeling data from an econometric approach, researchers again have to decide whether to use a static or a dynamic specification of the model. For static models in which current values of predictors affect current values of the outcome, researchers may estimate the model with ordinary least squares (OLS) in the *rare* case of no serial correlation. For efficiency gains on a static model, however, feasible generalized least squares (FGLS) is a better estimator. By contrast, in the case of a dynamic functional form, a lag structure can be introduced into the linear model's specification.

Starting with static models, the simplest kind of model (though rarely appropriate) would be to estimate the model using simple OLS. Returning to our energy policy data, our model specification here would be:

```
static.ols<-lm(Energy~rmn1173+grf0175+grf575+jec477+
    jec1177+jec479+embargo+hostages+oilc+
    Approval+Unemploy,data=pres.energy)
```

By typing summary(static.ols) we get our familiar output from a linear regression model. Beware, though, that if there is serial correlation in the disturbances, these estimates of the standard errors are incorrect:

```
Call:
lm(formula=Energy~rmn1173+grf0175+grf575+jec477+
  jec1177+
    jec479 + embargo + hostages + oilc + Approval +
     Unemploy,
    data = pres.energy)

Residuals:
     Min       1Q   Median       3Q      Max
-104.995  -12.921   -3.448    8.973  111.744

Coefficients:
             Estimate Std. Error t value Pr(>|t|)
(Intercept) 319.7442    46.8358   6.827 1.51e-10 ***
rmn1173      78.8261    28.8012   2.737  0.00687 **
grf0175      60.7905    26.7006   2.277  0.02406 *
grf575       -4.2676    26.5315  -0.161  0.87240
jec477       47.0388    26.6760   1.763  0.07966 .
jec1177      15.4427    26.3786   0.585  0.55905
jec479       72.0519    26.5027   2.719  0.00724 **
embargo      96.3760    13.3105   7.241 1.53e-11 ***
hostages     -4.5289     7.3945  -0.612  0.54106
oilc         -5.8765     1.0848  -5.417 2.07e-07 ***
Approval     -1.0693     0.2147  -4.980 1.57e-06 ***
Unemploy     -3.7018     1.3861  -2.671  0.00831 **
---
Signif. codes:  0 *** 0.001 ** 0.01 * 0.05 . 0.1   1

Residual standard error: 26.26 on 168 degrees of
 freedom
Multiple R-squared:  0.5923,  Adjusted R-squared:
 0.5656
F-statistic: 22.19 on 11 and 168 DF,  p-value:
 < 2.2e-16
```

Yet, we need to diagnose whether serial correlation is present in the residuals before we are content with the results. To do this, we need to load the lmtest package (first introduced in Chap. 6) to make a few diagnostics available. Loading this package, we can then compute a Durbin–Watson or Breusch–Godfrey test for autocorrelation:

```
library(lmtest)
dwtest(static.ols)
bgtest(static.ols)
```

For both the dwtest and bgtest commands, we simply provide the name of the model as the main argument. The **D**urbin-**W**atson **test** (computed with dwtest) tests for first-order serial correlation and is not valid for a model that includes a lagged dependent variable. Our test produces the following output:

```
Durbin-Watson test
```

```
data:  static.ols
DW = 1.1649, p-value = 1.313e-09
alternative hypothesis: true autocorrelation is greater
   than 0
```

The Durbin–Watson d statistic (1.1649 in this case), does not have a parametric distribution. Traditionally the value of d has been checked against tables based on Monte Carlo results to determine significance. R, however, does provide an approximate p-value with the statistic. For a Durbin–Watson test, the null hypothesis is that there is no autocorrelation, so our significant value of d suggests that autocorrelation is a problem.

Meanwhile, the results of our **B**reusch-**G**odfrey **test** (computed with bgtest) offer a similar conclusion. The Breusch–Godfrey test has a χ^2 distribution and can be used to test autocorrelation in a model with a lagged dependent variable. By default, the bgtest command checks for first-order serial correlation, though higher-order serial correlation can be tested with the order option. Our output in this case is:

```
Breusch-Godfrey test for serial correlation of
   order up to
1
```

```
data:  static.ols
LM test = 38.6394, df = 1, p-value = 5.098e-10
```

Again, the null hypothesis is that there is no autocorrelation, so our significant χ^2 value shows that serial correlation is a concern, and we need to do something to account for this.

At this point, we can draw one of two conclusions: The first possibility is that our *static model specification* is correct, and we need to find an estimator that is efficient in the presence of error autocorrelation. The second possibility is that we have overlooked a dynamic effect and need to respecify our model. (In other words, if there is a true spillover effect, and we have not modeled it, then the errors will appear to be serially correlated.) We will consider each possibility.

First, if we are confident that our static specification is correct, then our functional form is right, but under the Gauss–Markov theorem OLS is inefficient with error autocorrelation, and the standard errors are biased. As an alternative, we can use feasible generalized least squares (FGLS), which estimates the level of error correlation and incorporates this into the estimator. There are a variety of estimation techniques here, including the Prais–Winsten and Cochrane–Orcutt estimators. We proceed by illustrating the Cochrane–Orcutt estimator, though users should be wary of the model's assumptions.[9] In short, **Cochrane–Orcutt** reestimates the model several times, updating the estimate of error autocorrelation each time, until it converges to a stable estimate of the correlation. To implement this procedure in R, we need to install and then load the `orcutt` package:

```
install.packages("orcutt")
library(orcutt)
cochrane.orcutt(static.ols)
```

Once we have loaded this package, we insert the name of a linear model we have estimated with OLS into the `cochrane.orcutt` command. This then iteratively reestimates the model and produces our FGLS results as follows:

```
$Cochrane.Orcutt


Call:
lm(formula = YB ~ XB - 1)


Residuals:
    Min      1Q   Median      3Q      Max
-58.404  -9.352   -3.658   8.451  100.524


Coefficients:
                 Estimate Std. Error t value Pr(>|t|)
XB(Intercept)     16.8306    55.2297   0.305   0.7609
XBrmn1173         91.3691    15.6119   5.853 2.5e-08 ***
XBgrf0175         32.2003    16.0153   2.011   0.0460 *
XBgrf575          -7.9916    15.7288  -0.508   0.6121
XBjec477          29.6881    15.6159   1.901   0.0590 .
XBjec1177         -6.4608    15.6174  -0.414   0.6796
XBjec479         -20.0677    15.6705  -1.281   0.2021
XBembargo         34.5797    15.0877   2.292   0.0232 *
XBhostages       -16.9183    14.1135  -1.199   0.2323
XBoilc             0.8240     1.0328   0.798   0.4261
XBApproval        -0.2399     0.2742  -0.875   0.3829
XBUnemploy        -0.1332     4.3786  -0.030   0.9758
---
Signif. codes:  0 *** 0.001 ** 0.01 * 0.05 . 0.1   1

Residual standard error: 20.19 on 167 degrees of
  freedom
```

---

[9]In particular, at each stage of the iterative process, the linear model is estimated by regressing $y_t^* = y_t - \rho y_{t-1}$ on $\mathbf{x}_t^* = \mathbf{x}_t - \rho \mathbf{x}_{t-1}$ (Hamilton 1994, p. 223). This procedure assumes that the dynamic adjustment process is the same for the outcome and the input variables, which is unlikely. Hence, a dynamic specification such as an autoregressive distributive lag model would be more flexible.

```
Multiple R-squared:  0.2966,     Adjusted R-squared:
   0.2461
F-statistic:  5.87 on 12 and 167 DF,  p-value:
 1.858e-08
```

```
$rho
[1] 0.8247688
```

```
$number.interaction
[1] 15
```

The first portion of table looks like the familiar linear regression output (though the letters XB appear before the name of each predictor). All of these coefficients, standard errors, and inferential statistics have the exact same interpretation as in a model estimated with OLS, but our estimates now should be efficient because they were computed with FGLS. Near the bottom of the output, we see $rho, which shows us our final estimate of error autocorrelation. We also see $number.interaction, which informs us that the model was reestimated in 15 iterations before it converged to the final result. FGLS is intended to produce efficient estimates if a static specification is correct.

By contrast, if we believe a *dynamic specification* is correct, we need to work to respecify our linear model to capture that functional form. In fact, if we get the functional form wrong, our results are biased, so getting this right is critical. Adding a lag specification to our model can be made considerably easier if we install and load the dyn package. We name our model koyck.ols for reasons that will be apparent shortly:

```
install.packages("dyn")
library(dyn)
pres.energy<-ts(pres.energy)
koyck.ols<-dyn$lm(Energy~lag(Energy,-1)+rmn1173+
    grf0175+grf575+jec477+jec1177+jec479+embargo+
    hostages+oilc+Approval+Unemploy,data=pres.energy)
```

After loading dyn, the second line uses the ts command to declare that our data are time series data. In the third line, notice that we changed the linear model command to read, dyn$lm. This modification allows us to include lagged variables within our model. In particular, we now have added lag(Energy,-1), which is the lagged value of our dependent variable. With the lag command, we specify the variable being lagged and how many times to lag it. By specifying -1, we are looking at the immediately prior value. (Positive values represent future values.) The default lag is 0, which just returns current values.

We can see the results of this model by typing summary(koyck.ols):

```
Call:
lm(formula = dyn(Energy ~ lag(Energy, -1) + rmn1173 +
    grf0175 +
```

```
  grf575 + jec477 + jec1177 + jec479 + embargo +
    hostages +
  oilc + Approval + Unemploy), data = pres.energy)
```

```
Residuals:
     Min      1Q  Median       3Q      Max
  -51.282  -8.638  -1.825    7.085   70.472
```

```
Coefficients:
                   Estimate Std. Error t value Pr(>|t|)
(Intercept)        62.11485   36.96818   1.680  0.09479 .
lag(Energy, -1)     0.73923    0.05113  14.458  < 2e-16 ***
rmn1173           171.62701   20.14847   8.518 9.39e-15 ***
grf0175            51.70224   17.72677   2.917  0.00403 **
grf575              7.05534   17.61928   0.400  0.68935
jec477             39.01949   17.70976   2.203  0.02895 *
jec1177           -10.78300   17.59184  -0.613  0.54075
jec479             28.68463   17.83063   1.609  0.10958
embargo            10.54061   10.61288   0.993  0.32206
hostages           -2.51412    4.91156  -0.512  0.60942
oilc               -1.14171    0.81415  -1.402  0.16268
Approval           -0.15438    0.15566  -0.992  0.32278
Unemploy           -0.88655    0.96781  -0.916  0.36098
---
Signif. codes:  0 *** 0.001 ** 0.01 * 0.05 . 0.1   1
```

```
Residual standard error: 17.42 on 166 degrees of
 freedom
  (2 observations deleted due to missingness)
Multiple R-squared:  0.822,     Adjusted R-squared:
 0.8092
F-statistic: 63.89 on 12 and 166 DF,  p-value:
 < 2.2e-16
```

Our specification here is often called a Koyck model. This is because Koyck (1954) observed that when a lagged dependent variable is included as a predictor, each predictor will have spillover effects in subsequent months.

Consider two examples of predictor spillover effects. First, our coefficient for Nixon's speech is approximately 172. Here, we are interested in an *impulse effect* whereby the predictor increased to 1 in the month the speech was given, and then went back to 0. Therefore, in the month of November 1973 when the speech was given, the expected effect of this speech holding all else equal is a 172 story increase in energy policy coverage. However, in December 1973, November's level of coverage is a predictor, and November's coverage was shaped by the speech. Since our coefficient on the lagged dependent variable is approximately 0.74, and since $0.74 \times 172 \approx 128$, we therefore expect that the speech increased energy coverage in December by 128, *ceteris paribus*. Yet the effect would persist into January as well because December's value predicts January 1974s value. Since

$0.74 \times 0.74 \times 172 \approx 94$, we expect the effect of Nixon's speech to be a 94 story increase in energy coverage in January, *ceteris paribus*. This kind of decaying dynamic effect persists for an impulse effect in any of these variables, so this is a powerful way to specify a dynamic model. Also, bear in mind that a researcher could easily plot these decaying intervention effects over time to visualize the dynamic impact of an intervention. Such a graph is valid for a Koyck model and would resemble the output of Fig. 9.3.

Second, consider the effect of unemployment. We should not make much of this predictor's impact because the coefficient is not discernible, but it does serve as an example of interpreting a continuous predictor's dynamic effect. If we are interested in a *step effect*, we would like to know what the long-run impact would be if a predictor increased by a single unit and stayed at that higher level. So although it is not statistically discernible, the coefficient for unemployment is -0.89, meaning that a percentage point increase in unemployment decreases news attention to energy policy by nearly nine-tenths of a story, in the same month, on average, and *ceteris paribus*. But if unemployment stayed a percentage point higher, how would coverage change in the long run? If β_{13} is the coefficient on unemployment and β_2 is the coefficient on the lagged dependent variable, then the long-term effect is computed by (Keele and Kelly 2006, p. 189):

$$\frac{\beta_{13}}{1 - \beta_2} \tag{9.2}$$

We can compute this in R simply by referencing our coefficients:

```
koyck.ols$coefficients[13]/(1-koyck.ols$coefficients[2])
```

Our output is -3.399746, which means that a persistent 1 % point rise in unemployment would reduce TV news coverage of energy policy in the long term by 3.4 stories on average and all else equal. Again, this kind of long-term effect could occur for any variable that is not limited to a pulse input.

As a final strategy, we could include one or more lags of one or more predictors without including a lagged dependent variable. In this case, any spillover will be limited to whatever we directly incorporate into the model specification. For example, if we only wanted a dynamic effect of Nixon's speech and a static specification for everything else, we could specify this model:

```
udl.mod<-dyn$lm(Energy~rmn1173+lag(rmn1173,-1)+
    lag(rmn1173,-2)+lag(rmn1173,-3)+lag(rmn1173,-4)+
    grf0175+grf575+jec477+jec1177+jec479+embargo+
    hostages+oilc+Approval+Unemploy,data=pres.energy)
```

In this situation, we have included the current value of the Nixon's speech indictor, as well as four lags. For an intervention, that means that this predictor will have an effect in November 1973 and for 4 months afterwards. (In April 1974, however, the effect abruptly drops to 0, where it stays.) We see the results of this model by typing `summary(udl.mod)`:

```
Call:
lm(formula=dyn(Energy~rmn1173+lag(rmn1173,-1)+lag
    (rmn1173,-2)+lag(rmn1173,-3)+lag(rmn1173,-4)
    +grf0175+grf575+jec477+jec1177+jec479+embargo
    +hostages+oilc+Approval+Unemploy),data=pres.energy)

Residuals:
    Min       1Q  Median       3Q      Max
-43.654  -13.236  -2.931    7.033  111.035

Coefficients:
                   Estimate Std. Error t value Pr(>|t|)
(Intercept)        334.9988    44.2887   7.564 2.89e-12 ***
rmn1173            184.3602    34.1463   5.399 2.38e-07 ***
lag(rmn1173, -1)   181.1571    34.1308   5.308 3.65e-07 ***
lag(rmn1173, -2)   154.0519    34.2151   4.502 1.29e-05 ***
lag(rmn1173, -3)   115.6949    34.1447   3.388 0.000885 ***
lag(rmn1173, -4)    75.1312    34.1391   2.201 0.029187 *
grf0175             60.5376    24.5440   2.466 0.014699 *
grf575              -3.4512    24.3845  -0.142 0.887629
jec477              45.5446    24.5256   1.857 0.065146 .
jec1177             14.5728    24.2440   0.601 0.548633
jec479              71.0933    24.3605   2.918 0.004026 **
embargo             -9.7692    24.7696  -0.394 0.693808
hostages            -4.8323     6.8007  -0.711 0.478392
oilc                -6.1930     1.0232  -6.053 9.78e-09 ***
Approval            -1.0341     0.1983  -5.216 5.58e-07 ***
Unemploy            -4.4445     1.3326  -3.335 0.001060 **
---
Signif. codes:  0 *** 0.001 ** 0.01 * 0.05 . 0.1   1

Residual standard error: 24.13 on 160 degrees of freedom
  (8 observations deleted due to missingness)
Multiple R-squared:  0.6683,    Adjusted R-squared:   0.6372
F-statistic: 21.49 on 15 and 160 DF,  p-value: < 2.2e-16
```

As we would expect, the effect shrinks every month after the onset. For this unrestricted distributed lag model, we have to estimate several more parameters than the Koyck model requires, but in some cases it may make sense theoretically.

9.3 Vector Autoregression

The final approach that we will describe in this chapter is vector autoregression (VAR). The VAR approach is useful when studying several variables that are endogenous to each other because there is reciprocal causation among them. The basic framework is to estimate a linear regression model for each of the endogenous variables. In each linear model, include several lagged values of the outcome variable itself (say p lags of the variable) as well as p lags of all of the other endogenous variables. So for the simple case of two endogenous variables, x and y, in which we set our lag length to $p = 3$, we would estimate two equations that could be represented as follows:

$$y_t = \beta_0 + \beta_1 y_{t-1} + \beta_2 y_{t-2} + \beta_3 y_{t-3} + \beta_4 x_{t-1} + \beta_5 x_{t-2} + \beta_6 x_{t-3} + \epsilon_t \quad (9.3)$$

$$x_t = \gamma_0 + \gamma_1 x_{t-1} + \gamma_2 x_{t-2} + \gamma_3 x_{t-3} + \gamma_4 y_{t-1} + \gamma_5 y_{t-2} + \gamma_6 y_{t-3} + \delta_t$$

A fuller treatment on this methodology, including notation for models with more endogenous variables and examples of models that include exogenous variables as well, can be found in Brandt and Williams (2007). With this model, tests such as Granger causality tests can be used to assess if there is a causal effect from one endogenous variable to another (Granger 1969).

As an example of how to implement a VAR model in R, we turn to work by Brandt and Freeman (2006), who analyze weekly data regarding the Israeli–Palestinian conflict. Their data are drawn from the Kansas Event Data System, which automatically codes English-language news reports to measure political events, with a goal of using this information as an early warning to predict political change. The endogenous variables in these data are scaled political actions taken by either the USA, Israel, or Palestine, and directed to one of the other actors. This produces six variables **a2i**, **a2p**, **i2a**, **p2a**, **i2p**, and **p2i**. The abbreviations are "a" for American, "i" for Israeli, and "p" for Palestinian. As an example, **i2p** measures the scaled value of Israeli actions directed toward the Palestinians. The weekly data we will use run from April 15, 1979 to October 26, 2003, for a total of 1278 weeks.

To proceed, we need to install and load the `vars` package to make the relevant estimation commands available. We also need the `foreign` package because our data are in Stata format:[10]

```
install.packages("vars")
library(vars)
library(foreign)
levant.0 <- read.dta("levant.dta")
levant<- subset(levant.0,
    select=c("a2i","a2p","i2p","i2a","p2i","p2a"))
```

After loading the packages, we load our data on the third line, naming it `levant.0`. These data also contain three date-related indices, so for analysis purposes we actually need to create a second copy of the data that only includes our six endogenous variables without the indices. We do this using the `subset` command to create the dataset named `levant`.

A key step at this point is to choose the appropriate lag length, p. The lag length needs to capture all error processes and causal dynamics. One approach to

---

[10]This example requires the file `levant.dta`. Please download this file from the Dataverse (see page vii) or this chapter's online content (see page 155).

determining the appropriate lag length is to fit several models, choose the model with the best fit, and then see if the residuals show any evidence of serial correlation. The command VARselect automatically estimates several <u>v</u>ector <u>a</u>uto<u>r</u>egression models and **select**s which lag length has the best fit. Since our data are weekly, we consider up to 104 weeks' lags, or 2 years' worth of data, to consider all possible options. The following command can take a minute to run because 104 models are being estimated:

```
levant.select<-VARselect(levant,type="const",lag.max=104)
```

To find out which of the lag lengths fits best, we can type levant.select$ selection. Our output is simply the following:

```
AIC(n)   HQ(n)   SC(n)  FPE(n)
    60       4       1      47
```

This reports the chosen lag length for the Akaike information criterion, Hannan–Quinn information criterion, Schwarz criterion, and forecast prediction error. All four of these indices are coded so that lower values are better. To contrast extremes, the lowest value of the Schwarz criterion, which has a heavy penalty for additional parameters, is for the model with only one lag of the endogenous variables. By contrast, the best fit on the AIC comes from the model that requires 60 lags—perhaps indicating that annual seasonality is present. A much longer printout giving the value of each of the four fit indices for all 104 models can be seen by typing: levant.select$criteria. Ideally, our fit indices would have settled on models with similar lag lengths. Since they did not, and since we have 1278 observations, we will take the safer route with the long lag length suggested by the AIC.[11]

To estimate the <u>v</u>ector <u>a</u>uto<u>r</u>egression model with $p = 60$ lags of each endogenous variable, we type:

```
levant.AIC<-VAR(levant,type="const",p=60)
```

The VAR command requires the name of a dataset containing all of the endogenous variables. With the type option, we have chosen "const" in this case (the default). This means that each of our linear models includes a constant. (Other options include specifying a "trend," "both" a constant and a trend, or "none" which includes neither.) With the option p we choose the lag length. An option we do not use here is the exogen option, which allows us to specify exogenous variables.

Once we have estimated our model using VAR, the next thing we should do is diagnose the model using a special call to the plot function:

```
plot(levant.AIC,lag.acf=104,lag.pacf=104)
```

By using the name of our VAR model, levant.AIC, as the only argument in plot, R will automatically provide a diagnostic plot for each of the endogenous

---

[11] You are encouraged to examine the models that would have been chosen by the Hannan–Quinn criterion (4 lags) or the Schwarz criterion (1 lag) on your own. How do these models perform in terms of diagnostics? How would inferences change?

variables. With the options of lag.acf and lag.pacf, we specify that the ACF
and PACF plots that this command reports should show us 2 years' worth (104
weeks) of autocorrelation patterns. For our data, R produces six plots. R displays
these plots one at a time, and between each, the console will pose the following
prompt:

```
Hit <Return> to see next plot:
```

R will keep a plot on the viewer until you press the <u>Return</u> key, at which point it
moves on to the next graph. This process repeats until the graph for each outcome
has been shown.

   Alternatively, if we wanted to see the diagnostic plot for one endogenous variable
in particular, we could type:

```
plot(levant.AIC,lag.acf=104,lag.pacf=104,names="i2p")
```

Here, the names option has let us specify that we want to see the diagnostics for **i2p**
(Israeli actions directed towards Palestine). The resulting diagnostic plot is shown
in Fig. 9.5. The graph has four parts: At the top is a line graph that shows the true
values in a solid black line and the fitted values in a blue dashed line. Directly
beneath this is a line plot of the residuals against a line at zero. These first two
graphs can illustrate whether the model consistently makes unbiased predictions of
the outcome and whether the residuals are homoscedastic over time. In general, the
forecasts consistently hover around zero, though for the last 200 observations the
error variance does seem to increase slightly. The third graph, in the bottom left,
is the ACF for the residuals on **i2p**.[12] Lastly, in the bottom right of the panel, we
see the PACF for **i2p**'s residuals. No spikes are significant in the ACF and only one
spike is significant in the PACF over 2 years, so we conclude that our lag structure
has sufficiently filtered-out any serial correlation in this variable.

   When interpreting a VAR model, we turn to two tools to draw inferences
and interpretations from these models. First, we use Granger causality testing to
determine if one endogenous variable causes the others. This test is simply a block
F-test of whether all of the lags of a variable can be excluded from the model. For
a joint test of whether one variable affects the other variables in the system, we can
use the causality command. For example, if we wanted to test whether Israeli
actions towards Palestine caused actions by the other five directed dyads, we would
type:

```
causality(levant.AIC, cause="i2p")$Granger
```

The command here calls for the name of the model first (levant.AIC), and then
with the cause option, we specify which of the endogenous variables we wish to
test the effect of. Our output is as follows:

---

[12]Note that, by default, the graph R presents actually includes the zero-lag perfect correlation. If
you would like to eliminate that, given our long lag length and the size of the panel, simply load
the TSA package before drawing the graph to change the default.

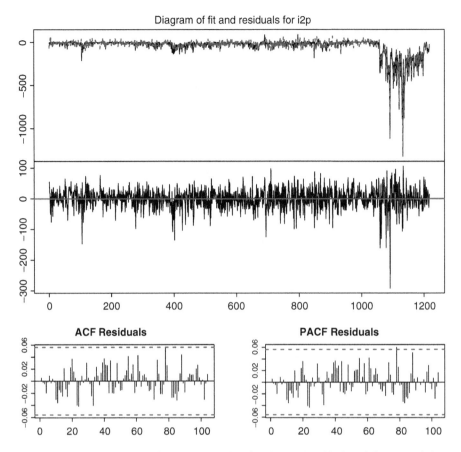

Fig. 9.5 Predicted values, residual autocorrelation function, and residual partial autocorrelation function for the Israel-to-Palestine series in a six-variable vector autoregression model

```
Granger causality H0: i2p do not Granger-cause
   a2i a2p i2a
p2i p2a

data:  VAR object levant.AIC
F-Test = 2.1669, df1 = 300, df2 = 5142, p-value
  < 2.2e-16
```

The null hypothesis is that the coefficients for all of the lags of **i2p** are zero when modeling each of the other five outcome variables. However, our F-test is significant here, as the minuscule p-value shows. Therefore, we would conclude that Israeli actions directed towards Palestine do have a causal effect on the other political action variables in the system.

We can proceed to test whether each of the other five variables Granger-cause the other predictors in the system by considering each one with the `causality` command:

```
causality(levant.AIC, cause="a2i")$Granger
causality(levant.AIC, cause="a2p")$Granger
causality(levant.AIC, cause="i2a")$Granger
causality(levant.AIC, cause="p2i")$Granger
causality(levant.AIC, cause="p2a")$Granger
```

The results are not reprinted here to preserve space. At the 95 % confidence level, though, you will see that each variable significantly causes the others, except for American actions directed towards Israel (**a2i**).

Finally to get a sense of the substantive impact of each predictor, we turn to impulse response analysis. The logic here is somewhat similar to the intervention analysis we graphed back in Fig. 9.3. An impulse response function considers a one-unit increase in one of the endogenous variables and computes how such an exogenous shock would dynamically influence all of the endogenous variables, given autoregression and dependency patterns.

When interpreting an impulse response function, a key consideration is the fact that shocks to one endogenous variable are nearly always correlated with shocks to other variables. We therefore need to consider that a one-unit shock to one variable's residual term is likely to create contemporaneous movement in the residuals of the other variables. The off-diagonal terms of the variance–covariance matrix of the endogenous variables' residuals, $\hat{\Sigma}$, tells us how much the shocks covary.

There are several ways to deal with this issue. One is to use theory to determine the *ordering* of the endogenous variables. In this approach, the researcher assumes that a shock to one endogenous variable is not affected by shocks to any other variable. Then a second variable's shocks are affected only by the first variable's, and no others. The researcher recursively repeats this process to identify a system in which all variables can be ordered in a causal chain. With a theoretically designed system like this, the researcher can determine how contemporaneous shocks affect each other with a structured Cholesky decomposition of $\hat{\Sigma}$ (Enders 2009, p. 309). A second option, which is the default option in R's `irf` command, is to assume that there is no theoretical knowledge of the causal ordering of the contemporaneous shocks and apply the method of *orthogonalization of the residuals*. This involves another Cholesky decomposition, in which we find A_0^{-1} by solving $A_0^{-1\prime}A_0 = \hat{\Sigma}$. For more details about response ordering or orthogonalizing residuals, see Brandt and Williams (2007, pp. 36–41 & 66–70), Enders (2009, pp. 307–315), or Hamilton (1994, pp. 318–324).

As an example of an impulse response function, we will graph the effect of one extra political event from Israel directed towards Palestine. R will compute our **i**mpulse **r**esponse **f**unction with the `irf` command, using the default orthogonalization of residuals. One of the key options in this command is `boot`, which determines whether to construct a confidence interval with **boot**straps. Generally, it is advisable to report uncertainty in predictions, but the process can take several minutes.[13] So if the reader wants a quick result, set `boot=FALSE`. To get the result with confidence intervals type:

```
levant.irf<-irf(levant.AIC,impulse="i2p",n.ahead=12,boot=TRUE)
```

We name our impulse response function `levant.irf`. The command requires us to state the name of our model (`levant.AIC`). The option `impulse` asks us to name the variable we want the effect of, the `n.ahead` option sets how far ahead we wish to forecast (we say 12 weeks, or 3 months), and lastly `boot` determines whether to create confidence intervals based on a bootstrap sample.

Once we have computed this, we can graph the impulse response function with a special call to `plot`:

```
plot(levant.irf)
```

The resulting graph is shown in Fig. 9.6. There are six panels, one for each of the six endogenous variables. The vertical axis on each panel lists the name of the endogenous variable and represents the expected change in that variable. The horizontal axis on each panel represents the number of months that have elapsed since the shock. Each panel shows a solid red line at zero, representing where a non-effect falls on the graph. The solid black line represents the expected effect in each month, and the red dashed lines represent each confidence interval. As the figure shows, the real impact of a shock in Israel-to-Palestine actions is dramatic to the Israel-to-Palestine series itself (**i2p**) on account of autoregression and feedback from effects to other series. We also see a significant jump in Palestine-to-Israel actions (**p2i**) over the ensuing 3 months. With the other four series, the effects pale in comparison. We easily could produce plots similar to Fig. 9.6 by computing the impulse response function for a shock in each of the six inputs. This is generally a good idea, but is omitted here for space.

9.4   Further Reading About Time Series Analysis

With these tools in hand, the reader should have some sense of how to estimate and interpret time series models in R using three approaches—Box–Jenkins modeling, econometric modeling, and vector autoregression. Be aware that, while this chapter uses simple examples, time series analysis is generally challenging. It can be difficult to find a good model that properly accounts for all of the trend and error processes, but the analyst must carefully work through all of these issues or the

---

[13]Beware that bootstrap-based confidence intervals do not always give the correct coverages because they confound information about how well the model fits with uncertainty of parameters. For this reason, Bayesian approaches are often the best way to represent uncertainty (Brandt and Freeman 2006; Sims and Zha 1999).

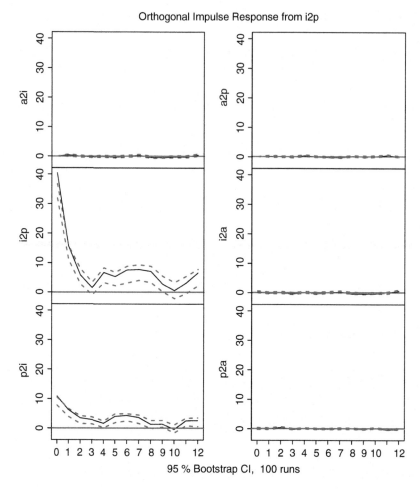

Fig. 9.6 Impulse response function for a one-unit shock in the Israel-to-Palestine series in a six-variable vector autoregression model

inferences will be biased. (See again, Granger and Newbold 1974.) So be sure to recognize that it often takes several tries to find a model that properly accounts for all issues.

It is also worth bearing in mind that this chapter cannot comprehensively address any of the three approaches we consider, much less touch on all types of time series analysis. (Spectral analysis, wavelet analysis, state space models, and error-correction models are just a handful of topics not addressed here.) Therefore, the interested reader is encouraged to consult other resources for further important details on various topics in time series modeling. Good books that cover a range of time series topics and include R code are: Cowpertwait and Metcalfe (2009), Cryer and Chan (2008), and Shumway and Stoffer (2006). For more depth on the theory behind time series, good volumes by Political Scientists include Box-Steffensmeier et al. (2014) and Brandt and Williams (2007). Other good books that cover time series theory include: Box et al. 2008, Enders (2009), Wei (2006), Lütkepohl (2005), and for an advanced take see Hamilton (1994). Several books focus on specific topics and applying the methods in R: For instance, Petris et al. (2009) covers dynamic linear models, also called state space models, and explains how to use the corresponding dlm package in R to apply these methods. Pfaff (2008) discusses cointegrated data models such as error-correction models and vector error-correction models, using the R package vars. Additionally, readers who are interested in time series cross section models, or panel data, should consult the plm package, which facilitates the estimation of models appropriate for those methods. Meanwhile, Mátyás and Sevestre (2008) offers a theoretical background on panel data methods.

9.5 Alternative Time Series Code

As mentioned in Sect. 9.1, we will now show alternative syntax for producing Figs. 9.3 and 9.4. This code is a little longer, but is more generalizable.[14] First off, if you do not have all of the packages, data objects, and models loaded from before, be sure to reload a few of them so that we can draw the figure:

```
library(TSA)
pres.energy<-read.csv("PESenergy.csv")
predictors<-as.matrix(subset(pres.energy,select=c(rmn1173,
    grf0175,grf575,jec477,jec1177,jec479,embargo,hostages,
    oilc,Approval,Unemploy)))
```

All three of the previous lines of code were run earlier in the chapter. By way of reminder, the first line loads the TSA package, the second loads our energy policy coverage data, and the third creates a matrix of predictors.

Now, to redraw either figure, we need to engage in a bit of data management:

```
months <- 1:180
static.predictors <- predictors[,-1]
dynamic.predictors <- predictors[,1, drop=FALSE]
y <- ts(pres.energy$Energy, frequency=12, start=c(1972, 1))
```

First, we define a month index, as before. Second, we subset our matrix predictors to those that have a static effect. Third, we isolate our dynamic predictor of the Nixon's speech. Fourth, we use the ts command to declare energy policy coverage to be a time series object. On this last line, we use the frequency option to specify that these are monthly data (hence the value 12) and the start option to note that these data begin in the first month of 1972.

---

[14] My thanks to Dave Armstrong for writing and suggesting this alternative code.

Next, we need to actually estimate our transfer function. Once we have done this, we can save several outputs from the model:

```
dynamic.mod<-arimax(y,order=c(1,0,0),xreg=static.predictors,
      xtransf=dynamic.predictors,transfer=list(c(1,0)))
b <- coef(dynamic.mod)
static.coefs <- b[match(colnames(static.predictors), names(b))]
ma.coefs <- b[grep("MA0", names(b))]
ar.coefs <- b[grep("AR1", names(b))]
```

The first line refits our transfer function. The second uses the `coef` command to extract the coefficients from the model and save them in a vector named `b`. The last three lines separate our coefficients into static effects (`static.coefs`), initial dynamic effects (`ma.coefs`), and decay terms (`ar.coefs`). In each line, we carefully reference the names of our coefficient vector, using the `match` command to find coefficients for the static predictors, and then the `grep` command to search for terms that contain `MA0` and `AR1`, respectively, just as output terms of a transfer function do.

With all of these elements extracted, we now turn specifically to redrawing Fig. 9.3, which shows the effect of the Nixon's speech intervention against the real data. Our intervention effect consists of two parts, the expected value from holding all of the static predictors at their values for the 58th month, and the dynamic effect of the transfer function. We create this as follows:

```
xreg.pred<-b["intercept"]+static.coefs%*%static.predictors[58,]
transf.pred <- as.numeric(dynamic.predictors%*%ma.coefs+
      ma.coefs*(ar.coefs^(months-59))*(months>59))
y.pred<-ts(xreg.pred+transf.pred,frequency=12,start=c(1972,1))
```

The first line simply makes the static prediction from a linear equation. The second uses our initial effects and decay terms to predict the dynamic effect of the intervention. Third, we add the two pieces together and save them as a time series with the same frequency and start date as the original series. With both `y` and `y.pred` now coded as time series of the same frequency over the same time span, it is now easy to recreate Fig. 9.3:

```
plot(y,xlab="Month", ylab="Energy Policy Stories",type="l")
lines(y.pred, lty=2,col='blue',lwd=2)
```

The first line simply plots the original time series, and the second line adds the intervention effect itself.

With all of the setup work we have done, reproducing Fig. 9.4 now only requires three lines of code:

```
full.pred<-fitted(dynamic.mod)
plot(full.pred,ylab="Energy Policy Stories",type="l",
      ylim=c(0,225))
points(y, pch=20)
```

The first line simply uses the `fitted` command to extract fitted values from the transfer function model. The second line plots these fitted values, and the third adds the points that represent the original series.

9.6   Practice Problems

This set of practice problems reviews each of the three approaches to time series modeling introduced in the chapter, and then poses a bonus question about the Peake and Eshbaugh-Soha energy data that asks you to learn about a new method. Questions #1–3 relate to single-equation models, so all of these questions use a dataset about electricity consumption in Japan. Meanwhile, question #4 uses US economic data for a multiple equation model.

1. Time series visualization: Wakiyama et al. (2014) study electricity consumption in Japan, assessing whether the March 11, 2011, Fukushima nuclear accident affected electricity consumption in various sectors. They do this by conducting an intervention analysis on monthly measures of electricity consumption in megawatts (MW), from January 2008 to December 2012. Load the foreign package and open these data in Stata format from the file comprehensiveJapanEnergy.dta. This data file is available from the Dataverse (see page vii) or this chapter's online content (see page 155). We will focus on household electricity consumption (variable name: **house**). Take the logarithm of this variable and draw a line plot of logged household electricity consumption from month-to-month. What patterns are apparent in these data?

2. Box–Jenkins modeling:

   a. Plot the autocorrelation function and partial autocorrelation function for logged household electricity consumption in Japan. What are the most apparent features from these figures?

   b. Wakiyama et al. (2014) argue that an ARIMA(1,0,1), with a Seasonal ARIMA(1,0,0) component fit this series. Estimate this model and report your results. (*Hint:* For this model, you will want to include the option seasonal=list(order=c(1,0,0), period=12) in the arima command.)

   c. How well does this ARIMA model fit? What do the ACF and PACF look like for the residuals from this model? What is the result of a Ljung–Box Q-test?

   d. Use the arimax command from the TSA package. Estimate a model that uses the ARIMA error process from before, the static predictors of temperature (**temp**) and squared temperature (**temp2**), and a transfer function for the Fukushima intervention (**dummy**).

   e. Bonus: The Fukushima indicator is actually a *step* intervention, rather than a *pulse*. This means that the effect *cumulates* rather than *decays*. Footnote 8 describes how these effects cumulate. Draw a picture of the cumulating effect of the Fukushima intervention on logged household electricity consumption.

3. Econometric modeling:

   a. Fit a static linear model using OLS for logged household electricity consumption in Japan. Use temperature (**temp**), squared temperature (**temp2**), and the Fukushima indicator (**dummy**) as predictors. Load the lmtest package, and compute both a Durbin–Watson and Breusch–Godfrey test for this linear model. What conclusions would you draw from each? Why do you think you get this result?

b. Reestimate the static linear model of logged household electricity consumption using FGLS with the Cochrane–Orcutt algorithm. How similar or different are your results from the OLS results? Why do you think this is?

c. Load the `dyn` package, and add a lagged dependent variable to this model. Which of the three econometric models do you think is the most appropriate and why? Do you think your preferred econometric model or the Box–Jenkins intervention analysis is more appropriate? Why?

4. Vector autoregression:

a. Enders (2009, p. 315) presents quarterly data on the US economy, which runs from the second quarter of 1959 to the first quarter of 2001. Load the `vars` and `foreign` packages, and then open the data in Stata format from the file `moneyDem.dta`. This file is available from the Dataverse (see page vii) or this chapter's online content (see page 155). Subset the data to only include three variables: change in logged real GDP (**dlrgdp**), change in the real M2 money supply (**dlrm2**), and change in the 3-month interest rate on US Treasury bills (**drs**). Using the `VARselect` command, determine the best-fitting lag length for a VAR model of these three variables, according to the AIC.

b. Estimate the model you determined to be the best fit according to the AIC. Examine the diagnostic plots. Do you believe these series are clear of serial correlation and that the functional form is correct?

c. For each of the three variables, test whether the variable Granger-causes the other two.

d. In monetary policy, the interest rate is an important policy tool for the Federal Reserve Bank. Compute an impulse response function for a percentage point increase in the interest rate (**drs**). Draw a plot of the expected changes in logged money supply (**dlrm2**) and logged real GDP (**dlrgdp**). (*Hint:* Include the option `response=c("dlrgdp","dlrm2")` in the `irf` function.) Be clear about whether you are orthogonalizing the residuals or making a theoretical assumption about response ordering.

5. Bonus: You may have noticed that Peake and Eshbaugh-Soha's (2008) data on monthly television coverage of the energy issue was used both as an example for count regression in Chap. 7 and as an example time series in this chapter. Brandt and Williams (2001) develop a Poisson autoregressive (PAR) model for time series count data, and Fogarty and Monogan (2014) apply this model to these energy policy data. Replicate this PAR model on these data. For replication information see: http://hdl.handle.net/1902.1/16677.

Chapter 10
Linear Algebra with Programming Applications

The R language has several built-in matrix algebra commands. This proves useful for analysts who wish to write their own estimators or have other problems in linear algebra that they wish to compute using software. In some instances, it is easier to apply a formula for predictions, standard errors, or some other quantity directly rather than searching for a canned program to compute the quantity, if one exists. Matrix algebra makes it straightforward to compute these quantities yourself. This chapter introduces the syntax and available commands for conducting matrix algebra in R.

The chapter proceeds by first describing how a user can input original data by hand, as a means of creating vectors, matrices, and data frames. Then it presents several of the commands associated with linear algebra. Finally, we work through an applied example in which we estimate a linear model with ordinary least squares by programming our own estimator.

As working data throughout the chapter, we consider a simple example from the 2010 US congressional election. We model the Republican candidate's share of the two-party vote in elections for the House of Representatives ($\mathbf{y}$) in 2010. The input variables are a constant ($\mathbf{x_1}$), Barack Obama's share of the two-party presidential vote in 2008 ($\mathbf{x_2}$), and the Republican candidate's financial standing relative to the Democrat in hundreds of thousands of dollars ($\mathbf{x_3}$). For simplicity, we model the nine House races in the state of Tennessee. The data are presented in Table 10.1.

Electronic supplementary material: The online version of this chapter (doi: 10.1007/978-3-319-23446-5_10) contains supplementary material, which is available to authorized users.

Table 10.1 Congressional election data from Tennessee in 2010

District	Republican (y)	Constant (x_1)	Obama (x_2)	Funding (x_3)
1	0.808	1	0.290	4.984
2	0.817	1	0.340	5.073
3	0.568	1	0.370	12.620
4	0.571	1	0.340	−6.443
5	0.421	1	0.560	−5.758
6	0.673	1	0.370	15.603
7	0.724	1	0.340	14.148
8	0.590	1	0.430	0.502
9	0.251	1	0.770	−9.048

Note: Data from Monogan (2013a)

10.1 Creating Vectors and Matrices

As a first task, when assigning values to a vector or matrix, we must use the traditional assignment command (<-). The command c **c**ombines several component elements into a *vector* object.[1] So to create a vector a with the specific values of 3, 4, and 5:

```
a <- c(3,4,5)
```

Within c, all we need to do is separate each element of the vector with a comma. As a more interesting example, suppose we wanted to input three of the variables from Table 10.1: Republican share of the two-party vote in 2010, Obama's share of the two-party vote in 2008, and Republican financial advantage, all as vectors. We would type:

```
Y<-c(.808,.817,.568,.571,.421,.673,.724,.590,.251)
X2<-c(.29,.34,.37,.34,.56,.37,.34,.43,.77)
X3<-c(4.984,5.073,12.620,-6.443,-5.758,15.603,14.148,0.502,
     -9.048)
```

Whenever entering data in vector form, we should generally make sure we have entered the correct number of observations. The length command returns how many observations are in a vector. To check all three of our vector entries, we type:

```
length(Y); length(X2); length(X3)
```

All three of our vectors should have length 9 if they were entered correctly. Observe here the use of the semicolon (;). If a user prefers to place multiple commands on a single line of text, the user can separate each command with a semicolon instead of putting each command on a separate line. This allows simple commands to be stored more compactly.

---

[1]Alternatively, when the combined elements are complex objects, c instead creates a list object.

If we want to create a vector that follows a **rep**eating pattern, we can use the `rep` command. For instance, in our model of Tennessee election returns, our constant term is simply a 9×1 vector of 1s:

```
X1 <- rep(1, 9)
```

The first term within `rep` is the term to be repeated, and the second term is the number of times it should be repeated.

Sequential vectors also are simple to create. A colon (`:`) prompts R to list sequential integers from the starting to the stopping point. For instance, to create an index for the congressional district of each observation, we would need a vector that contains values counting from 1 to 9:

```
index <- c(1:9)
```

As an aside, a more general command is the `seq` command, which allows us to define the intervals of a **seq**uence, as well as starting and ending values. For example, if for some reason we wanted to create a sequence from -2 to 1 in increments of 0.25, we would type:

```
e <- seq(-2, 1, by=0.25)
```

Any vector we create can be printed to the screen simply by typing the name of the vector. For instance, if we simply type `Y` into the command prompt, our vector of Republican vote share is printed in the output:

```
[1]  0.808 0.817 0.568 0.571 0.421 0.673 0.724
[8]  0.590 0.251
```

In this case, the nine values of the vector `Y` are printed. The number printed in the square braces at the start of each row offers the index of the first element in that row. For instance, the eighth observation of `Y` is the value 0.590. For longer vectors, this helps the user keep track of the indices of the elements within the vector.

10.1.1 Creating Matrices

Turning to matrices, we can create an object of class *matrix* in several possible ways. First, we could use the `matrix` command: In the simplest possible case, suppose we wanted to create a matrix with all of the values being the same. To create a 4×4 matrix b with every value equaling 3:

```
b <- matrix(3, ncol=4, nrow=4, byrow=FALSE)
```

The syntax of the `matrix` command first calls for the elements that will define the matrix: In this case, we listed a single scalar, so this number was repeated for all matrix cells. Alternatively, we could list a vector instead that includes enough entries to fill the entire matrix. We then need to specify the number of columns (`ncol`) and rows (`nrow`). Lastly, the `byrow` argument is set to `FALSE` by default. With the `FALSE` setting, R fills the matrix column-by-column. A `TRUE` setting fills the matrix row-by-row instead. As a rule, whenever creating a matrix, type the name of the matrix (b in this case) into the command console to see if the way R input the data matches what you intended.

A second simple option is to create a matrix from vectors that have already been entered. We can **bind** the vectors together as <u>c</u>olumn vectors using the cbind command and as <u>r</u>ow vectors using the rbind command. For example, in our model of Tennessee election returns, we will need to create a matrix of all input variables in which variables define the columns and observations define the rows. Since we have defined our three variable vectors (and each vector is ordered by observation), we can simply create such a matrix using cbind:

```
X<-cbind(1,X2,X3)
X
```

The cbind command treats our vectors as columns in a matrix. This is what we want since a predictor matrix defines rows with observations and columns with variables. The 1 in the cbind command ensures that all elements of the first column are equal to the constant 1. (Of course, the way we designed X1, we also could have included that vector.) When typing X in the console, we get the printout:

```
         X2       X3
[1,]  1 0.29    4.984
[2,]  1 0.34    5.073
[3,]  1 0.37   12.620
[4,]  1 0.34   -6.443
[5,]  1 0.56   -5.758
[6,]  1 0.37   15.603
[7,]  1 0.34   14.148
[8,]  1 0.43    0.502
[9,]  1 0.77   -9.048
```

These results match the data we have in Table 10.1, so our covariate matrix should be ready when we are ready to estimate our model.

Just to illustrate the rbind command, R easily would combine the vectors as rows as follows:

```
T<-rbind(1,X2,X3)
T
```

We do not format data like this, but to see how the results look, typing T in the console results in the printout:

```
       [,1]   [,2]   [,3]   [,4]    [,5]    [,6]    [,7]
      1.000  1.000  1.00   1.000   1.000   1.000   1.000
X2    0.290  0.340  0.37   0.340   0.560   0.370   0.340
X3    4.984  5.073 12.62  -6.443  -5.758  15.603  14.148
       [,8]   [,9]
      1.000  1.000
X2    0.430  0.770
X3    0.502 -9.048
```

Hence, we see that each variable vector makes a row and each observation makes a column. In the printout, when R lacks the space to print an entire row on a single line, it wraps all rows at once, thus presenting columns 8 and 9 later.

Third, we could create a matrix by using subscripting. (Additional details on vector and matrix subscripts are presented in Sect. 10.1.3.) Sometimes when creating a matrix, the user will know all of the values up front, but on other occasions a user must create a matrix and then fill in the values later. In the latter case, it is a good idea to create "blanks" to fill in by designating every cell as missing (or NA). The nice feature of this is that a user can easily identify a cell that was never filled-in. By contrast, if a matrix is created with some default numeric value, say 0, then later on it is impossible to distinguish a cell that has a default 0 from one with a true value of 0. So if we wanted to create a 3×3 matrix named blank to fill in later, we would write:

```
blank <- matrix(NA, ncol=3, nrow=3)
```

If we then wanted to assign the value of 8 to the first row, third column element, we would write:

```
blank[1,3] <- 8
```

If we then wanted to insert the value π ($= 3.141592\ldots$) into the second row, first column entry, we would write:

```
blank[2,1] <- pi
```

If we wanted to use our previously defined vector $\mathbf{a} = (3, 4, 5)'$ to define the second column, we would write:

```
blank[,2] <- a
```

We then could check our progress simply by typing blank into the command prompt, which would print:

```
         [,1] [,2] [,3]
[1,]       NA    3    8
[2,] 3.141593    4   NA
[3,]       NA    5   NA
```

To the left of the matrix, the row terms are defined. At the top of the matrix, the column terms are defined. Notice that four elements are still coded NA because a replacement value was never offered.

Fourth, in contrast to filling-in matrices after creation, we also may know the values we want at the time of creating the matrix. As a simple example, to create a 2×2 matrix $\mathbf{W}$ in which we list the value of each cell column-by-column:

```
W <- matrix(c(1,2,3,4), ncol=2, nrow=2)
```

Notice that our first argument is now a vector because we want to provide unique elements for each of the cells in the matrix. With four elements in the vector, we have the correct number of entries for a 2×2 matrix. Also, in this case, we ignored the byrow argument because the default is to fill-in by columns. By contrast, if we wanted to list the cell elements row-by-row in matrix $\mathbf{Z}$, we would simply set byrow to TRUE:

```
Z <- matrix(c(1,2,3,4), ncol=2, nrow=2, byrow=TRUE)
```

Type W and Z into the console and observe how the same vector of cell entries has been reorganized going from one cell to another.

Alternatively, suppose we wanted to create a 10×10 matrix **N** where every cell entry was a **r**andom draw from a **norm**al distribution with mean 10 and standard deviation 2, or $\mathcal{N}(10, 4)$:

```
N <- matrix(rnorm(100, mean=10, sd=2), nrow=10, ncol=10)
```

Because rnorm returns an object of the vector class, we are again listing a vector to create our cell entries. The rnorm command is drawing from the normal distribution with our specifications 100 times, which provides the number of cell entries we need for a 10×10 matrix.

Fifth, on many occasions, we will want to create a *diagonal matrix* that contains only elements on its main **diag**onal (from the top left to the bottom right), with zeros in all other cells. The command diag makes it easy to create such a matrix:

```
D <- diag(c(1:4))
```

By typing D into the console, we now see how this diagonal matrix appears:

```
     [,1] [,2] [,3] [,4]
[1,]   1    0    0    0
[2,]   0    2    0    0
[3,]   0    0    3    0
[4,]   0    0    0    4
```

Additionally, if one inserts a square matrix into the diag command, it will return a vector from the matrix's diagonal elements. For example, in a variance-covariance matrix, the diagonal elements are variances and can be extracted quickly in this way.

10.1.2 Converting Matrices and Data Frames

A final means of creating a matrix object is with the as.matrix command. This command can take an object of the *data frame* class and convert it to an object of the *matrix* class. For a data frame called mydata, for example, the command mydata.2 <- as.matrix(mydata) would coerce the data into matrix form, making all of the ensuing matrix operations applicable to the data. Additionally, typing mydata.3 <- as.matrix(mydata[,4:8]) would only take columns four through eight of the data frame and coerce those into a matrix, allowing the user to subset the data while creating a matrix object.

Similarly, suppose we wanted to take an object of the *matrix* class and create an object of the *data frame* class, perhaps our Tennessee electoral data from Table 10.1. In this case, the as.data.frame command will work. If we simply wanted to create a data frame from our covariate matrix **X**, we could type:

```
X.df <- as.data.frame(X)
```

If we wanted to create a data frame using all of the variables from Table 10.1, including the dependent variable and index, we could type:

```
tennessee <- as.data.frame(cbind(index,Y,X1,X2,X3))
```

In this case, the `cbind` command embedded in `as.data.frame` defines a matrix, which is immediately converted to a data frame. In all, then, if a user wishes to input his or her own data into R, the most straightforward way will be to define variable vectors, bind them together as columns, and convert the matrix to a data frame.

10.1.3 Subscripting

As touched on in the matrix creation section, calling elements of vectors and matrices by their subscripts can be useful for either extracting necessary information or for making assignments. To call a specific value, we can index a vector **y** by the *n*th element, using `Y[n]`. So the third element of vector **y**, or y_3, is called by:

```
Y[3]
```

To index an $n \times k$ matrix **X** for the value X_{ij}, where *i* represents the row and *j* represents the column, use the syntax `X[i,j]`. If we want to select all values of the *j*th column of **X**, we can use `X[,j]`. For example, to return the second column of matrix **X**, type:

```
X[,2]
```

Alternatively, if a column has a name, then the name (in quotations) can be used to call the column as well. For example:

```
X[,"X2"]
```

Similarly, if we wish to select all of the elements of the *i*th row of **X**, we can use `X[i,]`. For the first row of matrix **X**, type:

```
X[1,]
```

Alternatively, we could use a row name as well, though the matrix **X** does not have names assigned to the rows.

If we wish, though, we can create **row names** for matrices. For example:

```
rownames(X)<-c("Dist. 1","Dist. 2","Dist. 3","Dist. 4",
        "Dist. 5","Dist. 6","Dist. 7","Dist. 8","Dist. 9")
```

Similarly, the command `colnames` allows the user to define **column names**. To simply type `rownames(X)` or `colnames(X)` without making an assignment, R will print the row or column names saved for a matrix.

10.2   Vector and Matrix Commands

Now that we have a sense of creating vectors and matrices, we turn to commands that either extract information from these objects or allow us to conduct linear algebra with them. As was mentioned before, after entering a vector or matrix into R, in addition to printing the object onto the screen for visual inspection, it is also a good idea to check and make sure the dimensions of the object are correct. For instance, to obtain the **length** of a vector **a**:

```
length(a)
```

Similarly, to obtain the **dim**ensions of a matrix, type:

```
dim(X)
```

The `dim` command first prints the number of rows, then the number of columns. Checking these dimensions offers an extra assurance that the data in a matrix have been entered correctly.

For vectors, the elements can be treated as data, and summary quantities can be extracted. For instance, to add up the **sum** of a vector's elements:

```
sum(X2)
```

Similarly, to take the **mean** of a vector's elements (in this example, the mean of Obama's 2008 vote by district):

```
mean(X2)
```

And to take the **var**iance of a vector:

```
var(X2)
```

Another option we have for matrices and vectors is that we can sample from a given object with the command `sample`. Suppose we want a sample of ten numbers from **N**, our 10×10 matrix of random draws from a normal distribution:

```
set.seed(271828183)
N <- matrix(rnorm(100, mean=10, sd=2), nrow=10, ncol=10)
s <- sample(N,10)
```

The first command, `set.seed` makes this simulation more replicable. (See Chap. 11 for more detail about this command.) This gives us a vector named **s** of ten random elements from **N**. We also have the option of applying the `sample` command to vectors.[2]

The `apply` command is often the most efficient way to do vectorized calculations. For example, to calculate the means for all the columns in our Tennessee data matrix **X**:

```
apply(X, 2, mean)
```

---

[2]For readers interested in bootstrapping, which is one of the most common applications of sampling from data, the most efficient approach will be to install the `boot` package and try some of the examples that library offers.

In this case, the first argument lists the matrix to analyze. The second argument, 2 tells R to apply a mathematical function along the *columns* of the matrix. The third argument, `mean` is the function we want to apply to each column. If we wanted the mean of the *rows* instead of the columns, we could use a 1 as the second argument instead of a 2. Any function defined in R can be used with the `apply` command.

10.2.1 Matrix Algebra

Commands that are more specific to matrix algebra are also available. Whenever the user wants to save the output of a vector or matrix operation, the assignment command must be used. For example, if for some reason we needed the difference between each Republican share of the two-party vote and Obama's share of the two-party vote, we could assign vector **m** to the difference of the two vectors by typing:

```
m <- Y - X2
```

With arithmetic operations, R is actually pretty flexible, but a word on how the commands work may avoid future confusion. For addition (+) and subtraction (-): If the arguments are two vectors of the same length (as is the case in computing vector **m**), then R computes regular vector addition or subtraction where each element is added to or subtracted from its corresponding element in the other vector. If the arguments are two matrices of the same size, matrix addition or subtraction applies where each entry is combined with its corresponding entry in the other matrix. If one argument is a scalar, then the scalar will be added to each element of the vector or matrix.

Note: If two vectors of uneven length or two matrices of different size are added, an error message results, as these arguments are non-conformable. To illustrate this, if we attempted to add our sample of ten numbers from before, **s**, to our vector of Obama's 2008 share of the vote, x_2, as follows:

```
s + X2
```

In this case we would receive an output that we should ignore, followed by an error message in red:

```
[1] 11.743450  8.307068 11.438161 14.251645 10.828459
[6] 10.336895  9.900118 10.092051 12.556688  9.775185
Warning message:
In s + X2 : longer object length is not a multiple of shorter
object length
```

This warning message tells us the output is nonsense. Since the vector s has length 10, while the vector X2 has length 9, what R has done here is added the *tenth* element of s to the *first* element of X2 and used this as the tenth element of the output. The error message that follows serves as a reminder that a garbage input that breaks the rules of linear algebra produces a garbage output that no one should use.

By contrast, $*$, $/$, $\hat{}$ (exponents), exp (exponential function), and log all apply the relevant operation to each scalar entry in the vector or matrix. For our matrix of predictors from Tennessee, for example, try the command:

```
X.sq <- X^2
```

This would return a matrix that squares each separate cell in the matrix **X**. By a similar token, the simple multiplication operation ($*$) performs multiplication element by element. Hence, if two vectors are of the same length or two matrices of the same size, the output will be a vector or matrix of the same size where each element is the product of the corresponding elements. Just as an illustration, let us multiply Obama's share of the two-party vote by Republican financial advantage in a few ways. (The quantities may be silly, but this offers an example of how the code works.) Try for example:

```
x2.x3 <- X2*X3
```

The output vector is:

```
[1]   1.44536   1.72482   4.66940  -2.19062  -3.22448
[6]   5.77311   4.81032   0.21586  -6.96696
```

This corresponds to element-by-element scalar multiplication.

More often, the user actually will want to conduct proper matrix multiplication. In R, matrix multiplication is conducted by the $\%*\%$ operation. So if we had instead multiplied our two vectors of Obama vote share and Republican financial advantage in this way:

```
x2.x3.inner <- X2%*%X3
```

R would now return the *inner product*, or dot product ($\mathbf{x_2} \cdot \mathbf{x_3}$). This equals 6.25681 in our example. Another useful quantity for vector multiplication is the *outer product*, or tensor product ($\mathbf{x_2} \otimes \mathbf{x_3}$). We can obtain this by *transposing* the second vector in our code:

```
x2.x3.outer <- X2%*%t(X3)
```

The output of this command is a 9×9 matrix. To obtain this quantity, the transpose command (t) was used.[3] In matrix algebra, we may need to turn row vectors to column vectors or vice versa, and the transpose operation accomplishes this. Similarly, when applied to a matrix, every row becomes a column and every column becomes a row.

As one more example of matrix multiplication, the input variable matrix **X** has size 9×3, and the matrix **T** that lets variables define rows is a 3×9 matrix. In this case, we could create the matrix $\mathbf{P} = \mathbf{TX}$ because the number of columns of **T** is the same as the number of rows of **X**. We therefore can say that the matrices are *conformable for multiplication* and will result in a matrix of size 3×3. We can compute this as:

---

[3] An alternate syntax would have been X2%o%X3.

```
P <- T%*%X
```

Note that if our matrices are not conformable for multiplication, then R will return an error message.[4]

Beyond matrix multiplication and the transpose operation, another important quantity that is unique to matrix algebra is the **det**erminant of a square matrix (or a matrix that has the same number of rows as columns). Our matrix **P** is square because it has three rows and three columns. One reason to calculate the determinant is that a square matrix has an inverse only if the determinant is nonzero.[5] To compute the determinant of **P**, we type:

```
det(P)
```

This yields a value of 691.3339. We therefore know that **P** has an inverse.

For a square matrix that can be inverted, the *inverse* is a matrix that can be multiplied by the original to produce the identity matrix. With the `solve` command, R will either **solve** for the inverse of the matrix or convey that the matrix is noninvertible. To try this concept, type:

```
invP <- solve(P)
invP%*%P
```

On the first line, we created P^{-1}, which is the inverse of **P**. On the second line, we multiply $P^{-1}P$ and the printout is:

```
                      X2              X3
    1.000000e+00 -6.106227e-16 -6.394885e-14
X2  1.421085e-14  1.000000e+00  1.278977e-13
X3  2.775558e-17 -2.255141e-17  1.000000e+00
```

This is the basic form of the identity matrix, with values of 1 along the main diagonal (running from the top left to bottom right), and values of 0 off the diagonal. While the off-diagonal elements are not listed exactly as zero, this can be attributed to rounding error on R's part. The scientific notation for the second row, first column element for example means that the first 13 digits after the decimal place are zero, followed by a 1 in the 14th digit.

---

[4]A unique variety of matrix multiplication is called the Kronecker product ($H \otimes L$). The Kronecker product has useful applications in the analysis of panel data. See the `kronecker` command in R for more information.

[5]As another application in statistics, the likelihood function for a multivariate normal distribution also calls on the determinant of the covariance matrix.

10.3   Applied Example: Programming OLS Regression

To illustrate the various matrix algebra operations that R has available, in this section we will work an applied example by computing the ordinary least squares (OLS) estimator with our own program using real data.

10.3.1   Calculating OLS by Hand

First, to motivate the background to the problem, consider the formulation of the model and how we would estimate this by hand. Our population linear regression model for vote shares in Tennessee is: $\mathbf{y} = \mathbf{X}\boldsymbol{\beta} + \mathbf{u}$. In this model, $\mathbf{y}$ is a vector of the Republican vote share in each district, $\mathbf{X}$ is a matrix of predictors (including a constant, Obama's share of the vote in 2008, and the Republican's financial advantage relative the Democrat), $\boldsymbol{\beta}$ consists of the partial coefficient for each predictor, and $\mathbf{u}$ is a vector of disturbances. We estimate $\hat{\boldsymbol{\beta}} = (\mathbf{X}'\mathbf{X})^{-1}\mathbf{X}'\mathbf{y}$, yielding the sample regression function $\hat{\mathbf{y}} = \mathbf{X}\hat{\boldsymbol{\beta}}$.

To start computing by hand, we have to define $\mathbf{X}$. Note that we must include a vector of 1s in order to estimate an intercept term. In scalar form, our population model is: $y_i = \beta_1 x_{1i} + \beta_2 x_{2i} + \beta_3 x_{3i} + u_i$, where $x_{1i} = 1$ for all i. This gives us the predictor matrix:

$$\mathbf{X} = \begin{bmatrix} 1 & 0.29 & 4.984 \\ 1 & 0.34 & 5.073 \\ 1 & 0.37 & 12.620 \\ 1 & 0.34 & -6.443 \\ 1 & 0.56 & -5.758 \\ 1 & 0.37 & 15.603 \\ 1 & 0.34 & 14.148 \\ 1 & 0.43 & 0.502 \\ 1 & 0.77 & -9.048 \end{bmatrix}$$

Next, premultiply $\mathbf{X}$ by its transpose:

$$\mathbf{X}'\mathbf{X} = \begin{bmatrix} 1.000 & 1.000 & 1.000 & 1.000 & 1.000 & 1.000 & 1.000 & 1.000 & 1.000 \\ 0.290 & 0.340 & 0.370 & 0.340 & 0.560 & 0.370 & 0.340 & 0.430 & 0.770 \\ 4.984 & 5.073 & 12.620 & -6.443 & -5.758 & 15.603 & 14.148 & 0.502 & -9.048 \end{bmatrix} \begin{bmatrix} 1 & 0.29 & 4.984 \\ 1 & 0.34 & 5.073 \\ 1 & 0.37 & 12.620 \\ 1 & 0.34 & -6.443 \\ 1 & 0.56 & -5.758 \\ 1 & 0.37 & 15.603 \\ 1 & 0.34 & 14.148 \\ 1 & 0.43 & 0.502 \\ 1 & 0.77 & -9.048 \end{bmatrix}$$

which works out to:

$$\mathbf{X'X} = \begin{bmatrix} 9.00000 & 3.81000 & 31.68100 \\ 3.81000 & 1.79610 & 6.25681 \\ 31.68100 & 6.25681 & 810.24462 \end{bmatrix}$$

We also need $\mathbf{X'y}$:

$$\mathbf{X'y} = \begin{bmatrix} 1.000 & 1.000 & 1.000 & 1.000 & 1.000 & 1.000 & 1.000 & 1.000 & 1.000 \\ 0.290 & 0.340 & 0.370 & 0.340 & 0.560 & 0.370 & 0.340 & 0.430 & 0.770 \\ 4.984 & 5.073 & 12.620 & -6.443 & -5.758 & 15.603 & 14.148 & 0.502 & -9.048 \end{bmatrix} \begin{bmatrix} 0.808 \\ 0.817 \\ 0.568 \\ 0.571 \\ 0.421 \\ 0.673 \\ 0.724 \\ 0.590 \\ 0.251 \end{bmatrix}$$

which works out to:

$$\mathbf{X'y} = \begin{bmatrix} 5.4230 \\ 2.0943 \\ 28.0059 \end{bmatrix}$$

Inverse by Hand

The last quantity we need is the inverse of $\mathbf{X'X}$. Doing this by hand, we can solve by Gauss-Jordan elimination:

$$[\mathbf{X'X}|\mathbf{I}] = \left[\begin{array}{ccc|ccc} 9.00000 & 3.81000 & 31.68100 & 1.00000 & 0.00000 & 0.00000 \\ 3.81000 & 1.79610 & 6.25681 & 0.00000 & 1.00000 & 0.00000 \\ 31.68100 & 6.25681 & 810.24462 & 0.00000 & 0.00000 & 1.00000 \end{array} \right]$$

Divide row 1 by 9:

$$\left[\begin{array}{ccc|ccc} 1.00000 & 0.42333 & 3.52011 & 0.11111 & 0.00000 & 0.00000 \\ 3.81000 & 1.79610 & 6.25681 & 0.00000 & 1.00000 & 0.00000 \\ 31.68100 & 6.25681 & 810.24462 & 0.00000 & 0.00000 & 1.00000 \end{array} \right]$$

Subtract 3.81 times row 1 from row 2:

$$\left[\begin{array}{ccc|ccc} 1.00000 & 0.42333 & 3.52011 & 0.11111 & 0.00000 & 0.00000 \\ 0.00000 & 0.18320 & -7.15481 & -0.42333 & 1.00000 & 0.00000 \\ 31.68100 & 6.25681 & 810.24462 & 0.00000 & 0.00000 & 1.00000 \end{array} \right]$$

Subtract 31.681 times row 1 from row 3:

$$\begin{bmatrix} 1.00000 & 0.42333 & 3.52011 & 0.11111 & 0.00000 & 0.00000 \\ 0.00000 & 0.18320 & -7.15481 & -0.42333 & 1.00000 & 0.00000 \\ 0.00000 & -7.15481 & 698.72402 & -3.52011 & 0.00000 & 1.00000 \end{bmatrix}$$

Divide row 2 by 0.1832:

$$\begin{bmatrix} 1.00000 & 0.42333 & 3.52011 & 0.11111 & 0.00000 & 0.00000 \\ 0.00000 & 1.00000 & -39.05464 & -2.31077 & 5.45852 & 0.00000 \\ 0.00000 & -7.15481 & 698.72402 & -3.52011 & 0.00000 & 1.00000 \end{bmatrix}$$

Add 7.15481 times row 2 to row 3:

$$\begin{bmatrix} 1.00000 & 0.42333 & 3.52011 & 0.11111 & 0.00000 & 0.00000 \\ 0.00000 & 1.00000 & -39.05464 & -2.31077 & 5.45852 & 0.00000 \\ 0.00000 & 0.00000 & 419.29549 & -20.05323 & 39.05467 & 1.00000 \end{bmatrix}$$

Divide row 3 by 419.29549:

$$\begin{bmatrix} 1.00000 & 0.42333 & 3.52011 & 0.11111 & 0.00000 & 0.00000 \\ 0.00000 & 1.00000 & -39.05464 & -2.31077 & 5.45852 & 0.00000 \\ 0.00000 & 0.00000 & 1.00000 & -0.04783 & 0.09314 & 0.00239 \end{bmatrix}$$

Add 39.05464 times row 3 to row 2:

$$\begin{bmatrix} 1.00000 & 0.42333 & 3.52011 & 0.11111 & 0.00000 & 0.00000 \\ 0.00000 & 1.00000 & 0.00000 & -4.17859 & 9.09607 & 0.09334 \\ 0.00000 & 0.00000 & 1.00000 & -0.04783 & 0.09314 & 0.00239 \end{bmatrix}$$

Subtract 3.52011 times row 3 from row 1:

$$\begin{bmatrix} 1.00000 & 0.42333 & 0.00000 & 0.27946 & -0.32786 & -0.00841 \\ 0.00000 & 1.00000 & 0.00000 & -4.17859 & 9.09607 & 0.09334 \\ 0.00000 & 0.00000 & 1.00000 & -0.04783 & 0.09314 & 0.00239 \end{bmatrix}$$

Subtract .42333 times row 2 from row 1:

$$\begin{bmatrix} 1.00000 & 0.00000 & 0.00000 & 2.04838 & -4.17849 & -0.04792 \\ 0.00000 & 1.00000 & 0.00000 & -4.17859 & 9.09607 & 0.09334 \\ 0.00000 & 0.00000 & 1.00000 & -0.04783 & 0.09314 & 0.00239 \end{bmatrix} = [\mathbf{I}|(\mathbf{X'X})^{-1}]$$

As a slight wrinkle in these hand calculations, we can see that $(\mathbf{X'X})^{-1}$ is a little off due to rounding error. It should actually be a symmetric matrix.

Final Answer by Hand

If we postmultiply $(\mathbf{X'X})^{-1}$ by $\mathbf{X'y}$ we get:

$$(\mathbf{X'X})^{-1}\mathbf{X'y} = \begin{bmatrix} 2.04838 & -4.17849 & -0.04792 \\ -4.17859 & 9.09607 & 0.09334 \\ -0.04783 & 0.09314 & 0.00239 \end{bmatrix} \begin{bmatrix} 5.4230 \\ 2.0943 \\ 28.0059 \end{bmatrix} = \begin{bmatrix} 1.0178 \\ -1.0018 \\ 0.0025 \end{bmatrix} = \hat{\beta}$$

Or in scalar form: $\hat{y}_i = 1.0178 - 1.0018x_{2i} + 0.0025x_{3i}$.

10.3.2 Writing An OLS Estimator in R

Since inverting the matrix took so many steps and even ran into some rounding error, it will be easier to have R do some of the heavy lifting for us. (As the number of observations or variables rises, we will find the computational assistance even more valuable.) In order to program our own OLS estimator in R, the key commands we require are:

- Matrix multiplication: `%*%`
- Transpose: `t`
- Matrix inverse: `solve`

Knowing this, it is easy to program an estimator for $\hat{\beta} = (\mathbf{X'X})^{-1}\mathbf{X'y}$.

First we must enter our variable vectors using the data from Table 10.1 and combine the input variables into a matrix. If you have not yet entered these, type:

```
Y<-c(.808,.817,.568,.571,.421,.673,.724,.590,.251)
X1 <- rep(1, 9)
X2<-c(.29,.34,.37,.34,.56,.37,.34,.43,.77)
X3<-c(4.984,5.073,12.620,-6.443,-5.758,15.603,14.148,0.502,
    -9.048)
X<-cbind(X1,X2,X3)
```

To estimate OLS with our own program, we simply need to translate the estimator $(\mathbf{X'X})^{-1}\mathbf{X'y}$ into R syntax:

```
beta.hat<-solve(t(X)%*%X)%*%t(X)%*%Y
beta.hat
```

Breaking this down a bit: The `solve` command leads off because the first quantity is an inverse, $(\mathbf{X'X})^{-1}$. Within the call to `solve`, the first argument must be transposed (hence the use of `t`) and then it is postmultiplied by the non-transposed covariate matrix (hence the use of `%*%`). We follow up by postmultiplying the transpose of $\mathbf{X}$, then postmultiplying the vector of outcomes ($\mathbf{y}$). When we print our results, we get:

```
        [,1]
    1.017845630
X2 -1.001809341
X3  0.002502538
```

These are the same results we obtained by hand, despite the rounding discrepancies we encountered when inverting on our own. Writing the program in R, however, simultaneously gave us full control over the estimator, while being much quicker than the hand operations.

Of course an even faster option would be to use the canned lm command we used in Chap. 6:

```
tennessee <- as.data.frame(cbind(Y,X2,X3))
lm(Y~X2+X3, data=tennessee)
```

This also yields the exact same results. In practice, whenever computing OLS estimates, this is almost always the approach we will want to take. However, this procedure has allowed us to verify the usefulness of R's matrix algebra commands. If the user finds the need to program a more complex estimator for which there is not a canned command, this should offer relevant tools with which to accomplish this.

10.3.3   Other Applications

With these basic tools in hand, users should now be able to begin programming with matrices and vectors. Some intermediate applications of this include: computing standard errors from models estimated with optim (see Chap. 11) and predicted values for complicated functional forms (see the code that produced Fig. 9.3). Some of the more advanced applications that can benefit from using these tools include: feasible generalized least squares (including weighted least squares), optimizing likelihood functions for multivariate normal distributions, and generating correlated data using **Chol**esky decomposition (see the chol command). Very few programs offer the estimation and programming flexibility that R does whenever matrix algebra is essential to the process.

10.4   Practice Problems

For these practice problems, consider the data on congressional elections in Arizona in 2010, presented below in Table 10.2:

Table 10.2 Congressional election data from Arizona in 2010

District	Republican (y)	Constant (x_1)	Obama (x_2)	Funding (x_3)
1	0.50	1	0.44	−9.11
2	0.65	1	0.38	8.31
3	0.52	1	0.42	8.00
4	0.28	1	0.66	−8.50
5	0.52	1	0.47	−7.17
6	0.67	1	0.38	5.10
7	0.45	1	0.57	−5.32
8	0.47	1	0.46	−18.64

Note: Data from Monogan (2013a)

1. Create a vector consisting of the Republican share of the two-party vote (**y**) in Arizona's eight congressional districts. Using any means you prefer, create a matrix, **X**, in which the eight rows represent Arizona's eight districts, and the three columns represent a constant vector of ones (**x_1**), Obama's 2008 share of the vote (**x_2**), and the Republican's financial balance (**x_3**). Print out your vector and matrix, and ask R to compute the vector's length and matrix's dimensions. Are all of these outputs consistent with the data you see in Table 10.2?
2. Using your matrix, **X**, compute **X′X** using R's commands. What is your result?
3. Using R's commands, find the inverse of your previous answer. That is, compute $(\mathbf{X'X})^{-1}$. What is your result?
4. Using the data in Table 10.2, consider the regression model $y_i = \beta_1 x_{1i} + \beta_2 x_{2i} + \beta_3 x_{3i} + u_i$. Using R's matrix algebra commands, compute $\hat{\boldsymbol{\beta}} = (\mathbf{X'X})^{-1}\mathbf{X'y}$. What are your estimates of the regression coefficients, $\hat{\beta}_1$, $\hat{\beta}_2$, and $\hat{\beta}_3$? How do your results compare if you compute these using the lm command from Chap. 6?

Chapter 11
Additional Programming Tools

As the last several chapters have shown, R offers users flexibility and opportunities for advanced data analysis that cannot be found in many programs. In this final chapter, we will explore R's programming tools, which allow the user to create code that addresses any unique problem he or she faces.

Bear in mind that many of the tools relevant to programming have already been introduced earlier in the book. In Chap. 10, the tools for matrix algebra in R were introduced, and many programs require matrix processing. Additionally, logical (or Boolean) statements are essential to programming. R's logical operators were introduced in Chap. 2, so see Table 2.1 for a reminder of what each operator's function is.

The subsequent sections will introduce several other tools that are important for programming: probability distributions, new function definition, loops, branching, and optimization (which is particularly useful for maximum likelihood estimation). The chapter will end with two large applied examples. The first, drawing from Monogan (2013b), introduces *object-oriented programming* in R and applies several programming tools from this chapter to finding solutions from an insoluble game theoretic problem. The second, drawing from Signorino (1999), offers an example of *Monte Carlo analysis* and more advanced maximum likelihood estimation in R.[1] Together, the two applications should showcase how all of the programming tools can come together to solve a complex problem.

Electronic supplementary material: The online version of this chapter (doi: 10.1007/978-3-319-23446-5_11) contains supplementary material, which is available to authorized users.

[1] See also: Signorino (2002) and Signorino and Yilmaz (2003).

© Springer International Publishing Switzerland 2015
J.E. Monogan III, *Political Analysis Using R*, Use R!,
DOI 10.1007/978-3-319-23446-5_11

Table 11.1 Using probability distributions in R

Prefix	Usage	Suffix	Distribution
p	Cumulative distribution function	norm	Normal
d	Probability density function	logis	Logistic
q	Quantile function	t	t
r	Random draw from distribution	f	F
		unif	Uniform
		pois	Poisson
		exp	Exponential
		chisq	Chi-squared
		binom	Binomial

11.1   Probability Distributions

R allows you to use a wide variety of distributions for four purposes. For each distribution, R allows you to call the cumulative distribution function (CDF), probability density function (PDF), quantile function, and random draws from the distribution. All probability distribution commands consist of a prefix and a suffix. Table 11.1 presents the four prefixes, and their usage, as well as the suffixes for some commonly used probability distributions. Each distribution's functions take arguments unique to that probability distribution's parameters. To see how these are specified, use help files (e.g., ?punif, ?pexp, or ?pnorm).[2]

If you wanted to know the probability that a standard normal observation will be less than 1.645, use the *cumulative distribution function* (CDF) command pnorm:

```
pnorm(1.645)
```

Suppose you want to draw a scalar from the standard normal distribution: to draw $a \sim \mathcal{N}(0, 1)$, use the *random draw* command rnorm:

```
a <- rnorm(1)
```

To draw a vector with ten values from a χ^2 distribution with four degrees of freedom, use the random draw command:

```
c <- rchisq(10,df=4)
```

Recall from Chap. 10 that the sample command also allows us to simulate values, whenever we provide a vector of possible values. Hence, R offers a wide array of data simulation commands.

---

[2]Other distributions can be loaded through various packages. For example, another useful distribution is the multivariate normal. By loading the MASS library, a user can sample from the multivariate normal distribution with the mvrnorm command. Even more generally, the mvtnorm package allows the user to compute multivariate normal and multivariate t probabilities, quantiles, random deviates, and densities.

Suppose we have a given probability, 0.9, and we want to know the value of a χ^2 distribution with four degrees of freedom at which the probability of being less than or equal to that value is 0.9. This calls for the *quantile function*:

```
qchisq(.9,df=4)
```

We can calculate the probability of a certain value from the *probability mass function* (PMF) for a discrete distribution. Of a Poisson distribution with intensity parameter 9, what is the probability of a count of 5?

```
dpois(5,lambda=9)
```

Although usually of less interest, for a continuous distribution, we can calculate the value of the *probability density function* (PDF) of a particular value. This has no inherent meaning, but occasionally is required. For a normal distribution with mean 4 and standard deviation 2, the density at the value 1 is given by:

```
dnorm(1,mean=4,sd=2)
```

11.2 Functions

R allows you to create your own functions with the `function` command. The `function` command uses the basic following syntax:

```
function.name <- function(INPUTS){BODY}
```

Notice that the `function` command first expects the inputs to be listed in round parentheses, while the body of the function is listed in curly braces. As can be seen, there is little constraint in what the user chooses to put into the function, so a function can be crafted to accomplish whatever the user would like.

For example, suppose we were interested in the equation $y = 2 + \frac{1}{x^2}$. We could define this function easily in R. All we have to do is specify that our input variable is x and our body is the right-hand side of the equation. This will create a function that returns values for y. We define our function, named `first.fun`, as follows:

```
first.fun<-function(x){
    y<-2+x^{-2}
    return(y)
    }
```

Although broken-up across a few lines, this is all one big command, as the curly braces ({}) span multiple lines. With the `function` command, we begin by declaring that x is the name of our one input, based on the fact that our equation of interest has x as the name of the input variable. Next, inside the curly braces, we assign the output y as being the exact function of x that we are interested in. As a last step before closing our curly braces, we use the `return` command, which tells the function what the output result is after it is called. The `return` command is useful when determining function output for a couple of reasons: First,

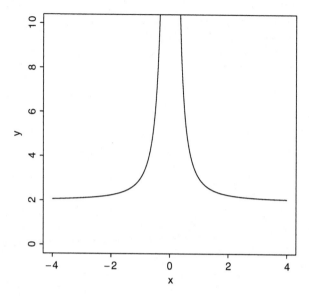

Fig. 11.1 Plot of the function $y = 2 + \frac{1}{x^2}$

if we define multiple objects inside of a command, this allows us to specify what should be printed in the output versus what was strictly internal to the function. Second, `return` allows us to report a list of items as an output, if we would like. Alternatively, we could have substituted the command `invisible`, which works the same way as `return`, except that it does not print the output on the screen, but simply stores the output.

With this function, if we want to know what value y takes when $x = 1$, we need only type: `first.fun(1)`. Since we used `return` instead of `invisible`, the printout simply reads:

```
[1] 3
```

Of course, the result that $y = 3$ here can easily be verified by hand. Similarly, we know that if $x = 3$, then $y = 2\frac{1}{9}$. To verify this fact, we can type: `first.fun(3)`. R will give us the corresponding printout:

```
[1] 2.111111
```

As a final task with this function, we can plot what it looks like by inserting a vector of x values into it. Consider the code:

```
my.x<-seq(-4,4,by=.01)
plot(y=first.fun(my.x),x=my.x,type="l",
     xlab="x",ylab="y",ylim=c(0,10))
```

This will produce the graph featured in Fig. 11.1.

As a more complicated example, consider a function that we will use as part of a larger exercise in Sect. 11.6. The following is an expected utility function for a political party in a model of how parties will choose an issue position when competing in sequential elections (Monogan 2013b, Eq. (6)):

$$EU_A(\theta_A, \theta_D) = \Lambda\{-(m_1 - \theta_A)^2 + (m_1 - \theta_D)^2 + V\} \qquad (11.1)$$
$$+ \delta\Lambda\{-(m_2 - \theta_A)^2 + (m_2 - \theta_D)^2\}$$

In this equation, the expected utility to a political party (party A) is the sum of two cumulative logistic distribution functions (the functions Λ), with the second downweighted by a discount term ($0 \le \delta \le 1$). Utility depends on the positions taken by party A and party D (θ_A and θ_D), a valence advantage to party A (V), and the issue position of the median voter in the first and second election (m_1 and m_2). This is now a function of several variables, and it requires us to use the CDF of the logistic distribution. To input this function in R, we type:

```
Quadratic.A<-function(m.1,m.2,p,delta,theta.A,theta.D){
    util.a<-plogis(-(m.1-theta.A)^2+
        (m.1-theta.D)^2+p)+
        delta*plogis(-(m.2-theta.A)^2+
        (m.2-theta.D)^2)
    return(util.a)
    }
```

The `plogis` command computes each relevant probability from the logistic CDF, and all of the other terms are named self-evidently from Eq. (11.1) (except that p refers to the valence term V). Although this function was more complicated, all we had to do is make sure we named every input and copied Eq. (11.1) entirely into the body of the function.

This more complex function, `Quadratic.A`, still behaves like our simple function. For instance, we could go ahead and supply a numeric value for every argument of the function like this:

```
Quadratic.A(m.1=.7,m.2=-.1,p=.1,delta=0,theta.A=.7,theta.D=.7)
```

Doing so prints an output of:

```
[1] 0.5249792
```

Hence, we now know that 0.52 is the expected utility to party A when the terms take on these numeric values. In isolation, this output does not mean much. In game theory, we are typically interested in how party A (or any player) can maximize its utility. Hence, if we take all of the parameters as fixed at the above values, except we allow party A to choose θ_A as it sees fit, we can visualize what A's best choice is. The following code produces the graph seen in Fig. 11.2:

```
positions<-seq(-1,1,.01)
util.A<-Quadratic.A(m.1=.7,m.2=-.1,p=.1,delta=0,
    theta.A=positions,theta.D=.7)
plot(x=positions,y=util.A,type="l",
    xlab="Party A's Position",ylab="Utility")
```

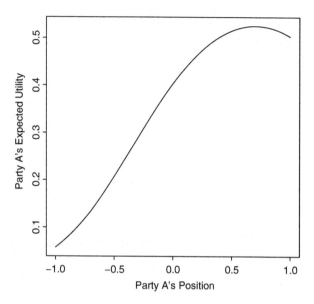

Fig. 11.2 Plot of an advantaged party's expected utility over two elections contingent on issue position

In the first line, we generate a range of positions party A may choose for θ_A. On the second line, we calculate a vector of expected utilities to party A at each of the issue positions we consider and setting the other parameters at their previously mentioned value. Lastly, we use the `plot` function to draw a line graph of these utilities. It turns out that the maximum of this function is at $\theta_A = 0.7$, so our previously mentioned utility of 0.52 is the best party A can do after all.

11.3 Loops

Loops are easy to write in R and can be used to repeat calculations that are either identical or vary only by a few parameters. The basic structure for a loop using the `for` command is:

```
for (i in 1:M) {COMMANDS}
```

In this case, M is the number of times the commands will be executed. R also supports loops using the `while` command which follow a similar command structure:

```
j <- 1
while(j < M) {
     COMMANDS
     j <- j + 1
     }
```

Whether a `for` loop or a `while` loop works best can vary by situation, so the user must use his or her own judgment when choosing a setup. In general, `while` loops tend to be better for problems where you would have to do something until a criterion is met (such as a convergence criterion), and `for` loops are generally better for things you want to repeat a fixed number of times. Under either structure, R will allow a wide array of commands to be included in a loop; the user's task is how to manage the loop's input and output efficiently.

As a simple demonstration of how loops work, consider an example that illustrates the law of large numbers. To do this, we can simulate **r**andom observations from the standard **norm**al distribution (easy with the `rnorm`) command. Since the standard normal has a population mean of zero, we would expect the sample mean of our simulated values to be near zero. As our sample size gets larger, the sample mean should generally be closer to the population mean of zero. A loop is perfect for this exercise: We want to repeat the calculations of simulating from the standard normal distribution and then taking the mean of the simulations. What differs from iteration to iteration is that we want our sample size to increase.

We can set this up easily with the following code:

```
set.seed(271828183)
store <- matrix(NA,1000,1)
for (i in 1:1000){
    a <- rnorm(i)
    store[i] <- mean(a)
    }
plot(store, type="h",ylab="Sample Mean",
    xlab="Number of Observations")
abline(h=0,col='red',lwd=2)
```

In the first line of this code, we call the command `set.seed`, in order to make our simulation experiment replicable. When R randomly draws numbers in any way, it uses a pseudo-random number generator, which is a list of 2.1 billion numbers that resemble random draws.[3] By choosing any number from 1 to 2,147,483,647, others should be able to reproduce our results by using the same numbers in their simulation. Our choice of 271,828,183 was largely arbitrary. In the second line of code, we create a blank vector named `store` of length 1000. This vector is where we will store our output from the loop. In the next four lines of code, we define our loop. The loop runs from 1 to 1000, with the index of each iteration being named `i`. In each iteration, our sample size is simply the value of `i`, so the first iteration simulates one observation, and the thousandth iteration simulates 1000 observations. Hence, the sample size increases with each pass of the loop. In each pass of the program, R samples from a $\mathcal{N}(0, 1)$ distribution and then takes the mean of that sample. Each mean is recorded in the `i`th cell of `store`. After the loop closes, we plot our sample means against the sample size and use `abline` to draw a red line

[3]Formally, this list makes-up draws from a standard uniform distribution, which is then converted to whatever distribution we want using a quantile function.

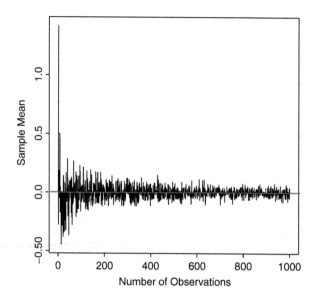

Fig. 11.3 The law of large numbers and loops in action

at the population mean of zero. The result is shown in Fig. 11.3. Indeed, our plot shows the mean of the sample converging to the true mean of zero as the sample size increases.

Loops are necessary for many types of programs, such as if you want to do a Monte Carlo analysis. In some (but not all) cases, however, loops can be slower than vectorized versions of commands. It may be worth trying the apply command, for instance, if it can accomplish the same goal as a loop. Which is faster often depends on the complexity of the function and the memory overhead for calculating and storing results. So if one approach is too slow or too complicated for your computer to handle, it may be worth trying the other.

11.4   Branching

R users have the option of executing commands conditional on a Boolean statement using the if command. This can be handy whenever the user only wants to implement something for certain cases, or if different data types should be treated differently. The basic syntax of an if statement is:

```
if (logical_expression) {
    expression_1
    ...
}
```

In this framework, the `logical_expression` is some Boolean statement, and `expression_1` represents whatever commands the user would like to apply whenever the logical expression is true.

As a toy example of how this works, suppose we wanted to simulate a process in which we draw two numbers from 1 to 10 (with repeated numbers allowed). The `sample` command allows us to simulate this process easily, and if we embed it in a `for` loop we can repeat the experiment several times (say, 100 trials). If we wanted to know in how many trials both numbers came up even, we could determine this with an `if` statement. Our code comes together like this:

```
even.count<-0
for (i in 1:100){
        a<-sample(c(1:10),2,replace=TRUE)
        if (sum(a%%2)==0){
                even.count<-even.count+1
                }
}
even.count
```

The first line creates a scalar named `even.count` and sets it at zero. The next line starts the loop that gives us 100 trials. The third line creates our sample of two numbers from 1 to 10, and names the sample a. The fourth line defines our `if` statement: We use the modulo function to find the remainder when each term in our sample is divided by two.[4] If the remainder for every term is zero, then all numbers are even and the sum is zero. In that case, we have drawn a sample in which numbers are even. Hence, when `sum(a%%2)==0` is true, then we want to add one to a running tally of how many samples of two even numbers we have. Therefore the fifth line of our code adds to our tally, but only in cases that meet our condition. (Notice that a recursive assignment for `even.count` is acceptable. R will take the old value, add one to it, and update the value that is saved.) Try this experiment yourself. As a hint, probability theory would say that 25 % of trials will yield two even numbers, on average.

Users also may make `if...else` branching statements such that one set of operations applies whenever an expression is true, and another set of operations applies when the expression is false. This basic structure looks like this:

```
if (logical_expression) {
      expression_1
        . . .
} else {
      expression_2
        . . .
}
```

---

[4]Recall from Chap. 1 that the modulo function gives us the remainder from division.

In this case, `expression_1` will only be applied in cases when the logical expression is true, and `expression_2` will only be applied in cases when the logical expression is false.

Finally, users have the option of branching even further. With cases for which the first logical expression is false, thereby calling the expressions following `else`, these cases can be branched again with another `if...else` statement. In fact, the programmer can nest as many `if...else` statements as he or she would like. To illustrate this, consider again the case when we simulate two random numbers from 1 to 10. Imagine this time we want to know not only how often we draw two even numbers, but also how often we draw two odd numbers and how often we draw one even number and one odd. One way we could address this is by keeping three running tallies (below named `even.count`, `odd.count`, and `split.count`) and adding additional branching statements:

```
even.count<-0
odd.count<-0
split.count<-0
for (i in 1:100){
     a<-sample(c(1:10),2,replace=TRUE)
     if (sum(a%%2)==0){
          even.count<-even.count+1
          } else if (sum(a%%2)==2){
               odd.count<-odd.count+1
                    } else{
                         split.count<-split.count+1
                         }
}
even.count
odd.count
split.count
```

Our `for` loop starts the same as before, but after our first `if` statement, we follow with an `else` statement. Any sample that did not consist of two even numbers is now subject to the commands under `else`, and the first command under `else` is... another `if` statement. This next `if` statement observes that if both terms in the sample are odd, then the sum of the remainders after dividing by two will be two. Hence, all samples with two odd entries now are subject to the commands of this new `if` statement, where we see that our `odd.count` index will be increased by one. Lastly, we have a final `else` statement—all samples that did not consist of two even or two odd numbers will now be subject to this final set of commands. Since these samples consist of one even and one odd number, the `split.count` index will be increased by one. Try this out yourself. Again, as a hint, probability theory indicates that on average 50 % of samples should consist of one even and one odd number, 25 % should consist of two even numbers, and 25 % should consist of two odd numbers.

11.5 Optimization and Maximum Likelihood Estimation

The `optim` command in R allows users to find the minimum or maximum of a function using a variety of numerical **optim**ization methods.[5] In other words, `optim` has several algorithms that efficiently search for the highest or lowest value of a function, several of which allow the user to constrain the possible values of input variables. While there are many uses of optimization in Political Science research, the most common is *maximum likelihood estimation* (MLE).[6]

The `optim` command, paired with R's simple function definition (discussed in Sect. 11.2), allows R to use readily the full flexibility of MLE. If a canned model such as those described in Chaps. 1–7 does not suit your research, and you want to derive your own estimator using MLE, then R can accommodate you.

To illustrate how programming an MLE works in R, consider a simple example—the estimator for the probability parameter (π) in a binomial distribution. By way of reminder, the motivation behind a binomial distribution is that we are interested in some trial that takes on one of two outcomes each time, and we repeat that trial multiple times. The simplest example is that we flip a coin, which will come up heads or tails on each flip. Using this example, suppose our data consist of 100 coin flips, and 43 of the flips came up heads. What is the MLE estimate of the probability of heads? By intuition or derivation, you should know that $\hat{\pi} = \frac{43}{100} = 0.43$. We still will estimate this probability in R to practice for more complicated cases, though.

To more formally define our problem, a binomial distribution is motivated by completing n Bernoulli trials, or trials that can end in either a success or a failure. We record the number of times we succeed in our n trials as y. Additionally, by definition our probability parameter (π) must be greater than or equal to zero and less than or equal to one. Our likelihood function is:

$$L(\pi \,|\, n, y) = \pi^y (1 - \pi)^{n-y} \tag{11.2}$$

For ease of calculation and computation, we can obtain an equivalent result by maximizing our log-likelihood function:

$$\ell(\pi \,|\, n, y) = \log L(\pi \,|\, n, y) = y \cdot \log(\pi) + (n - y) \log(1 - \pi) \tag{11.3}$$

We can easily define our log-likelihood function in R with the `function` command:

```
binomial.loglikelihood <- function(prob, y, n) {
    loglikelihood <- y*log(prob) + (n-y)*log(1-prob)
    return(loglikelihood)
}
```

---

[5]See Nocedal and Wright (1999) for a review of how these techniques work.

[6]When using maximum likelihood estimation, as an alternative to using `optim` is to use the `maxLik` package. This can be useful for maximum likelihood specifically, though `optim` has the advantage of being able to maximize or minimize other kinds of functions as well, when appropriate.

Now to estimate $\hat{\pi}$, we need R to find the value of π that maximizes the log-likelihood function given the data. (We call this term prob in the code to avoid confusion with R's use of the command pi to store the geometric constant.) We can do this with the optim command. We compute:

```
test <- optim(c(.5),            # starting value for prob
   binomial.loglikelihood,       # the log-likelihood function
   method="BFGS",                # optimization method
   hessian=TRUE,                 # return numerical Hessian
   control=list(fnscale=-1),     # maximize instead of minimize
   y=43, n=100)                  # the data
print(test)
```

Remember that everything after a pound sign (#) is a comment that R ignores, so these notes serve to describe each line of code. We always start with a vector of starting values with all parameters to estimate (just π in this case), name the log-likelihood function we defined elsewhere, choose our optimization method (**B**royden-**F**letcher-**G**oldfarb-**S**hanno is often a good choice), and indicate that we want R to return the numerical Hessian so we can compute standard errors later. The fifth line of code is vitally important: By default optim is a *minimizer*, so we have to specify fnscale=-1 to make it a *maximizer*. Any time you use optim for *maximum* likelihood estimation, this line will have to be included. On the sixth line, we list our data. Often, we will call a matrix or data frame here, but in this case we need only list the values of y and n.

Our output from print(test) looks like the following:

```
$par
[1] 0.4300015

$value
[1] -68.33149

$counts
function gradient
      13        4

$convergence
[1] 0

$message
NULL

$hessian
          [,1]
[1,] -407.9996
```

To interpret our output: The par term lists the estimates of the parameters, so our estimate is $\hat{\pi} = 0.43$ (as we anticipated). The log-likelihood for our final solution is -68.33149, and is presented under value. The term counts tells us how often optim had to call the function and the gradient. The term convergence will be coded 0 if the optimization was successfully completed; any other value is an error code. The message item may return other necessary information from the optimizer. Lastly, the hessian is our matrix of second derivatives of the log-likelihood function. With only one parameter here, it is a simple 1×1 matrix. In general, if the user wants *standard errors* from an estimated maximum likelihood model, the following line will return them:

```
sqrt(diag(solve(-test$hessian)))
```

This line is based on the formula for standard errors in maximum likelihood estimation. All the user will ever need to change is to replace the word test with the name associated with the call to optim. In this case, R reports that the standard error is $SE(\hat{\pi}) = 0.0495074$.

Finally, in this case in which we have a single parameter of interest, we have the option of using our defined log-likelihood function to draw a picture of the optimization problem. Consider the following code:

```
ruler <- seq(0,1,0.01)
loglikelihood <- binomial.loglikelihood(ruler, y=43, n=100)
plot(ruler, loglikelihood, type="l", lwd=2, col="blue",
    xlab=expression(pi),ylab="Log-Likelihood",ylim=c(-300,-70),
    main="Log-Likelihood for Binomial Model")
abline(v=.43)
```

The first line defines all values that π possibly can take. The second line inserts into the log-likelihood function the vector of possible values of π, plus the true values of y and n. The third through fifth lines are a call to plot that gives us a line graph of the log-likelihood function. The last line draws a vertical line at our estimated value for $\hat{\pi}$. The result of this is shown in Fig. 11.4. While log-likelihood functions with many parameters usually cannot be visualized, this does remind us that the function we have defined can still be used for purposes other than optimization, if need be.

11.6 Object-Oriented Programming

This section takes a turn towards the advanced, by presenting an application in object-oriented programming. While this application does synthesize many of the other tools discussed in this chapter, novice users are less likely to use object-oriented programming than the features discussed so far. That said, for advanced uses object-oriented work can be beneficial.

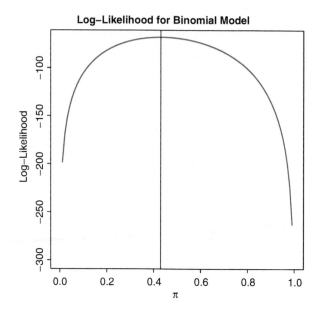

Fig. 11.4 Binomial log-likelihood across all possible values of probability parameter π when the data consist of 43 successes in 100 trials

As was mentioned in Chap. 1, R is an object-oriented environment. This means that you, as a researcher, have the opportunity to use sophisticated programming tools in your own research. In object-oriented programming, you create a *class* of item that has a variety of features. You then can create items within the class (called *objects* or *variables*) that will have unique features. In R, you can create classes from the object systems S3 or S4.

To illustrate, a "linear model" is a class of objects created by the lm command. It is an S3 class. Back in Chap. 6, we estimated a model that we named mod.hours, which was an object of the linear model class. This object had features including coefficients, residuals, and cov.unscaled. In all S3-class objects, we can call a feature by writing the object name, the dollar sign, and the name of the feature we want. For example, mod.hours$coefficients would list the vector of coefficients from that model. (S4 uses slightly different referencing, described later.) When you define your own objects, you may use either S3 or S4 object system. The following example saves our outputs in the S3 object system, though footnotes illustrate how you could use the S4 object system if you preferred.

11.6.1   Simulating a Game

As a working example of object-oriented programming, we consider a somewhat simplified version of the work presented in Monogan (2013b).[7] We touched on this model in Sect. 11.2, introducing one actor's utility function. In brief, this article develops a game theoretic model of how two parties will choose a position on an issue according to the spatial proximity model of politics. The spatial model, described somewhat in Chap. 7, assumes that issue positions can be represented as locations in space. Voters choose parties that take issue positions closer to their own position in issue space, so parties try to maximize votes by strategically choosing their issue positions.

In the game we consider, the substantive motivation is the fact that public opinion shows strong trends on certain policy issues because of demographic trends or generational differences. Issues like this include environmental policy, immigration policy, and protections for gay rights. We assume that two parties will compete in two elections. However, to consider the fact that parties should be mindful of the future and may be held to account for past issue positions, the position they take in the first election is the position they are stuck with in the second election. We also assume that the issue position of the median voter changes from one election to the next in a way that parties anticipate, since on these issues public opinion trends are often clear.

Another feature is that one party has an advantage in the first election (due to incumbency or some other factor), so for this reason the players are party *A* (a party with a non-issue valence *advantage* in the first election) and party *D* (a disadvantaged party). The second election is assumed to be less valuable than the first, because the reward is farther away. Finally, voters also consider factors unknown to the parties, so the outcome of the election is probabilistic rather than certain. In this game, then, parties try to maximize their probability of winning each of the two elections. How do they position themselves on an issue with changing public opinion?

The tricky feature of this game is that it cannot be solved algebraically (Monogan 2013b, p. 288). Hence, we turn to R to help us find solutions through simulation. The first thing we need to do is clean up and define the expected utility functions for parties *A* and *D*:

```
rm(list=ls())
Quadratic.A<-function(m.1,m.2,p,delta,theta.A,theta.D){
    util.a<-plogis(-(m.1-theta.A)^2+
        (m.1-theta.D)^2+p)+
        delta*plogis(-(m.2-theta.A)^2+
```

---

[7]To see the full original version of the program, consult http://hdl.handle.net/1902.1/16781. Note that here we use the S3 object family, but the original code uses the S4 family. The original program also considers alternative voter utility functions besides the quadratic proximity function listed here, such as an absolute proximity function and the directional model of voter utility (Rabinowitz and Macdonald 1989).

```
                (m.2-theta.D)^2)
        return(util.a)
        }
Quadratic.D<-function(m.1,m.2,p,delta,theta.A,theta.D){
        util.d<-(1-plogis(-(m.1-theta.A)^2+
                (m.1-theta.D)^2+p))+
            delta*(1-plogis(-(m.2-theta.A)^2+
                (m.2-theta.D)^2))
        return(util.d)
        }
```

We already considered the function Quadratic.A in Sect. 11.2, and it is formally defined by Eq. (11.1). Quadratic.D is similar in structure, but yields differing utilities. Both of these functions will be used in the simulations we do.

Our next step is to define a long function that uses our utility functions to run a simulation and produces an output formatted the way we want.[8] All of the following code is one big function definition. Comments after pound signs (#) again are included to help distinguish each party of the function body. The function, called simulate, simulates our game of interest and saves our results in an object of class game.simulation:

```
simulate<-function(v,delta,m.2,m.1=0.7,theta=seq(-1,1,.1)){

        #define internal parameters, matrices, and vectors
        precision<-length(theta)
        outcomeA<-matrix(NA,precision,precision)
        outcomeD<-matrix(NA,precision,precision)
        bestResponseA<-rep(NA,precision)
        bestResponseD<-rep(NA,precision)
        equilibriumA<- 'NA'
        equilibriumD<- 'NA'

        #matrix attributes
        rownames(outcomeA)<-colnames(outcomeA)<-rownames(outcomeD)<-
            colnames(outcomeD)<-names(bestResponseA)<-
            names(bestResponseD)<-theta

        #fill-in the utilities for all strategies for party A
        for (i in 1:precision){
                for (j in 1:precision){
                    outcomeA[i,j]<-Quadratic.A(m.1,m.2,v,delta,
                        theta[i],theta[j])
                    }
```

---

[8]If you preferred to use the S4 object system for this exercise instead, the next thing we would need to do is define the object class before defining the function. If we wanted to call our object class simulation, we would type: setClass("simulation", representation(outcomeA="matrix", outcomeD="matrix", bestResponseA="numeric", bestResponseD="numeric", equilibriumA="character", equilibriumD="character")). The S3 object system does not require this step, as we will see when we create objects of our self-defined game.simulation class.

```
        }

    #utilities for party D
    for (i in 1:precision){
            for (j in 1:precision){
                outcomeD[i,j]<-Quadratic.D(m.1,m.2,v,delta,
                    theta[i],theta[j])
                }
        }

    #best responses for party A
    for (i in 1:precision){
        bestResponseA[i]<-which.max(outcomeA[,i])
        }

    #best responses for party D
    for (i in 1:precision){
        bestResponseD[i]<-which.max(outcomeD[i,])
        }

    #find the equilibria
    for (i in 1:precision){
        if (bestResponseD[bestResponseA[i]]==i){
            equilibriumA<-dimnames(outcomeA)[[1]][
                bestResponseA[i]]
            equilibriumD<-dimnames(outcomeD)[[2]][
                bestResponseD[bestResponseA[i]]]
            }
    }

    #save the output
    result<-list(outcomeA=outcomeA,outcomeD=outcomeD,
        bestResponseA=bestResponseA,bestResponseD=bestResponseD,
        equilibriumA=equilibriumA,equilibriumD=equilibriumD)
    class(result)<-"game.simulation"
    invisible(result)
}
```

As a general tip, when writing a long function, it is best to test code outside of the `function` wrapper. For bonus points and to get a full sense of this code, you may want to break this function into its components and see how each piece works. As the comments throughout show, each set of commands does something we normally might do in a function. Notice that when the arguments are defined, both m.1 and `theta` are given default values. This means that in future uses, if we do not specify the values of these inputs, the function will use these defaults, but if we do specify them, then the defaults will be overridden. Turning to the arguments within the function, it starts off by defining internal parameters and setting their attributes. Every set of commands thereafter is a loop within a loop to repeat certain commands and fill output vectors and matrices.

The key addition here that is unique to anything discussed before is in the definition of the `result` term at the end of the function. Notice that in doing this, we first define the output as a `list`, in which each component is named. In this case, we already named our objects the same as the way we want to label them in the output list, but that may not always be the case.[9] We then use the `class` command to declare that our output is of the `game.simulation` class, a concept we are now creating. The `class` command formats this as an object in the S3 family. By typing `invisible(result)` at the end of the function, we know that our function will return this `game.simulation`-class object.[10]

Now that this function is defined, we can put it to use. Referring to the terms in Eq. (11.1), suppose that $V = 0.1$, $\delta = 0$, $m_1 = 0.7$, and $m_2 = -0.1$. In the code below, we create a new object called `treatment.1` using the `simulate` function when the parameters take these values, and then we ask R to print the output:

```
treatment.1<-simulate(v=0.1,delta=0.0,m.2=-0.1)
treatment.1
```

Notice that we did not specify `m.1` because 0.7 already is the default value for that parameter. The output from the printout of `treatment.1` is too lengthy to reproduce here, but on your own screen you will see that `treatment.1` is an object of the `game.simulation` class, and the printout reports the values for each attribute.

If we are only interested in a particular feature from this result, we can ask R to return only the value of a specific slot. For an S3 object, which is how we saved our result, we can call an attribute by naming the object, using the $ symbol, and then naming the attribute we want to use. (This contrasts from S4 objects, which use the @ symbol to call slots.) For example, if we only wanted to see what the equilibrium choices for parties A and D were, we could simply type:

```
treatment.1$equilibriumA
treatment.1$equilibriumD
```

Each of these commands returns the same output:

```
[1]  "0.7"
```

So, substantively, we can conclude that the equilibrium for the game under these parameters is $\theta_A = \theta_D = 0.7$, which is the ideal point of the median voter in the first

---

[9]For example, in the phrase `outcomeA=outcomeA`, the term to the left of the equals sign states that this term in the list will be named `outcomeA`, and the term to the right calls the object of this name from the function to fill this spot.

[10]The code would differ slightly for the S4 object system. If we defined our `simulation` class as the earlier footnote describes, here we would replace the definition of `result` as follows: `result<-new("simulation",outcomeA=outcomeA, outcomeD=outcomeD,bestResponseA=bestResponseA, bestResponseD=bestResponseD, equilibriumA=equilibriumA, equilibriumD=equilibriumD)`. Replacing the `list` command with the new command assigns the output to our `simulation` class and fills the various slots all in one step. This means we can skip the extra step of using the `class` command, which we needed when using the S3 system.

election. Substantively, this should make sense because setting $\delta = 0$ is a special case when the parties are not at all concerned about winning the second election, so they position themselves strictly for the first election.[11]

To draw a contrast, what if we conducted a second simulation, but this time increased the value of δ to 0.1? We also could use finer-grained values of the positions parties could take, establishing their position out to the hundredths decimal place, rather than tenths. We could do this as follows:

```
treatment.2<-simulate(v=0.1,delta=0.1,m.2=-0.1,
     theta=seq(-1,1,.01))
treatment.2$equilibriumA
treatment.2$equilibriumD
```

We accomplished the finer precision by substituting our own vector in for `theta`. Our output values of the two equilibrium slots are again the same:

```
[1] "0.63"
```

So we know under this second treatment, the equilibrium for the game is $\theta_A = \theta_D = 0.63$. Substantively, what happened here is we increased the value of winning the second election to the parties. As a result, the parties moved their issue position a little closer to the median voter's issue preference in the second election.

11.7 Monte Carlo Analysis: An Applied Example

As an applied example that synthesizes several of the tools developed in this chapter, we now conduct a Monte Carlo analysis. The basic logic of Monte Carlo analysis is that the researcher generates data knowing the true population model. The researcher then asks whether a certain method's sample estimates have good properties, given what the population quantities are. Common treatments in a Monte Carlo experiment include: choice of estimator, sample size, distribution of predictors, variance of errors, and whether the model has the right functional form (e.g., ignoring a nonlinear relationship or omitting a predictor). By trying various treatments, a user can get a comparative sense of how well an estimator works.

In this case, we will introduce Signorino's (1999) strategic multinomial probit model as the estimator we will use in our Monte Carlo experiment. The idea behind this approach is that, when a recurring political situation can be represented with a game (such as militarized international disputes), we can develop an empirical model of the outcomes that can occur (such as war) based on the strategy of the game. Each possible outcome has a *utility function* for each player, whether the player be an individual, a country, or another actor. The utility represents how much

---

[11]If we had instead saved `treatment.1` as an `S4` simulation object as the prior footnotes described, the command to call a specific attribute would instead be: `treatment.1@equilibriumA`.

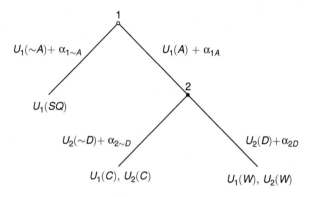

Fig. 11.5 Strategic deterrence model

benefit the player gets from the outcome. In this setup, we use observable predictors to model the utilities for each possible outcome. This kind of model is interesting because the population data-generating process typically has nonlinearities in it that are not captured by standard approaches. Hence, we will have to program our own likelihood function and use `optim` to estimate it.[12]

To motivate how the strategic multinomial probit is set up, consider a substantive model of behavior between two nations, an aggressor (1) and a target (2). This is a two-stage game: First, the aggressor decides whether to attack (A) or not (~A); then, the target decides whether to defend (D) or not (~D). Three observable consequences could occur: if the aggressor decides not to attack, the **status quo** holds; if the aggressor attacks, the target may choose to **capitulate**; finally, if the target defends, we have **war**. The game tree is presented in Fig. 11.5. At the end of each branch are the utilities to players (1) and (2) for **status quo** (SQ), **capitulation** (C), and **war** (W), respectively. We make the assumption that these players are rational and therefore choose the actions that maximize the resulting payoff. For example, if the target is weak, the payoff of war $U_2(W)$ would be terribly negative, and probably lower than the payoff for capitulation $U_2(C)$. If the aggressor knows this, it can deduce that in the case of attack, the target would capitulate. The aggressor therefore would know that if it chooses to attack, it will receive the payoff $U_1(C)$ (and not $U_1(W)$). If the payoff of capitulation $U_1(C)$ is bigger than the payoff of the status quo $U_1(SQ)$ for the aggressor, the rational decision is to attack (and the target's rational decision is to capitulate). Of course, the goal is to get a sense of what will happen as circumstances change across different dyads of nations.

In general, we assume the utility functions respond to observable specific circumstances (the value of the disputed resources, the expected diplomatic price due to sanctions in case of aggression, the military might, and so forth). We

---

[12]Readers interested in doing research like this in their own work should read about the games package, which was developed to estimate this kind of model.

will also assume that the utilities for each country's choice are stochastic. This introduces uncertainty into our payoff model, representing the fact that this model is incomplete, and probably excludes some relevant parameters from the evaluation. In this exercise, we will consider only four predictors X_i to model the utility functions, and assume that the payoffs are linear in these variables.

In particular, we consider the following parametric form for the payoffs:

$$U_1(SQ) = 0$$
$$U_1(C) = X_1\beta_1$$
$$U_1(W) = X_2\beta_2 \tag{11.4}$$
$$U_2(C) = 0$$
$$U_2(W) = X_3\beta_3 + X_4\beta_4$$
$$\alpha \sim \mathcal{N}(0, 0.5)$$

Each nation makes its choice based on which decision will give it a bigger utility. This is based on the known information, plus an unknown private disturbance (α) for each choice. This private disturbance adds a random element to actors' decisions. We as researchers can look at past conflicts, measure the predictors (X), observe the outcome, and would like to infer: How important are X_1, X_2, X_3, and X_4 in the behavior of nation-dyads? We have to determine this based on whether each data point resulted in **status quo**, **capitulation**, or **war**.

11.7.1 Strategic Deterrence Log-Likelihood Function

We can determine estimates of each $\hat{\beta}$ using maximum likelihood estimation. First, we have to determine the probability (p) the target (2) will defend if attacked:

$$p = P(D) = P(U_2(D) + \alpha_{2D} > U_2(\sim D) + \alpha_{2\sim D})$$
$$= P(U_2(D) - U_2(\sim D) > \alpha_{2\sim D} - \alpha_{2D}) \tag{11.5}$$
$$= \Phi(X_3\beta_3 + X_4\beta_4)$$

Where Φ is the cumulative distribution function for a standard normal distribution. If we know p, we can determine the probability (q) that the aggressor (1) will attack:

$$q = P(A) = P(U_1(A) + \alpha_{1A} > U_a(\sim A) + \alpha_{1\sim A})$$
$$= P(U_1(A) - U_1(\sim A) > \alpha_{1\sim A} - \alpha_{1A}) \tag{11.6}$$
$$= \Phi(pX_2\beta_2 + (1-p)X_1\beta_1)$$

Notice that p is in the equation for q. This nonlinear feature of the model is not accommodated by standard canned models.

Knowing the formulae for p and q, we know the probabilities of status quo, capitulation, and war. Therefore, the likelihood function is simply the product of the probabilities of each event, raised to a dummy of whether the event happened, multiplied across all observations:

$$L(\boldsymbol{\beta}|\mathbf{y}, \mathbf{X}) = \prod_{i=1}^{n} (1 - q)^{D_{SQ}} \times (q(1 - p))^{D_C} \times (pq)^{D_W} \tag{11.7}$$

Where D_{SQ}, D_C, and D_W are dummy variables equal to 1 if the case is status quo, capitulation, or war, respectively, and 0 otherwise. The log-likelihood function is:

$$\ell(\boldsymbol{\beta}|\mathbf{y}, \mathbf{X}) = \sum_{i=1}^{n} D_{SQ} \log(1 - q) + D_C \log q(1 - p) + D_W \log(pq) \tag{11.8}$$

We are now ready to begin programming this into R. We begin by cleaning up and then defining our log-likelihood function as llik, which again includes comments to describe parts of the function's body:

```
rm(list=ls())

llik=function(B,X,Y) {
   #Separate data matrices to individual variables:
   sq=as.matrix(Y[,1])
   cap=as.matrix(Y[,2])
   war=as.matrix(Y[,3])
   X13=as.matrix(X[,1])
   X14=as.matrix(X[,2])
   X24=as.matrix(X[,3:4])

   #Separate coefficients for each equation:
   B13=as.matrix(B[1])
   B14=as.matrix(B[2])
   B24=as.matrix(B[3:4])

   #Define utilities as variables times coefficients:
   U13=X13 %*% B13
   U14=X14 %*% B14
   U24=X24 %*% B24

   #Compute probability 2 will fight (P4) or not (P3):
   P4=pnorm(U24)
   P3=1-P4

   #Compute probability 1 will attack (P2) or not (P1):
   P2=pnorm((P3*U13+P4*U14))
   P1=1-P2

   #Define and return log-likelihood function:
   lnpsq=log(P1)
   lnpcap=log(P2*P3)
```

```
    lnpwar=log(P2*P4)
    llik=sq*lnpsq+cap*lnpcap+war*lnpwar
    return(sum(llik))
}
```

While substantially longer than the likelihood function we defined in Sect. 11.5, the
idea is the same. The function still accepts parameter values, independent variables,
and dependent variables, and it still returns a log-likelihood value. With a more
complex model, though, the function needs to be broken into component steps.
First, our data are now matrices, so the first batch of code separates the variables
by equation from the model. Second, our parameters are all coefficients stored in
the argument B, so we need to separate the coefficients by equation from the model.
Third, we matrix multiply the variables by the coefficients to create the three utility
terms. Fourth, we use that information to compute the probabilities that the target
will defend or not. Fifth, we use the utilities, plus the probability of the target's
actions, to determine the probability the aggressor will attack or not. Lastly, the
probabilities of all outcomes are used to create the log-likelihood function.

11.7.2 Evaluating the Estimator

Now that we have defined our likelihood function, we can use it to simulate data and
fit the model over our simulated data. With any Monte Carlo experiment, we need
to start by defining the number of experiments we will run for a given treatment
and the number of simulated data points in each experiment. We also need to define
empty spaces for the outputs of each experiment. We type:

```
set.seed(3141593)
i<-100      #number of experiments
n<-1000     #number of cases per experiment
beta.qre<-matrix(NA,i,4)
stder.qre<-matrix(NA,i,4)
```

We start by using set.seed to make our Monte Carlo results more replicable.
Here we let i be our number of experiments, which we set to be 100. (Though
normally we might prefer a bigger number.) We use n as our number of cases. This
allows us to define beta.qre and stder.qre as the output matrices for our
estimates of the coefficients and standard errors from our models, respectively.

With this in place, we can now run a big loop that will repeatedly simulate a
dataset, estimate our strategic multinomial probit model, and then record the results.
The loop is as follows:

```
for(j in 1:i){
    #Simulate Causal Variables
    x1<-rnorm(n)
    x2<-rnorm(n)
    x3<-rnorm(n)
    x4<-rnorm(n)
```

```
#Create Utilities and Error Terms
u11<-rnorm(n,sd=sqrt(.5))
u13<-x1
u23<-rnorm(n,sd=sqrt(.5))
u14<-x2
u24<-x3+x4+rnorm(n,sd=sqrt(.5))
pR<-pnorm(x3+x4)
uA<-(pR*u14)+((1-pR)*u13)+rnorm(n,sd=sqrt(.5))

#Create Dependent Variables
sq<-rep(0,n)
capit<-rep(0,n)
war<-rep(0,n)
sq[u11>=uA]<-1
capit[u11<uA & u23>=u24]<-1
war[u11<uA & u23<u24]<-1
Nsq<-abs(1-sq)

#Matrices for Input
stval<-rep(.1,4)
depvar<-cbind(sq,capit,war)
indvar<-cbind(x1,x2,x3,x4)

#Fit Model
strat.mle<-optim(stval,llik,hessian=TRUE,method="BFGS",
    control=list(maxit=2000,fnscale=-1,trace=1),
    X=indvar,Y=depvar)

#Save Results
beta.qre[j,]<-strat.mle$par
stder.qre[j,]<-sqrt(diag(solve(-strat.mle$hessian)))
}
```

In this model, we set $\beta = 1$ for every coefficient in the population model. Otherwise, Eq. (11.4) completely defines our population model. In the loop the first three batches of code all generate data according to this model. First, we generate four independent variables, each with a standard normal distribution. Second, we define the utilities according to Eq. (11.4), adding in the random disturbance terms (α) as indicated in Fig. 11.5. Third, we create the values of the dependent variables based on the utilities and disturbances. After this, the fourth step is to clean our simulated data; we define starting values for optim and bind the dependent and independent variables into matrices. Fifth, we use optim to actually estimate our model, naming the within-iteration output strat.mle. Lastly, the results from the model are written to the matrices beta.qre and stder.qre.

After running this loop, we can get a quick look at the average value of our estimated coefficients ($\hat{\beta}$) by typing:

```
apply(beta.qre,2,mean)
```

In this call to apply, we study our matrix of regression coefficients in which each row represents one of the 100 Monte Carlo experiments, and each column represents one of the four regression coefficients. We are interested in the coefficients, so we type 2 to study the columns, and then take the mean of the columns. While your results may differ somewhat from what is printed here, particularly if you did not set the seed to be the same, the output should look something like this:

```
[1] 1.0037491 1.0115165 1.0069188 0.9985754
```

In short, all four estimated coefficients are close to 1, which is good because 1 is the population value for each. If we wanted to automate our results a little more to tell us the bias in the parameters, we could type something like this:

```
deviate <- sweep(beta.qre, 2, c(1,1,1,1))
colMeans(deviate)
```

On the first line, we use the sweep command, which **sweep**s out (or subtracts) the summary statistic of our choice from a matrix. In our case, beta.qre is our matrix of coefficient estimates across 100 simulations. The 2 argument we enter separately indicates to apply the statistic by column (e.g., by coefficient) instead of by row (which would have been by experiment). Lastly, instead of listing an empirical statistic we want to subtract away, we simply list the true population parameters to subtract away. On the second line, we calculate the bias by taking the **Mean** deviation by **col**umn, or by parameter. Again, the output can vary with different seeds and number generators, but in general it should indicate that the average values are not far from the true population values. All of the differences are small:

```
[1]   0.003749060   0.011516459   0.006918824  -0.001424579
```

Another worthwhile quantity is the mean absolute error, which tells us how much an estimate differs from the population value on average. This is a bit different in that overestimates and underestimates cannot wash out (as they could with the bias calculation). An unbiased estimator still can have a large error variance and a large mean absolute error. Since we already defined deviate before, now we need only type:

```
colMeans(abs(deviate))
```

Our output shows small average absolute errors:

```
[1]   0.07875179 0.08059979 0.07169820 0.07127819
```

To get a sense of how good or bad this performance is, we should rerun this Monte Carlo experiment using another treatment for comparison. For a simple comparison, we can ask how well this model does if we increase the sample size. Presumably, our mean absolute error will decrease with a larger sample, so in each experiment we can simulate a sample of 5000 instead of 1000. To do this, rerun all of the code from this section of the chapter, but replace a single line. When defining the number of cases—the third line after the start of Sect. 11.7.2—instead of typing n<-1000, type instead: n<-5000. At the end of the program, when the mean absolute errors are reported, you will see that they are smaller. Again, they will vary from session to session, but the final output should look something like this:

[1] 0.03306102 0.02934981 0.03535597 0.02974488

As you can see, the errors are smaller than they were with 1000 observations. Our sample size is considerably bigger, so we would hope that this would be the case. This gives us a nice comparison.

With the completion of this chapter, you now should have the toolkit necessary to program in R whenever your research has unique needs that cannot be addressed by standard commands, or even user-contributed packages. With the completion of this book, you should have a sense of the broad scope of what R can do for political analysts, from data management, to basic models, to advanced programming. A true strength of R is the flexibility it offers users to address whatever complexities and original problems they may face. As you proceed to use R in your own research, be sure to continue to consult with online resources to discover new and promising capabilities as they emerge.

11.8   Practice Problems

1. Probability distributions: Calculate the probability for each of the following events:

   a. A standard normally distributed variable is larger than 3.
   b. A normally distributed variable with mean 35 and standard deviation 6 is larger than 42.
   c. $X < 0.9$ when x has the standard uniform distribution.

2. Loops: Let $h(x, n) = 1 + x + x^2 + \cdots + x^n = \sum_{i=0}^{n} x^i$. Write an R program to calculate $h(0.9, 25)$ using a for loop.

3. Functions: In the previous question, you wrote a program to calculate $h(x, n) = \sum_{i=0}^{n} x^i$ for $x = 0.9$ and $n = 25$. Turn this program into a more general function that takes two arguments, x and n, and returns $h(x, n)$. Using the function, determine the values of $h(0.8, 30)$, $h(0.7, 50)$, and $h(0.95, 20)$.

4. Maximum likelihood estimation. Consider an applied example of Signorino's (1999) strategic multinomial probit method. Download a subset of nineteenth century militarized interstate disputes, the Stata-formatted file war1800.dta, from the Dataverse (see page vii) or this chapter's online content (see page 205). These data draw from sources such as EUGene (Bueno de Mesquita and Lalman 1992) and the Correlates of War Project (Jones et al. 1996). Program a likelihood function for a model like the one shown in Fig. 11.5 and estimate the model for these real data. The three outcomes are: **war** (coded 1 if the countries went to war), **sq** (coded 1 if the status quo held), and **capit** (coded 1 if the target country capitulated). Assume that $U_1(SQ)$ is driven by **peaceyrs** (number of years since the dyad was last in conflict) and **s_wt_rel** (S score for political similarity of states, weighted for aggressor's region). $U_1(W)$ is a function of **balanc** (the aggressor's military capacity relative to the combined capacity of

the dyad). $U_2(W)$ is a function of a constant and **balanc**. $U_1(C)$ is a constant, and $U_2(C)$ is zero.

   a. Report your estimates and the corresponding standard errors.

   b. Which coefficients are statistically distinguishable from zero?

   c. <u>Bonus:</u> Draw the predicted probability of **war** if **balanc** is manipulated from its minimum of 0 to its maximum of 1, while **peaceyrs** and **s_wt_re1** are held at their theoretical minima of 0 and -1, respectively.

- <u>Just for fun:</u> If you draw the same graph of predicted probabilities, but allow **balanc** to go all the way up to 5, you can really illustrate the kind of non-monotonic relationship that this model allows. Remember, though, that you do not want to interpret results outside of the range of your data. This is just a fun illustration for extra practice.

5. Monte Carlo analysis and optimization: Replicate the experiment on Signorino's (1999) strategic multinomial probit from Sect. 11.7. Is there much difference between your average estimated values and the population values? Do you get similar mean absolute errors to those reported in that section? How do your results compare when you try the following treatments?

   a. Suppose you decrease the standard deviation of x1, x2, x3, and x4 to 0.5 (as opposed to the original treatment which assumed a standard deviation of 1). Do your estimates improve or get worse? What happens if you cut the standard deviation of these four predictors even further, to 0.25? What general pattern do you see, and why do you see it? (*Remember:* Everything else about these treatments, such as the sample size and number of experiments, needs to be the same as the original control experiment. Otherwise all else is not being held equal.)

   b. <u>Bonus:</u> What happens if you have an omitted variable in the model? Change your log-likelihood function to exclude x4 from your estimation procedure, but continue to include x4 when you simulate the data in the for loop. Since you only estimate the coefficients for x1, x2, and x3, how do your estimates in this treatment compare to the original treatment in terms of bias and mean absolute error?

References

Alvarez RM, Levin I, Pomares J, Leiras M (2013) Voting made safe and easy: the impact of e-voting on citizen perceptions. Polit Sci Res Methods 1(1):117–137

Bates D, Maechler M, Bolker B, Walker S (2014) lme4: linear mixed-effects models using Eigen and S4. R package version 1.1-7. http://www.CRAN.R-project.org/package=lme4

Becker RA, Cleveland WS, Shyu M-J (1996) The visual design and control of Trellis display. J Comput Graph Stat 5(2):123–155

Beniger JR, Robyn DL (1978) Quantitative graphics in statistics: a brief history. Am Stat 32(1):1–11

Berkman M, Plutzer E (2010) Evolution, creationism, and the battle to control America's classrooms. Cambridge University Press, New York

Black D (1948) On the rationale of group decision-making. J Polit Econ 56(1):23–34

Black D (1958) The theory of committees and elections. Cambridge University Press, London

Box GEP, Tiao GC (1975) Intervention analysis with applications to economic and environmental problems. J Am Stat Assoc 70:70–79

Box GEP, Jenkins GM, Reinsel GC (2008) Time series analysis: forecasting and control, 4th edn. Wiley, Hoboken, NJ

Box-Steffensmeier JM, Freeman JR, Hitt MP, Pevehouse JCW (2014) Time series analysis for the social sciences. Cambridge University Press, New York

Brambor T, Clark WR, Golder M (2006) Understanding interaction models: improving empirical analyses. Polit Anal 14(1):63–82

Brandt PT, Freeman JR (2006) Advances in Bayesian time series modeling and the study of politics: theory testing, forecasting, and policy analysis. Polit Anal 14(1):1–36

Brandt PT, Williams JT (2001) A linear Poisson autoregressive model: the Poisson AR(p) model. Polit Anal 9(2):164–184

Brandt PT, Williams JT (2007) Multiple time series models. Sage, Thousand Oaks, CA

Bueno de Mesquita B, Lalman D (1992) War and reason. Yale University Press, New Haven

Carlin BP, Louis TA (2009) Bayesian methods for data analysis. Chapman & Hall/CRC, Boca Raton, FL

Chang W (2013) R graphics cookbook. O'Reilly, Sebastopol, CA

Cleveland WS (1993) Visualizing data. Hobart Press, Sebastopol, CA

Cowpertwait PSP, Metcalfe AV (2009) Introductory time series with R. Springer, New York

Cryer JD, Chan K-S (2008) Time series analysis with applications in R, 2nd edn. Springer, New York

Downs A (1957) An economic theory of democracy. Harper and Row, New York

Eliason SR (1993) Maximum likelihood estimation: logic and practice. Sage, Thousand Oaks, CA

© Springer International Publishing Switzerland 2015

J.E. Monogan III, *Political Analysis Using R*, Use R!,

DOI 10.1007/978-3-319-23446-5

Enders W (2009) Applied econometric time series, 3rd edn. Wiley, New York

Fitzmaurice GM, Laird NM, Ware JH (2004) Applied longitudinal analysis. Wiley-Interscience, Hoboken, NJ

Fogarty BJ, Monogan JE III (2014) Modeling time-series count data: the unique challenges facing political communication studies. Soc Sci Res 45:73–88

Gelman A, Hill J (2007) Data analysis using regression and multilevel/hierarchical models. Cambridge University Press, New York

Gelman A, Carlin JB, Stern HS, Rubin DB (2004) Bayesian data analysis, 2nd edn. Chapman & Hall/CRC, Boca Raton, FL

Gibney M, Cornett L, Wood R, Haschke P (2013) Political terror scale, 1976–2012. Retrieved December 27, 2013 from the political terror scale web site: http://www.politicalterrorscale.org

Gill J (2001) Generalized linear models: a unified approach. Sage, Thousand Oaks, CA

Gill J (2008) Bayesian methods: a social and behavioral sciences approach, 2nd edn. Chapman & Hall/CRC, Boca Raton, FL

Granger CWJ (1969) Investigating causal relations by econometric models and cross spectral methods. Econometrica 37:424–438

Granger CWJ, Newbold P (1974) Spurious regressions in econometrics. J Econ 26:1045–1066

Gujarati DN, Porter DC (2009) Basic econometrics, 5th edn. McGraw-Hill/Irwin, New York

Halley E (1686) An historical account of the trade winds, and monsoons, observable in the seas between and near the tropicks, with an attempt to assign the phisical cause of the said winds. Philos Trans 16(183):153–168

Hamilton JD (1994) Time series analysis. Princeton University Press, Princeton, NJ

Hanmer MJ, Kalkan KO (2013) Behind the curve: clarifying the best approach to calculating predicted probabilities and marginal effects from limited dependent variable models. Am J Polit Sci 57(1):263–277

Honaker J, King G, Blackwell M (2011) Amelia II: a program for missing data. J Stat Softw 45(7):1–47

Hotelling H (1929) Stability in competition. Econ J 39(153):41–57

Huber PJ (1967) The behavior of maximum likelihood estimates under nonstandard conditions. In: LeCam LM, Neyman J (eds) Proceedings of the 5th Berkeley symposium on mathematical statistics and probability, volume 1: statistics University of California Press, Berkeley, CA

Iacus SM, King G, Porro G (2009) cem: software for coarsened exact matching. J Stat Softw 30(9):1–27

Iacus SM, King G, Porro G (2011) Multivariate matching methods that are monotonic imbalance bounding. J Am Stat Assoc 106(493):345–361

Iacus SM, King G, Porro G (2012) Causal inference without balance checking: coarsened exact matching. Polit Anal 20(1):1–24

Imai K, van Dyk DA (2004) Causal inference with general treatment regimes: generalizing the propensity score. J Am Stat Assoc 99(467):854–866

Jones DM, Bremer SA, Singer JD (1996) Militarized interstate disputes, 1816–1992: rationale, coding rules, and empirical patterns. Confl Manag Peace Sci 15(2):163–213

Kastellec JP, Leoni EL (2007) Using graphs instead of tables in political science. Perspect Polit 5(4):755–771

Keele L, Kelly NJ (2006) Dynamic models for dynamic theories: the ins and outs of lagged dependent variables. Polit Anal 14(2):186–205

King G (1989) Unifying political methodology. Cambridge University Press, New York

King G, Honaker J, Joseph A, Scheve K (2001) Analyzing incomplete political science data: an alternative algorithm for multiple imputation. Am Polit Sci Rev 95(1):49–69

Koyck LM (1954) Distributed lags and investment analysis. North-Holland, Amsterdam

Laird NM, Fitzmaurice GM (2013) Longitudinal data modeling. In: Scott MA, Simonoff JS, Marx BD (eds) The Sage handbook of multilevel modeling. Sage, Thousand Oaks, CA

LaLonde RJ (1986) Evaluating the econometric evaluations of training programs with experimental data. Am Econ Rev 76(4):604–620

Little RJA, Rubin DB (1987) Statistical analysis with missing data, 2nd edn. Wiley, New York

Long JS (1997) Regression models for categorical and limited dependent variables. Sage, Thousand Oaks, CA

Lowery D, Gray V, Monogan JE III (2008) The construction of interest communities: distinguishing bottom-up and top-down models. J Polit 70(4):1160–1176

Lütkepohl H (2005) New introduction to multiple time series analysis. Springer, New York

Martin AD, Quinn KM, Park JH (2011) MCMCpack: Markov chain Monte Carlo in R. J Stat Softw 42(9):1–21

Mátyás L, Sevestre P (eds) (2008) The econometrics of panel data: fundamentals and recent developments in theory and practice, 3rd edn. Springer, New York

McCarty NM, Poole KT, Rosenthal H (1997) Income redistribution and the realignment of American politics. American enterprise institute studies on understanding economic inequality. AEI Press, Washington, DC

Monogan JE III (2011) Panel data analysis. In: Badie B, Berg-Schlosser D, Morlino L (eds) International encyclopedia of political science. Sage, Thousand Oaks, CA

Monogan JE III (2013a) A case for registering studies of political outcomes: an application in the 2010 House elections. Polit Anal 21(1):21–37

Monogan JE III (2013b) Strategic party placement with a dynamic electorate. J Theor Polit 25(2):284–298

Nocedal J, Wright SJ (1999) Numerical optimization. Springer, New York

Owsiak AP (2013) Democratization and international border agreements. J Polit 75(3):717–729

Peake JS, Eshbaugh-Soha M (2008) The agenda-setting impact of major presidential TV addresses. Polit Commun 25:113–137

Petris G, Petrone S, Campagnoli P (2009) Dynamic linear models with R. Springer, New York

Pfaff B (2008) Analysis of Integrated and cointegrated time series with R, 2nd edn. Springer, New York

Playfair W (1786/2005) In: Wainer H, Spence I (eds) Commercial and political atlas and statistical breviary. Cambridge University Press, New York

Poe SC, Tate CN (1994) Repression of human rights to personal integrity in the 1980s: a global analysis. Am Polit Sci Rev 88(4):853–872

Poe SC, Tate CN, Keith LC (1999) Repression of the human right to personal integrity revisited: a global cross-national study covering the years 1976–1993. Int Stud Q 43(2):291–313

Poole KT, Rosenthal H (1997) Congress: a political-economic history of roll call voting. Oxford University Press, New York

Poole KT, Lewis J, Lo J, Carroll R (2011) Scaling roll call votes with wnominate in R. J Stat Softw 42(14):1–21

Rabinowitz G, Macdonald SE (1989) A directional theory of issue voting. Am Polit Sci Rev 83:93–121

Robert CP (2001) The Bayesian choice: from decision-theoretic foundations to computational implementation, 2nd edn. Springer, New York

Rubin DB (1987) Multiple imputation for nonresponse in surveys. Wiley, New York

Rubin DB (2006) Matched sampling for causal effects. Cambridge University Press, New York

Scott MA, Simonoff JS, Marx BD (eds) (2013) The Sage handbook of multilevel modeling. Sage, Thousand Oaks, CA

Sekhon JS, Grieve RD (2012) A matching method for improving covariate balance in cost-effectiveness analyses. Health Econ 21(6):695–714

Shumway RH, Stoffer DS (2006) Time series analysis and its applications with R examples, 2nd edn. Springer, New York

Signorino CS (1999) Strategic interaction and the statistical analysis of international conflict. Am Polit Sci Rev 93:279–297

Signorino CS (2002) Strategy and selection in international relations. Int Interact 28:93–115

Signorino CS, Yilmaz K (2003) Strategic misspecification in regression models. Am J Polit Sci 47:551–566

Sims CA, Zha T (1999) Error bands for impulse responses. Econometrica 67(5):1113–1155

Singh SP (2014a) Linear and quadratic utility loss functions in voting behavior research. J Theor Polit 26(1):35–58

Singh SP (2014b) Not all election winners are equal: satisfaction with democracy and the nature of the vote. Eur J Polit Res 53(2):308–327

Singh SP (2015) Compulsory voting and the turnout decision calculus. Polit Stud 63(3):548–568

Tufte ER (2001) The visual display of quantitative information, 2nd edn. Graphics Press, Cheshire, CT

Tukey JW (1977) Exploratory data analysis. Addison-Wesley, Reading, PA

Wakiyama T, Zusman E, Monogan JE III (2014) Can a low-carbon-energy transition be sustained in post-Fukushima Japan? Assessing the varying impacts of exogenous shocks. Energy Policy 73:654–666

Wei WWS (2006) Time series analysis: univariate and multivariate methods, 2nd edn. Pearson, New York

White H (1980) A heteroskedasticity-consistent covariance matrix estimator and a direct test for heteroskedasticity. Econometrica 48(4):817–838

Yau N (2011) Visualize this: the FlowingData guide to design, visualization, and statistics. Wiley, Indianapolis

Index

© Springer International Publishing Switzerland 2015   237
J.E. Monogan III, *Political Analysis Using R*, Use R!,
DOI 10.1007/978-3-319-23446-5

input code, 4
installing R , 2
invisible, 208, 220
IQR, 56
irf, 180, 181
is, 22
is.data.frame, 22
is.matrix, 22
is.na, 22, 81, 129, 134
Israeli-Palestinian conflict weekly actions data,
        158, 176

J
Japanese electricity consumption data, 185
Jarque-Bera test, 92
jitter, 87
jpeg, 50

K
kronecker, 197
kurtosis, 91

L
lag, 172, 174
LATEX, 83
legend, 46, 107, 122, 152
length, 149, 188, 194, 220
levels, 25
lines, 43, 46, 107, 109, 122, 166, 184
list, 17, 188, 220
list, 146, 220
Ljung-Box Q-test, 162
lm, 42, 79, 81, 168, 202, 218
    dyn$lm, 172, 174
    coefficients, 174
    fitted.values, 43, 85
    product terms, 81
    residuals, 85, 90, 91
lmer, 129
logistic regression, 101, 102
    AIC, 102, 104
    Bayesian, 138
    deviance, 102
    odds ratio, 106
    percent correctly predicted, 102
    predicted probabilities, 106
    z-ratio, 102
ls, 9, 129, 134, 141, 148, 226

M
mad, 60

match, 184
matching
    average treatment effect on the treated, 145
    balance, 141
    Coarsened Exact Matching, 140
matrix, 17, 187, 192
    addition, 195
    commands for, 194
    creating, 189
    determinant, 197
    diagonal, 192
    formula for OLS, 198
    indices, 149, 166, 183, 184, 191, 193, 220,
        226
    inverse, 197, 199, 201, 217, 227
    Kronecker product, 197
    matrix algebra, 195
    matrix formula for OLS, 201
    multiplication (%*%), 166, 184, 196, 197,
        201, 226
    print, 190–192
matrix, 149, 189, 191, 192, 194, 211, 220,
        227
maximum likelihood estimation, 215
    likelihood function, 215, 226
    log-likelihood function, 215, 217, 226
    optimizing, 216, 227
    programming, 215
    standard errors, 217
MCMClogit, 138, 139
MCMCmetrop1R, 134
MCMCregress, 134
mean, 54, 194, 211, 228
measurement models, 147
median, 56
merge, 28
mtext, 46, 107
multilevel models, 128
    linear, 128
    logistic, 131

N
NA, 14, 22, 81, 129, 134, 191, 211, 220, 227
na.omit, 22, 81
names, 220
    data, 19
    linear regression, 85
    vector, 39
naming objects, 5
National Supported Work Demonstration, 53,
        63, 141
National Survey of High School Biology
        Teachers, 79, 128, 134